ETHICS

Studying the Art of Moral Appraisal

Ronnie L. Littlejohn

Belmont University

UNIVERSITY
PRESS OF
AMERICA

Lanham • New York • London

Copyright © 1993 by
University Press of America®, Inc.
4720 Boston Way
Lanham, Maryland 20706

3 Henrietta Street
London WC2E 8LU England

Library of Congress Cataloging-in-Publication Data

Littlejohn, Ronnie, 1949–
Ethics : studying the art of moral appraisal / by Ronnie L. Littlejohn.
p.   cm.
Includes bibliographical references and index.
1. Ethics. I. Title. II. Title: Moral appraisal.
BJ1031.L58   1993   170—dc20   92–2481 CIP

ISBN 0–8191–8918–9 (pbk. : alk. paper)

The paper used in this publication meets the minimum requirements of
American National Standard for Information Sciences—Permanence
of Paper for Printed Library Materials, ANSI Z39.48–1984.

I wish to dedicate this work to my father, Alpha Omega Littlejohn, a man who lived a virtuous life and taught me what it means to be a moral person.

CONTENTS

Preface

In this work, I have tried to provide a clear presentation of some very technical work done in the philosophy of human action and other events, as well as to introduce a few of the most important discussions in the history of ethics about the theoretical issues arising from the practice of moral appraisal. The text introduces a student to the study of ethics by making philosophical observations on the actual practice of moral appraisal and its language. One goal is to enable a student to appreciate the structure of moral evaluation under any theoretical description whatever. What I mean by this is that whether one is a utilitarian, a deontologist, or a virtue ethicist, there are some common structures in the appraisal process. Each of these theoretical models must decide who is morally appraisable; what events are to be appraised; when justifications and excuses are acceptable and when they are merely rationalizations; and so forth. Such components of moral practice reoccur in all theoretical systems.

As for the classical theoretical systems typically introduced in an ethics course, and the key figures associated with the development of these understandings, I have treated such issues as second-order reflections on the way human persons practice moral appraisals. I try to show that moral practice may yield more than one reflective interpretation, and that privileging one of these requires a justification argument of its own. These discussions are gathered in a chapter to themselves. During the course of the work, I have pointed to questions about moral practice which may yield theoretical responses, thus guiding the student to the next level of reflection.

In the history of the study of ethics it has often been the case that the main objective has been to offer theories about how moral appraisal *should* be done, or what *should* be valued, or *should* be said. My own feeling is that the introduction to ethics has too often simply offered competing theories or alternative answers to these fundamental questions without adequately helping the student know how to decide between the theoretical answers which are offered, or even if some decision must be made. The result is that students sometimes leave an ethics course very confused about the actual process of moral appraisal and how it is done. To be sure, the students may have acquired some historical knowledge about which philosopher said what. They may even be able to know when a person is making an appraisal on "utilitarian" grounds or from a "subjectivist" stance. But I believe such accomplishments cannot be the sole outcomes of the introduction to ethics. In fact, it should not even be the principal responsibility of such a course of study.

This book redirects attention toward a different approach which I believe will provide greater personal benefit to the student, while also accomplishing the general education objective of introducing classical theories, philosophers, and their arguments about moral practice. Although this book introduces some theoretical reflection on important ethical issues, *the principal concern is to teach ethics by describing how persons do in fact make moral appraisals.* My goal is to describe what is done in moral appraisal, not to impose a theory of morality on actual practice. I want to get clear about what we do in moral appraisal, with as little interference with the actual practice of moral evaluation as is possible.

This conception of how a study of ethics should proceed is open to the objection that what persons actually and ordinarily do in moral appraisal is perhaps not what they *should* do. I believe this is an important objection. However, I do not wish to deny that our understanding of morality might be improved by theoretical reflection.[1] What I want to hold is that unless the groundwork is done first, our theories--no matter how pleasing--are not likely to advance our ability to accomplish the ends for which moral appraisal seems to be designed: the creation of a thoroughly humane community of persons. A description of what we actually do in moral evaluation may not be the last word on what it *should be like,* but we can be sure that if a moral concept is used, or a distinction about persons is made, or an excuse works well in everyday life, then there is something significant to be noticed by philosophers. If persons did not consider such practical moves meaningful and helpful, then they would fall out of use and language. Accordingly, no adequate ethical theory should ignore what we ordinarily do.

My own view is that probably all attempts at offering comprehensive moral theories have tried to offer coherent accounts of how we ordinarily proceed in moral practice. So, I am certainly willing to entertain the claim that constructing a comprehensive theory of moral appraisal may be both possible and desirable. But I must insist that any theory which we develop must be one which can, at a very minimum, account for our normal moral experience and language. Accordingly, it seems best to begin with the language we use and our actual practice, and then see what kind of theory emerges. This is to turn the common pedagogy of ethics inside out. Instead of studying various theories, and using the one to critique another, I wish to encourage first the description of actual moral practice and only later the formation of a theory which captures what persons do. It is my continued insistence on the need for addressing such theoretical issues which separates what this work does from a sociology of morals.

Professors who use this book in an introductory ethics course may find a good anthology to be a very effective companion. The articles which appear in anthologies and cover key topics about which there is considerable moral reflection are typically preoccupied with just the kinds of issues and structures which are exposed and treated in this text. For example, consider an essay such as Judith Thompson's "A Defense of Abortion," which has been widely anthologized. One way of reading this essay is to suggest that it first deals with the issue of what moral concept or rule the practice of abortion is to be taken under. Is the fetus a person? Is abortion the taking of a human life? Thompson holds that even under the description of the fetus as person, the appraisal of abortion must deal with prioritization of moral value concepts (the right of the woman to say how her body is to be used), and the possible excusing conditions for abortion. In all of this, I believe she is quite correct. Furthermore, I think she is exhibiting moral practice at its best. What I try to do in this textbook is to uncover how prioritization works and what kinds of excusing conditions replicate in moral grammar. Accordingly, the interchange which can occur between this work and the many fine anthologies available on the market now can be quite instructive for students of ethics.

At this time I wish to acknowledge a debt of gratitude to many of my students at Belmont University. These students have provided numerous insights and suggestions for the improvement of this book. This has been especially true of

---

[1]J. L. Austin, "A Plea for Excuses," in <u>Philosophical Papers,</u> edited by J.O. Urmson and G.J. Warnock (Oxford: Oxford University Press, 1970), p. 185.

those who worked so diligently on it during the Fall and Spring semesters from 1989 to the present . Although they are certainly to be praised for making the book better, they are not to be blamed for its remaining deficiencies.   Also, I want to express my appreciation to Peter French, of Trinity University in San Antonio for his encouragement and guidance, as well as to all those who labored with me in the National Endowment of Humanities Seminar on "The Spectrum of Responsibility" during the Summer 1990. Specifically, I want to mention Ken Pahel of Knox College, Eddy Wilson of the University of the South, Parker English of Ball State, and Cheshire Calhoun of the College of Charleston for their support and helpful criticisms and suggestions. I want to thank also Robert Kuschwitz of Georgetown College and Tom Buford of Furman University for their support and suggestions. Finally, I wish to salute Ludwig Wittgenstein, whose creative genius nudged my faltering abilities to undertake the task of furthering some of his work, if ever so slightly.

Introduction: Ethics as the Study of Moral Appraisal

The word "Philosophy" comes from a combination of two Greek words: *philos* meaning "love" and *sophia* meaning "wisdom." So, etymologically "philosophy" means the love of wisdom. However, noting the origin of a word in the history of language does not always help us understand how it is currently used, and therefore what it means, in today's practice.

In contemporary usage "philosophy" marks the rational activity of formulating and understanding questions which are of fundamental concern to human persons. If I ask, "What kind of government does Japan have?" I am not asking a philosophical question. It is one which could be answered by a political scientist or a historian. If I inquire, "Is Japan's government best at encouraging the development of business enterprises?" then an international economist could probably provide an answer. Yet, if I ask, "Is Japan's the best government ?" then I am asking a philosophical question, just as if I inquired, "What is the best form of government anyway?"

Consider another approach. If I ask you, "What do you want to do when you graduate?" I am not asking you a philosophical question. If you answer that you wish to be a ballerina, I may inquire "How do you become a ballerina?" You may certainly tell me how one becomes a ballerina, without necessarily making any philosophical claims or playing the role of philosopher. You may describe the years of intensive training in dance, the numerous recitals, the need to cultivate a love for the theater, and so forth. However, if I entreat you to tell me, "Will being a ballerina make you happy?" then I am asking a philosophical question, although some psychologists may yet consider this entreaty proper to their discipline too. If I ask, "What is happiness anyway?" then I am definitely on philosophical ground.

When I said that philosophy deals with fundamental questions, I was using the word *fundamental* to mean basic, or primary, or essential. Consider that choosing what you want to do after graduation depends on the more basic determination of what will make you happy, and that in turn relies on your philosophical understanding of what happiness is. So, philosophical understandings are basic or fundamental to our practical life decisions in this sense.

Philosophical questions may be divided into several categories. There are those which have to do with matters such as how we know what is true, and what knowledge and truth are in themselves. This set of philosophical questions, and the answers offered to them, is called *epistemology*. Philosophers deal also with questions about reality (called *metaphysics*), as well as questions about values (called *axiology*). *Axiology* is occupied with questions and issues related to matters such as what human persons value, why they value what they do, and how they express appraisals or judgments of value. Traditionally, axiology is divided into two main subdivisions: *aesthetics* and *ethics*. *Aesthetics* is the philosophical effort to explore what is considered to be a work of art and how the appraisal of art works is practiced (e.g., "That's a beautiful painting"). *Ethics* is the philosophical discipline which makes a systematic effort to understand the practice of moral appraisal. Such a study includes identifying what concepts and rules are essential to this practice and how they are employed. It also requires that one come to some understanding about the types of entities which are appraised morally, and those which are not. Ethics focuses additionally on what constitutes an actual description of moral responsibility and what different types of such descriptions may be found in actual practice. Human persons make moral appraisals about topics like what ways of living are of value and which are not, and why some forms of conduct and some types of persons are more to be valued and encouraged than others. Ethics studies how we make these appraisals, what entities are appraised in this manner, and what is the importance of this practice to human persons. It also engages in the presentation of theoretical questions arising out of the practice of making appraisals of such entities.

An analogy may help in understanding the basic approach to the study of morality which is followed in this book. Suppose that we arranged a group of 4 or 5 persons to play a card game, for instance, "21" or "Black Jack." If there were some observers who watched how the game was played, but had no previous knowledge of it, they could still make many accurate observations about its rules and practice. After a few minutes, the observers could identify the basic procedures of the game. For example, they would note that each new hand began by dealing one card down, and one card facing up, etc. They would recognize that the game followed certain standards or rules, such as that "no player should turn up the hole card of an opponent," and that "the person coming nearest to 21 without going over was the winner," and such. They would also take note of certain common and recurring exceptions in the game. For example, that the ace card could count as "1" or "11." It is this procedure of describing what takes place in practice which we will follow in the study of moral appraisal as well. There are some definite implications of this approach, some of which I wish to discuss now.

1) Learning what is actually done in making a moral appraisal provides an inside look into what takes place when morality is transmitted to each new generation. We notice that moral education is provided, in part, simply by teaching a person a language. When one learns a language, one learns the uses of its component concepts, some of which are used to attach moral blame or praise, or to diminish such blame or enhance the offered praise. Learning the use of a moral concept is learning how to make a moral appraisal. There is a sense in which moral education is just that simple. When a child learns a language he learns what is to be blamed or praised, and what counts as an excuse, and so forth.

If we ask, "How do we acquire our morality?" no one description will do. Many accounts may be offered and all may be true. a) We may say that we *learned* it or were *taught* it, meaning that it came to us through the instruction of others or in just learning language. As we move from one community into another (e.g., school, job, etc.) we learn different moral concepts and how to use them. b) We may also say that we *became convinced* of some moral views, meaning that we appraise or evaluate certain conduct and persons in ways to which we have given rational consent, because we think that there are better reasons to practice morality as we do, rather than the way others do. c) The experience of a religious conversion may also be a way of coming to have the moral practices we do. It may not be like recognizing that a conclusion follows from a set of premises, but it may still constitute being from thenceforward disposed to appraise morally as one does. d) Some ways of moral practice may be imposed on us; we submit to practice the judgments and evaluations which we are told to.

Any moral practice whatever includes excuses and justifications which are entertained and rejected. Moral practice privileges the importance of having good moral credit in the community to which one belongs. So, giving careful attention to moral practice will make it possible for us to uncover many of these components in the educational process and thereby improve our own abilities in moral evaluation.

2)   A second implication of the descriptive approach taken toward ethics in this text is that it helps us to understand how a community defines its values: the things which matter most to it, and the way of life which is considered best. What matters to persons, what is considered necessary for a fulfilling and satisfying life is expressed in his moral practice. If one considers that the most important thing a person does is to define his own identity, then one's moral practice may be the most significant thing we can know about a person, for in it we learn what he values. Moral language, particularly language about one's character, is indispensable to this endeavor. A person who says, "I am an artist" is defining himself, but no more so than one who uses moral concepts to affirm, "I am kind" or "I am generous." Indeed, others may consider it more significant to their flourishing and fulfillment to know whether a person is kind or generous than to know whether the person's vocation is an artist. The study of ethics will provide some insight into how this process is done.

3)   Another implication of a descriptive approach to the study of moral appraisal is that it minimizes any anxiety which a student may have about the nature of an ethics course as an exercise in indoctrination. Students embarking on their first course in ethics sometimes fear having another person's point of view on morality "forced down their throats." It is right to consider such indoctrination an enemy.   R. M. Hare said,

> Indoctrination only begins when we are trying to stop the growth in our children of the capacity to think for themselves about moral questions. If all the time that we are influencing them we are saying to ourselves, 'perhaps in the end they will decide that the best way to live is quite different from what I am teaching them; and they will have a perfect right to decide that, 'then we are not to be accused of indoctrinating.[2]

Ethics education indefensibly becomes indoctrination when the goal is to stop, or even to discourage, the students from thinking for themselves, and to require acquiescence to the views of the teacher instead. Indoctrination of this sort is morally blameworthy because it is an affront to the personhood of the students, and this in itself is sufficient reason to avoid it. But also of significance is another consideration. If one goal of an ethics course is to make it possible for students to function more effectively as moral agents, to understand what considerations are necessary to the evaluation of the conduct and character of others, then they must be capable of participating in moral practice without depending upon someone else to tell them what to notice. Students must be aware of the way the moral community makes appraisals in order to figure out for themselves what it would be most praiseworthy for them to do and what they should avoid in order to be the type of person who has access to the relationships needed by all persons within that community.   None of these abilities can be acquired if the student receives only "doctrine" from the teacher, and no understanding of the practice of morality. So this implies that a descriptive approach to ethics yields a direct benefit to the students.

---

[2]R.M. Hare, "Adolescents into Adults," Aims in Education, edited by T.H.B. Hollins (Manchester: Manchester University Press, 1964), p. 52.

4) There is one final implication which I believe should be mentioned as derived from the descriptive approach to ethics. A descriptive approach to morality discloses that some moral standards and concepts, as well as some responsibility descriptions assigning blame and praise, are rather nonnegotiable in the moral community of human persons.   Such disclosure allows an ethics teacher to call attention to the seriousness with which the community takes some conduct, and being a certain sort of person. The result is that ethics teachers may legitimately be concerned not only with whether their students are skillful in the process of moral evaluation, but also the teacher may stress the importance of which standards and concepts their students actually hold. Consider in this respect that ethicists have wrestled with the tension between two competing understandings of their role. The one says that an ethics class should teach different ethical theories and interfere as little as possible in the personal moral practice of the student. The other says that an ethics teacher's job is not complete unless the student is led to embrace appropriate personal moral standards. In defense of this latter approach, Edmund Pincoffs observed about Fagin, a widely known figure in literature, that his training of Oliver Twist was bad, not because he aimed to make it impossible for Oliver to think for himself, but because he made him into a thief and an artful dodger.[3]

It would seem that one thing to be avoided in ethics instruction is making one's students into morally objectionable persons. That is, ethics teachers do not want their students to know only how to manipulate moral practice. Ethics teachers have the positive obligation to foster the espousal of high moral standards by their students, and this is best done by watching the workings of the human moral community to see how it proceeds. If students are to have a well-founded respect for the concepts and powers of discrimination which are to be found in the way the community practices morality, then they must first learn to appreciate its description.

This book is structured to take such an approach to the study of moral practice seriously. Chapter One identifies a few of the many types of language usage, including that of value appraisal. Several different types of value appraisals are discussed and some of the distinguishing characteristics of moral appraisals are identified.

Chapter Two makes observations about which types of beings are characteristically the subjects of moral appraisal. A look at our moral language makes us aware of the difference between entities whose conduct is appraised morally, and those which are not. What emerges from this description is a rough outline of the traits necessary for an entity to be considered a person; where being a person is a status conferred by a community. Moral language also reveals a class of entities which are given moral consideration by human persons, but about which we have no language of character description or conduct appraisal.

Chapter Three takes note of the range of conduct about which we make appraisals. In this chapter we notice that moral language is used both of a person's intentional actions, as well as of the things which a person was willing to have happen as a result of an intentional action. We also find that moral appraisals are made of the things a person attempts to do, even if unsuccessfully; and the omissions a person makes, when an action, or, at the very least, an attempt was

---

[3]Edmund L. Pincoffs, Quandaries and Virtues: Against Reductivism in Ethics (Lawrence, Kansas: University of Kansas Press, 1986), p. 145.

called for. Moral discourse is likewise shown to include as appraisable not only the conduct of individual persons, but also the many ways in which a person may be involved with others in conduct for which he is morally accountable: as a multiple agent, an intervening agent, and in a group.

Chapter Four is concerned with the conditions under which persons are not appraisable morally. A description of moral practice reveals that there are times when we recognize that it is not appropriate to use moral language about a person's conduct or character. This chapter identifies the conditions under which a person has an exemption from moral accountability, and how value appraisal language may shift from moral concepts to the language of clinical practice to exemplify the nonappraisability of the person.

Chapter Five describes the ways persons use language to defend their conduct by offering justifications. The most common types of justification appeals which persons use to defend the moral rightness of their conduct are exposed. We notice that persons often defend their conduct by saying that those wishing to blame them have misdescribed what happened. Likewise, when persons are sometimes blamed for not having done the best they could have, the defense is that they did what was required.

Chapter Six describes the ways persons use language to admit wrongdoing, but lessen their blame through the offering of excuses. The chapter discusses a partial grammar of excuses used to diminish blame whenever persons are accountable for some untoward conduct.

Chapter Seven uncovers some rationalizations which occur in ordinary language, displaying both failed justifications and excuses of various types.

Chapter Eight describes the way virtue and vice language is used to describe events as well as the moral character of individual persons.

Chapter Nine summarizes a few of the major theoretical questions raised by the practice of moral appraisal, questions which do not seem to be clarified by a description of our use of moral language. Nested within the complexity of moral appraisal one finds many of the issues addressed by the traditional ethical theories, and some of these are discussed in this chapter.

The Conclusion challenges a person to join in active reflection on the process of moral appraisal, exploring the considerations uncovered through a description of moral language, and employing the claims supported by theoretical argument.

For Discussion

1) The author suggests that we can learn something about moral appraisal (e.g., its procedures, standards, recognized excuses, and justifications) simply by paying attention to how this art is practiced and making a description of it.

Arrange a group of 4 or 5 persons who are playing a card game like "Black Jack" or "Bridge"; or a board game such as "Monopoly" or "Chess." Have some observers watch how the play proceeds. After a few minutes, have the observers identify the procedures, standards (rules and concepts), and exceptions for the game. See how accurate they are. Do you think it is fair to compare this type of activity with the approach the author is suggesting for a study of ethics?

2) How would the descriptions of the observers in #1 be different if they were participants in the game and not just spectators? Do you think that the fact that an ethics student is always a participant in the practice of moral appraisal has any

bearing on what the student will describe? Do you see any problems posed by the fact that a study of moral appraisal is always undertaken by those who participate in the process? Are any of these problems controllable? Can any negative effects be minimized? How?

3) Some persons argue against following a descriptive approach to ethics by holding that such a method trivializes this discipline and makes it unworthy of a place in a philosophy curriculum.   Study the illustration below, taken from Sir Arthur Conan Doyle's story, "The Dancing Men" and comment on both Sherlock Holmes' ability to draw out findings from his observations of ordinary things about Dr. Watson's behavior and the doctor's reaction.   Would you compare Dr. Watson's reaction to that made by persons who consider the descriptive approach to ethics to be overly simplistic?

Holmes had been seated for some hours in silence with his long, thin back curved over a chemical vessel in which he was brewing a particularly malodorous product. His head was sunk upon his breast, and he looked from my point of view like a strange, lank bird, with dull grey plumage and a black top-knot.

"So, Watson," said he, suddenly, "you do not propose to invest in South African securities?"

I gave a start of astonishment. Accustomed as I was to Holmes' curious faculties, this sudden intrusion into my most intimate thoughts was utterly inexplicable.

"How on earth do you know that?" I asked.

"Now, Watson, confess yourself utterly taken aback," said he.

"I am."

"I ought to make you sign a paper to that effect."

"Why?"

"Because in five minutes you will say that it is all so absurdly simple."

"I am sure that I shall say nothing of the kind."

"You see, my dear Watson"--he propped his test-tube in the rack and began to lecture with the air of a professor addressing his class--"Now, it was not really difficult, by an inspection of the groove between your left forefinger and thumb, to feel sure that you did not propose to invest your small capital in the goldfields."

"I see no connection."

"Very likely not; but I can quickly show you a close connection. Here are the missing links of the very simple chain: 1. You had chalk between your left finger and thumb when you returned from the club last night. 2. You put chalk there when you play billiards to steady the cue. 3. You never play billiards except with Thurston. 4. You told me four weeks ago that Thurston had an option on some South African property which would expire in a month, and which he desired you to share with him. 5. Your checkbook is locked in my drawer, and you have not asked for the key. 6. You do not propose to invest your money in this manner."

"How absurdly simple!" I cried.

4) Do you think that someone may be trained to see things in the activity of moral evaluation which other persons would overlook until these features were explained? Would you consider this another benefit of the descriptive approach to ethics?

Chapter One: The Spectrum of Appraisability

Types of Language Usage

Language is one of the truly remarkable features of being a person. It makes possible communication with others and helps us both order and create the world of experience. We may *order* the world of experience through language in many ways. Consider just one. We use general or class terms to organize what otherwise would be very confusing. We have words like fruits, chairs, coins, and clothes. These words work hard for us. They make many of our day-to-day activities much easier to accomplish. For example, think about how "Go to the store and buy some fruit" helps us order our shopping trip. Some of the ways in which we can *create* phenomena by the use of language are giving orders, telling a story, singing a song, presenting data or reporting the results of an experiment, or even making up a joke. We also use language creatively to describe the appearance of an object, report an event's occurrence, ask, thank, greet, curse, and evaluate persons or objects.

As we discussed earlier, philosophers have traditionally considered the field of ethics to belong to the study of values (axiology). As such, moral language is a type of evaluative discourse, similar to what is done in aesthetics. Ethics evaluates the conduct of a person, whereas aesthetics evaluates productions and creations of persons, such as in art or music. In a perfectly straightforward sense, moral language is the way we have of indicating what is necessary for a fulfilling and satisfying life. Our moral language expresses what we believe contributes to such a life, as well as what we believe to interfere with it. Since human persons share many of the same biological and emotional needs, wants, and interests, then we may reasonably expect to find that there will be a significant common terrain of moral concepts and standards among the linguistic and cultural families of humanity. Cultures and communities are in large measure created and defined by their moral language because such grammar tells us what they value and what they wish to discourage and blame. Arriving at a well-defined set of moral concepts may take generations; and those concepts which served a culture or community earlier in its history may be revised or discarded as other aspects of the culture change.

This way of conceiving the categorization of "evaluative language" is helpful for distinguishing ethics from aesthetics, but it is somewhat oversimplified. There are many other types of evaluations of a person's conduct which are not moral ones. These additional practices may be classified as etiquette, personal taste, and law.[4] This whole schema is made even more complex because the same language may be used to make appraisals which fit under one or more of these categories. In this chapter, we want to observe what the various different value descriptions of conduct look like, what they emphasize, and what they take into account .

---

[4]There is a discussion of these distinctions in many introductory ethics texts. One that you may find useful is Ethical Issues in Professional Life, edited by Joan C. Callahan (New York: Oxford University Press, 1988), pp. 10-15.

Value Appraisal of Conduct

An event may be describable under an etiquette, taste, moral, or legal appraisal, or even as more than one of these at the same time. In our ordinary language, appraisal descriptions often are layered. For example, the male executive who refers to his female secretary as "honey" and "doll" may be displaying poor business etiquette. The Chairperson of the Board may offer the appraisal, "You should not address your secretary like that." The Chairperson may mean that it is bad manners to do this in today's business climate. However, the Chairperson may think that the executive is acting in such a way as to raise moral concern as well. The Chairperson may wish to indicate to the executive that speaking in this way to his secretary is a way of denigrating her personhood, and that such conduct should be discouraged. If so, when he says, "You should not address your secretary like that" he may mean it is morally blameworthy to do so; it is not just an issue of bad manners. But how would we know which type of appraisal was intended? Probably we could not know without asking the Chairperson. Does it matter that we determine which was meant? If the conduct is altered, maybe we would say that one description was as "good" as another. If so, by "good" we mean "effective in producing a change from undesirable to desirable behavior toward another person."

Consider this evaluative appraisal. "You should shake hands when you are introduced." This looks like an etiquette rule. The etiquette for introductions in some communities includes shaking hands. However, suppose we ask what might happen if someone does not shake hands when introduced. Has this person committed a breach of morality or of etiquette? Or is it possible to do both simultaneously? Of course, I suspect that the answer is that we could do both.

If instead of "not shaking hands" I "*refuse* to shake hands" this means that *intentionally* and *deliberately* I decided not to shake hands; then the description of my omission has changed. Sometimes we find persons using such intensifiers to try to mark the difference between an etiquette appraisal and a moral one, under the notion that morally notable conduct is more significant or intense than that which is merely a breach of etiquette. In effect such a strategy implies that this use of "refuse" is designed to mark not just a breach of etiquette, but a moral wrong.

On the other hand, it seems that the intensification of the appraisal is not, by itself, sufficient to tell me whether the omission is a breach of etiquette or of morality. To be sure, the introduction of "refuse" means that this omission is *more to be praised or blamed* than if it lacked such deliberate intentional consideration. But it does not necessarily tell us whether it is an intensified breach of etiquette, or of morality. Neither does the use of the intensifier considered alone tell us that every "refusing to shake hands" would always be *blameworthy*. In certain circumstances, it might be important for someone to show a conscientious disapproval of another person or of the person's action by refusing to shake hands, and we might say, "Good for you! You refused to shake his hand." And this could be a moral or etiquette approval. In a given community shaking hands might display horribly bad manners, and refusing to do so would be praised as exemplifying a cultured style.

If I say, "You should not have painted your house purple," I may be making an appraisal based on my personal taste (i.e., "I do not like the color purple"). However, what if I am calling attention to your disregard for the interests and desires of your neighbors (i.e., "Painting your house purple ruined the property values of the neighborhood, which adversely effects the well-being of your neighbors, and no one should do that")? If that is what I am considering, then I am making a moral appraisal, even though the description itself is opaque, and may be taken in more than one way. In order to clarify that I am making a moral appraisal, and not merely one of personal taste, I may say something like the following: "The color you paint your house is a matter of personal taste, up to a point, but not beyond that point. You may paint your house as it suits you, unless how you paint it causes harm to others." So, an appraisal which seems to be only a matter of personal taste may instead be a moral evaluation under an alternative description of the context, or circumstances, or depending on what considerations we want a person to note.

Of course, this appraisal may have multiple meanings at the same time. I may express both my personal dislike for the color of your house, and my moral assessment of the implications of your having painted it as you did; and I may do so by the same evaluative expression. There are certainly ways that etiquette and personal taste appraisals may sometimes praise or blame, recommend, obligate, or prohibit the same conduct that moral appraisals do.

Distinguishing Moral and Nonmoral Value Appraisals

We can see why there is often a great deal of confusion about what kind of value appraisal a person is making. This opaqueness belongs to language itself and it seems not to be erasable completely, that is to say that no value judgment whatever may finally be reducible to one and only one appraisal function or type. Whether it is possible to do so or not must be debated at a theoretical level and cannot be resolved by description alone.

Two important questions arise now. 1) Are there some recurring considerations or common characteristics which occur in evaluative language usage which will help us know when we are using the appraisal to make a moral evaluation? 2) Is it necessary to know this?

I would like to respond to the second question first. In Aristotle's Nicomachean Ethics, it seems to me that he makes no special effort to distinguish between the various types of value appraisals. Rather, he seems to consider all of them to belong to the proper subject matter of ethics.[5] The style of one's life, as usually addressed by what we call etiquette and taste, was not radically distinguished by Aristotle from what we might call morality. A study of his list of virtues and vices will reveal that the "moral virtues" seem to be treated alongside those which seem more characteristic of "etiquette" or even "personal taste." However, I am not sure that we want to continue this way of seeing things. It does seem to be the case that there are times when it is both important to emphasize that we are making a moral appraisal and even necessary that we do so, in order to achieve and/or preserve the relationships we want and need as human persons.

Let me illustrate what I mean. Consider that even the most careful observance of etiquette does not insure that a person is morally praiseworthy. No matter how *charming* a person may be, if he has moral faults these may take preeminence in any consideration we make about whether to have relationships with

---

[5]See Aristotle's discussion of virtues of social intercourse in Nicomachean Ethics, Book IV, Ch. 5, 1126ff. in Introduction to Aristotle, edited by Richard McKeon (Chicago: The University of Chicago Press, 1973).

him and what kind we will have.   Russell may be an impeccable *professional* speaking under an etiquette description. Let us say that he always wears power suits, is never late for meetings, runs a good conference, makes a fine presentation, etc. However, our moral appraisal of him might be very different. He might be a *liar,* a *cheat,* or an *adulterer.* Now, what is so interesting about this is that we can now take note of something which is often overlooked. Our use of evaluative language discloses that we consider it possible for Russell to be both an impeccable professional and yet a liar, cheat, or adulterer.

Our first reaction is to say that these latter descriptions are much more significant to any decision we make about our relationship to Russell. But this may not be the right way to frame the issue. Closer examination of common practice indicates that the relative importance of the appraisal descriptions depends on what kind of relationships we want or need to have with Russell and whether to have any at all. If all that one desires is a business relationship with him, his professionalism is privileged as most important. We may never inquire about his private conduct; and if we find that some of his nonprofessional conduct is morally blameworthy, we frequently still conclude that such a finding has nothing to do with our relationship to him.   On the other hand, if we know that he is a liar, or cheat, or adulterer, we may well conclude that a person of this kind of character may not be desirable for having personal relationships with, let us say if we were considering whether to date him, or to go on a family outing with him. Such difficulties raised by common practice extend quite far. For example, it is common for persons to ask whether the "private" life of a politician should be considered in whether to vote for him for an office, especially if he has proven competent and effective as a professional.

There are two very important assumptions which may be enticed out of the practice of continuing to be interested in the private lives of those to whom we relate primarily at a professional level. First, the very fact that we do this suggests that we are not very confident about our knowledge of how to mark the lines between professional and private conduct for evaluative purposes.   Second, our attention to the evaluations which can be made of the private lives of those with whom we have only a professional relationship also discloses that we do not believe that the persons themselves can hold these two arenas altogether separate.

But perhaps this discussion has surfaced a way of talking about how moral appraisals are generally made about conduct which is of extreme importance and significance to persons. While it is true that what we consider to be important or significant is somewhat relative to the context, nevertheless there is a way in which moral appraisals are made about conduct which is most needed to make it possible for us to have lives of meaning and fulfillment simply *persons qua persons.* Whatever else we MAY want or desire because of contextual variations such as whether one has a business or personal relationship with another person, still we will CERTAINLY need and desire some things simply because we are human persons. This claim does not negate the observation that determining what is important or significant is context-dependent.   It only points to the most fundamental of contexts which all persons share.

For example, human persons do not merely want to be free from *murder, cruelty, torture* in order to live a full and satisfying life. They actually need such freedom.   They want, but also need, to encourage *kindness, trust, justice* , and to discourage *lying, stealing,* and such. All of this is because there are certain biological, social, and emotional givens about the most basic context of being human persons which must be protected and insured in order for them to have lives of meaning and fulfillment. There are ways of violating these desires, interests and needs arising out of these givens which must be discouraged. There are ways of satisfying these desires, interests and needs which must be encouraged. Moral appraisal is the primary method which persons use to accomplish these tasks. More than any other single thing that human beings do, it is our capacity to make moral appraisal which breeds the excellence of life all human persons crave.

Consider that these observations are reinforced by noticing that moral appraisals require justifications or excuses for any untoward conduct. That is, if we say, "Bill, you lied," then Bill is expected to offer a justification to show that he did not lie, or an excuse which explains why he lied and that his blame should be diminished. If he cannot do either of these things, then we will probably withhold, or at least alter, certain relationships with him.

If an appraisal of someone's conduct **requires** that they offer an excuse or a justification, then the appraisal is not merely a matter of personal taste. We are signaling the other person that his conduct is not something that we are going to let pass without further consideration. But personal taste judgments are not these sorts of things. If I say, "It's wrong to eat snails," you may agree or disagree with me. If you disagree, and choose to eat them, I may ask, "Why do you eat those horrible things?" You may simply reply, "Because I like them," or "Because I want to." For me, this reply will settle it. "Well, to each his own," I may say. I do not expect you to offer any further justification, only to state that snails are your preference, or perhaps that you just wanted to try them. I will let it pass. You certainly will need no excuse. But if I say "It's wrong to murder," and you plan to go ahead anyway, then you had better have some really sound excuse for doing so, because I am not going to let this conduct get by. In part, what makes me let one of these judgments pass without justification or excuse, and the other not, is that *my access to relationships I want and need to have a fulfilling and satisfying life depends on my avoiding such conduct.* If you murder another person this access is altered in a way which is not true if you only eat snails. I might find it repulsive that you eat snails. I may not want to watch. But you do not owe me a justification or excuse. However, if you murder, more is at stake that just giving me a weak stomach, and you will owe me some description of responsibility.

Consider another way of approaching this same point. I do not feel the need to know whether someone likes chocolate more than vanilla. Unless something is emotionally wrong with me, such preferences are not relevant considerations in whether I prefer having a relationship with her or not. But I think it is very important to know whether she is telling me the truth or not. If I find out Beth happens to like vanilla, not chocolate, she will not have to provide a justification or an excuse to me. Except in some rather bizarre circumstances, her preference for vanilla will not be something I consider in determining what relationships to have with her. In fact, if I were to tell you that I did not want to be around Beth because she likes vanilla ice cream rather than chocolate, you would certainly think I was acting bizarre. You would probably consider that something was wrong with me; not Beth. However, if I tell you that I prefer not having a relationship with Beth because she is a liar, that will make good sense to you. You will understand that preference well and probably not question it. You may wonder whether she is a liar or not, but you will not wonder why someone would like to avoid a liar. If I find out she told you a lie, and you tell me "Beth is a liar," that will make a great deal of difference to me. I might say, "Oh, really! Then I'll be very careful."

Some evidence that we have this description right lies simply in noting the fact that we do have a concept for marking that someone knowingly tells falsehoods ("liar"); whereas, we have no such concept for things like "vanilla-liking". The use of the moral concept word "liar" tells me that she may deceive me, leaving out or distorting information I need. Because information may be very crucial to me in some situations, I need to know whether I can count on a person to provide it truthfully. It is important both to me and to others that I be able to mark the differences between persons with regard to such important conduct, so the concept of "liar" is used to do this. That it is *much less important* to do so on the matter of ice cream preference is implied by the fact that there is no concept by which to perform this function.

The Language of Moral Appraisal

We are now ready to return to the first question which arose when we noted the complex way in which value appraisals are intertwined. Are there some recurring considerations or common characteristics which occur in evaluative language usage which will help us know when we are using the appraisal to make a moral evaluation? We can begin to answer this question by looking closely at the way language is used when engaging in the practice of moral appraisal.

Some moral evaluations make use of **value indicator words** (e.g., *right, wrong, should, ought, good, and bad*). But these are free-floating value indicators. What I mean by this is that they occur in all types of value appraisals, and not just in moral ones. So, it is impossible to distinguish a moral appraisal from a nonmoral one based on the use of these indicators alone. They may as easily be employed in an etiquette or personal taste appraisal, as in a moral one. The purpose of such indicators seems to be to indicate simply THAT a value appraisal is being made, not what kind of appraisal is being offered. Strictly considered, from the grammatical point of view, both of the following use free-floating value indicator words: "It is wrong to talk with your mouth full." "It is wrong to rape your date." One of these is a moral appraisal, the other is not. But we cannot distinguish between the two based on the use of the value indicator *wrong* .

Moral appraisals sometimes use **intensity discriminator terms** (e.g., *negligent, inadvertent, deliberate, intentional, reckless, careless*, etc.) An intensity discriminator word describes the *manner of the conduct,* which it is important to take notice of when making a value appraisal. In the case of a moral evaluation, for example, it is significant to mark not only that "Will hurt Susan," but whether "Will hurt Susan *deliberately* ," or "Will hurt Susan *accidently* ." However, etiquette and personal taste judgments may use the same intensifying discriminators as found in moral discourse. After all, a person could excuse a poor choice of dress by saying, "I am sorry, I did not wear pants to the party deliberately." These words are relevant in all value appraisals because we use them to intensify or diminish blame or praise by calling attention to how an act, attempt, or omission is discriminated from others like it. So, again, they may function in all value discourse, and not merely in moral appraisal.

A description of moral appraisal reveals the use of some significant expressions which may be called **conduct discriminator words.** Some examples of these are *murder, lying, stealing, adultery.* Others are *honest, callous, vindictive, benevolent.* Some conduct discriminators seem to be etiquette concepts (e.g., *graceful* or *pretentious*). Others may be called **moral concepts.** In our example above, we recognized that "It is wrong to talk with your mouth full" is an etiquette appraisal; whereas "It is wrong to rape your date" is a moral one. How do we see the difference? One way of answering this is to say simply that "Rape" is a moral concept word.

We use moral concept discriminators to say something like, "Mary, that was spiteful." We may also say of Mary, "She is *spiteful* ." We may say not only that Mike's action was honest but that "Mike is *honest." Honesty* used in this sense is a **virtue** word which praises a person; **vice** words, such as *spiteful* blame persons. Virtue and vice terms are moral concepts which appraise persons and not merely conduct.

The same language may be employed in self-evaluation too. We may say, "I was so *callous* in the way I treated Becky." Or, "I have become so *callous* that such conduct does not bother me anymore." These are forms of self-appraisal which use the same concepts we employ of others' conduct and character, only they are self-attributions.

These concepts are important because they actually create and constitute the moral world. Without moral concepts there would be only bodily movements or omissions to move. The world would be morally neutral. Every language has moral concepts and these are used to mark conduct which is to be discouraged or encouraged and praised. The creation of moral concepts is such marking. Only as conduct becomes marked is there a world which has *lies, thefts, murders, courage, kindness, altruism,* and so forth. Unlike value indicator words and intensifying discriminators, which float freely among all type of evaluative discourse, these concepts specifically constitute moral discourse. "Raping" one's date is not just bad manners; it is a moral offence. A person's conduct appraised under this concept must either provide a justification according to which the conduct was not "Rape"; or else if the conduct is admitted as rape, then the person must offer an excuse to diminish blame in order to have continued access to the relationships he needs and desires.

Moral concept terms are a type of shorthand we use for actually making a moral appraisal. Some of these are blaming concepts, others are praising concepts. If we say, "Judy is *lying,* " we are disapproving of her action. About this there is no doubt. We do not ask whether it was right of her to do so, although we may consider whether she has an excuse which diminishes her blame for doing so. If Judy tells a lie and admits this, she may offer an excuse for lying which may diminish the degree of blame placed on her, but she is not completely exonerated. When we say she lied, we are not merely stating that she communicated a falsehood. We are saying that she communicated a falsehood of a particular sort, one for which she should be blamed. The use of this concept is our signal to others and to her that she deserves blame. *Lying* is different from *misinformation* . One can provide *misinformation* absent the intent to deceive. One can simply not know the facts or have them wrong.

In cases of serious actions, such as killing, language is rich with intensifying discriminators and moral concepts. We may say Joe's killing of his partner was *manslaughter* , or that it was *self-defense* , or *euthanasia* . The point is that although *manslaughter* and *murder* are both moral concepts, they do not mark the same manner of killing; as do neither *self-defense* and *murder*; or for that matter *self-defense* and *manslaughter.* Some persons try to identify *murder* and *euthanasia* , but these are not the same either. Consider that although one might both *murder* and *euthanatize* intentionally and deliberately, the purposes of the killings are very different. I suggest that it is that difference which we wish to mark. There are no exact synonyms. If we have several moral concepts, it is probably because we wish to mark differences which are morally important.

Comparing various moral communities reveals that the moral language used by a given community is rich or poor in certain kinds of moral concepts and intensifying discriminators because members of that community, in trying to manage their relationships, have specific needs to take note of certain features of conduct which other communities may not. These become embodied in language. For example, if we were the sorts of creatures who lived in the kind of environment in which every desire we have were fulfilled immediately, then there would be no *perseverance* , *patience,* or *persistence* , and these would not be moral concepts of virtue. If we were immune to pain both psychologically and physically, then there would be no *cruelty*, *spite,* or *vindictiveness*, and these would not be moral concepts of vice. What seems noteworthy about all of this is that languages consistently reveal a much larger vocabulary of moral concepts which blame, than of those which praise. It seems that we are more concerned with how things can go wrong, than how they can go right? Of course, someone might claim theoretically both that such virtues and vices still exist even though we have no language about them, and also that we have the moral concepts we do because they mark the moral facts of reality. But this is a question to which we can return later in this work. (**Cf. Are Moral Appraisal Standards Objective or Subjective? in Ch. 9**)

There are some very interesting implications of all of this. One is that some moral concepts are **not** found in connection with certain intensifying discriminators. We do not say, "Joe *accidently murdered* his partner," or "Joe *carelessly murdered* his partner." The reason we do not say such things is to be found in the concept of "murder" itself. The sort of killing we mark by the concept of "murder" is not something that can be done "accidently" or "carelessly." Killings--just as killings, let us say--can be done in either of these sorts of ways, but "murder" cannot.

Another interesting implication of our description is that it is probable that a person who lived completely alone would not develop a moral vocabulary that looked much like what we use, because our present moral appraisal discourse is thick with concepts and intensifying discriminators which mark considerations which have to do with the interests, desires, and needs of other human persons with whom we must have contact daily. A hermit's vocabulary for moral appraisal would be almost exclusively self-referential, and many of our moral concepts and intensifying discriminators would be empty and meaningless. Of course, the vocabulary could include some non self-referential language; for example, concepts which mark his conduct toward trees, rivers, animals or such. Or, regarding another scenario, if he had at one time lived in a community and learned its language, but was now a hermit.

The hermit's situation would be different than that of a person who tried to live and move in the moral community, but was invisible. About such an invisible person, we would still use our moral grammar, and if such a one *wanted to be admitted* into the relationships human persons value, he would have to find a way of using moral language, and show us how to use it of his conduct.

A third interesting implication of our description of moral language is that ordinary language may already capture most of what is worth noting morally. J. L.

Austin writes,

> ...our common stock of words embodies all the distinctions men
> have found worth drawing, and the connexions they have found
> worth marking, in the lifetimes of many generations: these surely
> are likely to be more numerous, more sound, since they have stood
> up to the long test of the survival of the fittest, and more subtle, at
> least in all ordinary and reasonably practical matters, than any that
> you or I are likely to think up in our arm-chairs of an afternoon--the
> most favoured alternative method.[6]

The words used in moral appraisals did not simply pop into language. They are
there to enable our appreciation for considerations about how persons relate to
others. They help us understand the appraisals others are making of our conduct,
or our character, or of the conduct of other persons with whom we are acquainted.
We may appraise ourselves by using such language; or give others some idea of
what they should expect from us by using moral concepts of ourselves, as well as
appraise other persons in the community using the common stock of language
which may be called moral discourse.

INTENSIFYING DISCRIMINATORS

Adverbs

purposely	bitterly	harshly	malignantly
acrimoniously	virulently	willfully	fervently
ardently	avidly	earnestly	impatiently
benignantly	recklessly	impulsively	gently
modestly	perversely	negligently	heedlessly
whimsically	rashly	rancorously	carelessly
mistakenly	accidently	incidentally	brazenly
voluntarily	intentionally	tactlessly	thoughtlessly

Idioms

couldn't help it	didn't mean to	didn't realize	under duress
after deliberation	under the influence	under orders	under threat
with care	with good graces	with a will to	with intent to
to no end	to an excess	to a fault	to the full
to someone's face	out of character	out of the blue	on the sly
on principle	on one's conscience	off the handle	of no avail
of one's own accord	in good faith	in a hurry	for all I know
for no rhyme/reason	above board	by the book	by chance
by mistake/accident	by surprise	at random	at risk
at the drop of a hat	at liberty to	to aggravate	as an affront

---

[6] Austin, "Plea for Excuses," p. 182.

MORAL CONCEPTS

Virtues

amiable	benevolent	brave	charitable
conscientious	courageous	decent	dedicated
dependable	disciplined	enterprising	fair
forgiving	generous	good-tempered	helpful
honest	just	kind	magnanimous
tolerant	prudent	reasonable	reliable
respected	self-disciplined	tactful	truthful
altruistic	sensitive	loyal	sincere
appreciative	self-confident	understanding	hospitable

Vices

cruel	dastardly	lustful	vindictive
promiscuous	revengeful	belligerent	negligent
quarrelsome	opinionated	peevish	patronizing
dictatorial	thoughtless	pretentious	callous
self-indulgent	stubborn	envious	malignant
arrogant	bullying	domineering	lazy
mercenary	nefarious	petulant	pompous
self-indulgent	vindictive	jealous	deceptive
deceitful	depraved	mean	noxious
pernicious	unprincipled	villainous	cowardly
hateful	ill-tempered	sullen	surly

Conduct

kill	slay	murder	execute	euthanatize
steal	pilfer	borrow	plunder	loot
lie	fib	deceive	mislead	misrepresent
injure	harm	abuse	mistreat	honor
cherish	commend	esteem	respect	

*This list is only meant to be a sampling of moral vocabulary. Other lists are provided elsewhere in this book. Try to add to this table from your own description of moral language.

Types of Standards Used in Making Moral Appraisals

By looking at moral appraisals offered in ordinary language, we can move backward to some reflection and grouping of what types of standards are implied under which a description of moral responsibility can take place. Notice the standards in the cases below.

Case * 1

Peter, forty-five, is married to Leslie, forty-three, and they have three teenage children. Generally speaking, they have a pretty good marriage, except for their sex life. Although they both know it is poor, they don't discuss it very often. Over a period of several months Leslie notices a change in Peter, and she finally asks him if there's anything wrong. Peter blurts out that he is in love with another woman with whom he's had a relationship for several months. Leslie is so angry and hurt that she immediately demands that he leave the house and states that she wants a divorce. "A relationship, you call it," she says, "well, I call it adultery."

This is an example of a value judgment which relies upon the use of a **moral concept** as the standard (in this case, *adultery*). The judgment may be cast as is it is in this case, "I call it adultery," where there are no value indicator reminders, such as the word "wrong." The concept "adultery" is sufficient to make us aware that moral blame is being assigned. Of course, the judgment may be worded with such a reminder (e.g., "What you are doing is wrong; it is adultery." or "Adultery is wrong, and that's what you did.") Likewise, the use of a moral concept term in order to mark a virtue or vice about a particular person may or may not take a value indicator word: "Bill is kind," or it may use one "Bill, you should be kind." [7]

A moral concept like "adultery" is a way we discriminate one undesirable way of relating to other persons sexually. It singles out this particular kind of such relating as different from other ways of doing so. The use of this concept is to make a blaming appraisal. To hear that an action one is considering is "adulterous" should be enough to cause any person to give pause to reconsider.

A description of moral practice discloses what happens when a person does not rethink an action called "adulterous," or recognize that to commit adultery would be blameworthy. What it shows is that more than one thing may be happening. 1) The person does not understand what "adultery" is. That is he does not appreciate that it is a blaming concept in our moral language. 2) The person does not think that the proposed conduct fits under the description of adultery. 3) The person is not appraisable because of some condition discussed later in this work. He has not learned to use the language, or is unable to grasp the significance of his conduct under moral descriptions. See the discussion of the conditions removing one from moral appraisability covered later in this work. 4) The person is morally bankrupt and vicious because he rejects the notion that adultery indicates moral fault. He sees himself as exempt from moral appraisal by others, or recognizes that it is a blaming concept but does not care.

In moral appraisal, sometimes the task is to see whether a person's conduct may be captured under the description of a moral concept. In some cases, it is clear that this can be done. In others, the person whose conduct is being appraised may try to substitute another concept entirely, or show why the conduct is not to be taken under the moral concept we are using. In still other situations, we may attempt to ensnare an event and bring it under a concept. We often employ an

---

[7] Hector-Neri Castaneda, The Structure of Morality (Springfield: Thomas, 1974), p. 13.

analogy to do this. "If this is not adultery, then it is so much like adultery that it should be treated as wrong, because adultery is wrong."

As we listen to moral language, we learn that it often either utilizes moral concepts, or aims at the clarification and formation of new moral concepts by making specific appraisal judgments which might be based on moral rules or even on nonmoral appraisal descriptions which one is trying to convert to a moral concept.[8]

Case * 2

Finally, Sam is an upperclassman. He knows virtually everyone in his dorm, especially all the people on his floor. The beginning of the school year is always exciting, and seeing the freshmen arrive looking like they are in a daze, reminds him of when he first came to college. There is always some joking with freshmen, that's just part of college. It's fun. But as Sam is with a group of other guys who live on his floor, they are planning to take Waldo, a freshman none of them likes, into the park not far from campus, strip him, and paint him red and blue (the school colors). "Whoa," says Sam. "I think that's a little much. We shouldn't really harm or injure others just because of a prank."

This is an example of an appraisal judgment which relies upon a **moral rule.** Moral rules often contain moral concepts, as in "Persons should not *murder* " or "Do not be *cruel* ." In this case, perhaps a moral rule which expresses a moral concept under which we might describe the conduct above would be "*Hazing* is wrong" or "We should not engage in *hazing.*" In our example, the rule is "We should not *harm or injure* other persons". These are much more general concepts. But since "hazing" is a type of harm or injury, this rule may still be appropriate for this case.

There are certain common traits which characterize the form of moral rules as they manifest themselves in ordinary language, and the rule upon which the judgment in Case Two is based reveals these traits quite clearly. The rule for Case #2 may be expressed in this way: *"We should not cause harm or injury to other persons."* The basic traits of this rule seem to be as follows.

1) **The rule is universal in scope.** Ordinary moral discourse privileges moral rules with the broadest possible range of application. The rule in our example does not contain personal names or addressee limitations. It does not say "'Bill' or 'Joe' or 'Pete' should not cause harm or injury to others." It is meant to apply universally to all persons. No restriction on the class of persons to whom it is directed is included. The expectation is that everyone is subject to this rule. Accordingly, any violation of the rule would require from anyone a justification or an excuse.

Some ethical theories hold that in order for a rule to gain universal scope, it must be totally impartial. However, it is unclear based simply on a description of moral language whether this is true or not. It is clear that we find rules which are

---

[8]See Ibid., pp. 13ff and G.J. Warnock, The Object of Morality (London: Methuen & Co. Ltd., 1971), pp. 86ff.

meant to be universal in scope, but the theoretical explanation for why these come to be recognized varies, and some of the theoretical dimensions of this problem are discussed later. **(Chapter 9: Can Ultimate Moral Standards be Justified Rationally?)**

2) **The rule is practicable.** Moral rules employed in practice only obligate those things within our control to perform, and they do not prohibit conduct which is beyond the ability or control of persons to avoid. The rule in our example prohibits conduct which we could perform, but should not. The conduct is avoidable. It is possible for us to omit causing harm or injury. Rules used in ordinary moral language must be practicable, or else they fall into disuse and vanish. Consider that it might be desirable to have a rule which said, "Parents should outlive their children." The motive behind forming such a rule could be that parents will be able to watch after their children, provide for them, and see to their security during the entire life cycle of the child. But we do not have a moral rule which obligates parents to outlive their children. And the reason probably has nothing to do with whether we believe it would be desirable or not for parents to be able to take care of their children's needs. The reason is more likely that "outliving one's children" is not something over which parents can exercise much control. So, what we find in moral language is that a moral rule must be practicable before it is created. We could also say that if a rule were proposed, and we later discovered the conduct it required was incapable of practice or impossible to omit, then it would quickly fall into disuse and vanish from language.

3) **The rule is imperative in form.** Moral rules used as standards for appraisal judgments are not advisory in form. The rule in our case study, for example, does not *suggest or recommend* that one avoid causing harm or injury; it *requires* that we do so. Interestingly enough, ordinary moral discourse uses rules which are both imperative and yet contain statements of conditions and exceptions which make them much more concrete and narrow their range of application. What this means is that we do find moral rules in ordinary language which already contain the exceptions or excuses which have been found to diminish blame to such a negligible degree as no longer to count as blameworthy. For example, the rule "Do not cause harm, suffering, or injury" is certainly different, and not as useful as is the rule: "Do not cause unnecessary or needless harm, suffering, or injury." The addition of "unnecessary" or "needless" is important and may be traced to well-established exceptions to the more general rule.

Let me explain. If we started with the rule "Do not cause harm or injury," what would we do with a surgeon who causes an injury to the patient whenever the scalpel is used? Obviously, we do not wish to treat this as a moral wrong under this rule. The injury may be necessary in order to do the patient a greater good. And we can well imagine what it is like to recognize this exception.

Descriptive ethics does not tell us how many times an exception to a rule must be noticed before the rule is altered, but it certainly reveals that this is done, and that it is done in order to preserve, not destroy the imperative tone of the rule. In some cases, perhaps where the issue is not very serious, maybe only one exception is necessary. In other cases, maybe the same type of excuse or exception needs to be noted repeatedly before it gives birth to a reshaped rule. There does not seem to be a rule for altering rules embodied in ordinary language, although it would be an interesting theoretical task to see if one could be constructed. But one very intriguing point does emerge from our descriptive approach.

Concrete rules are more functional in the practice of moral appraisal than are highly general ones; and it seems to be the case that the greater the frequency of the situations which are rule-governed, the more concrete the rules will be which are employed, and the more rules there are which will be available for use in making appraisals.   In his theoretical discussion of rule formation Richard Brandt takes note of what we already find occurring in ordinary moral practice. He holds that our moral rules should be made as concrete as possible, especially in crucial action-guiding situations.

> At what level of abstraction should the rules regulating act-types be framed? Should there, for instance, be a basic rule forbidding carrying a revolver? Or is it enough if there is a rule prohibiting risking injury to others? One advantage to abstract rules is increased applicability--perhaps world-wide. Abstract rules can also be few in number, and that is an advantage since the basic motivations have to be established by conditioning. On the other hand, the conditions and exceptions of the abstract rule, as well as the inference from it to the concrete application,may be too complex for the average person.   A reasonable compromise is to propose that the code contain fairly concrete rules for frequent situations, especially ones for which predictability of behavior is important to many persons. [9]

We can also notice that in moral language, rules may be equally effective for the purposes of appraisal and yet expressed in different ways. We could profitably say, "Do not cause harm or injury, *except* as a temporary condition to a greater benefit." Or,   "Do not cause needless harm, suffering, or injury." Or, "Do not cause unnecessary harm, suffering, or injury." Or, "Do not cause harm, suffering, or injury for their own sake." Making this descriptive observation does not mean that all of these rules communicate the same thing, only that each of them may have a certain usefulness in doing moral appraisal, and that one may be as effective for the desired ends as is the other, depending on the context. In actual practice, if one rule formulation does not work, we often change the formulation. Or else, we may simply change to another rule under which the appraisal may be made.   For example, in Case #2 above, we may appraise this conduct under the rule prohibiting harm or injury; or under a rule which obligates us to conduct ourselves toward other persons as we would like to be treated; or under a rule which requires that we treat all persons with respect; or by a rule prohibiting hazing or harassment.

Moral practice shows that there is not always one and only one rule by which to make an appraisal of some conduct; on the contrary, it shows that a constellation of rules may be applicable to any given situation.

4. **The rule is compatible with other rules and with the moral concepts employed in a community**. Moral rules which logically or inevitably contradict each other do not both survive in a unified and coherent grammar of morality.   One or both rules will be altered.   Or, excuses and exceptions will enter into the rule formulation. Sometimes one or both of the moral rules will fall into disuse and vanish if they are in contradiction, depending on the

---

[9]Warnock, p. 290.

nature and seriousness of the conduct over which they are meant to expedite appraisal. The rule in our case does not prohibit conduct which some other rule obligates; neither does it obligate conduct prohibited by some other rule. So, it stands well within a coherent moral grammar.

A word of caution is in order at this point. In common moral discourse we recognize that there may be situations in which our moral rules may obligate us to conduct ourselves in a way which would break some other rule *governing that situation* (e.g., there may be times when telling the truth might mean causing harm or injury). In fact, such situations have a name in ethics. They are called *dilemmas*. What must not be overlooked here is that a dilemma is not generated by the rules themselves, but by the situational peculiarities of the context. Later in this book, we shall discuss the theoretical position of the moral absolutists. Moral absolutists hold that there really never are such cases of irremovable conflict; there are no genuine moral dilemmas, only apparent ones. But whether the absolutists are right or not, this is not relevant to the point we are now making. That point is that such conflicts between moral rules which occur in dilemmas, if there are any, are generated by the situation, not by any formal characteristic or flaw in the moral rules themselves.

Some final remarks about the use of moral rules are in order. It is very interesting to watch how moral rules actually function in the making of appraisals. Some rules *obligate* persons to conduct themselves in a specified way. They will be blamed if they do not do as the rule prescribes. They will have done what is expected if they conduct themselves as the rule commands. Other rules *prohibit* persons from conducting themselves in certain ways. They will be blamed if they perform the conduct prohibited. They will have done their duty if they avoid the prohibited behavior. An interesting feature of how moral rules function in language is that when one describes what persons are obligated to perform and prohibited from doing, one notices that a zone of behavior arises which is neither obligated or prohibited and is usually morally permitted to us, at our discretion. This is a zone of moral permission.[10] So, moral rules also *permit* persons to conduct themselves in various ways. In such cases, one may choose to act, attempt, or omit as one wishes. The zone of moral permission may be wide or narrow, depending on the moral grammar of the community.

Some conduct which we are permitted to do falls into the area which is known in ethics as supererogation. **Supererogatory** *conduct includes actions, attempts, and omissions which go above and beyond our general moral obligations or prohibitions as expressed in moral rules and concepts.* Heroes and *saints* are moral concept words used to mark some types of supererogatory conduct. Moral language about heroes and saints is reserved for those who exhibit conduct which is beyond what they are obligated to do, or which shows restraint above that which is expected of the general moral community. One of the most intriguing features of language about supererogation is that persons can omit all supererogatory conduct and still be virtuous. The use of virtue language does not require that one be a hero or a saint.

Consider an example of supererogatory conduct. There is no moral rule of universal scope that says "Persons should sacrifice their lives for the sake of

---

[10]This area may belong to personal taste.

others." This is not an obligation in ordinary moral language. In fact, what we find in language is a well-established vocabulary about self-defense which makes it clear that this is not regarded as a general moral obligation for all persons. However, we do not find the prohibition, "Persons should never sacrifice their lives for the sake of others" either. Since moral language neither obligates nor prohibits this conduct as a rule, then it belongs to the zone of moral permission in which we may choose as we wish, assuming that no other moral obligation or prohibition is involved. Choosing to give one's life for the sake of others, when not obligated to do so, is supererogatory.

Case * 3

Karmen is a twenty-seven year old woman who lives across from your aging grandmother. You see her when you go to visit. She lives with her handicapped father and her five children. Her kids are poorly clothed and malnourished, and her father is unable to help. In fact, he too is badly in need of care. For the past few weeks, you have noticed that whenever you stop by to take the kids some clothes or some dinner, that Karmen is not there. When you ask your grandmother about this, she says Karmen goes partying with a different man every night, returns in the early hours of the morning, and sleeps most of the rest of the day. "She should provide for the health and care of her children and father," you say. "She knows that she has obligations to meet."

This is an example of a moral appraisal which relies upon a **special role moral standard.** Such obligations and prohibitions may be used when appraising conduct on the basis of the roles we occupy in life, or the groups to which we belong, and not simply by virtue of the fact that we are human persons. Unlike rules of the sort discussed under Case #2, these obligations and prohibitions are not universal in scope. One of the best ways to think of the important difference between special role standards and those which are universal in scope is to imagine that all persons belong to what might be called the **general moral community**. This community consists of a language about *persons qua persons*. But in addition, moral practice discloses the use of concepts and rules which apply only to some persons and not to others. Typically in such cases there is some differentiating role or group identification associated with the use and application of these special standards of appraisal.

With these categories in place we can better describe what we find in ordinary practice. What we find is that a person not only belongs to the general moral community, but also to one or more sub-communities, each of which may have moral concepts and rules under which to appraise the character of its members. One way of identifying the sub-communities to which one belongs is to speak of the roles one has in life. Another way of identifying the sub-communities to which one belongs is to take notice of the moral standards used to appraise a particular person, not all other persons as well. [11]

A person may occupy many different roles in life. The most basic role that all persons occupy is simply the role of being a person, and there is a language of moral concepts and rules which apply to persons just as persons. This is the language of the **general moral community**. Other roles which a person may occupy include those of student, parent, professor, club member, lawyer, doctor, soldier, coach, friend, and many others. With each of these roles comes a set of moral standards which extend the range and type of appraisal which can be done of a person. These are **special role communities**. The same person may occupy more than one of these roles at the same time: a person may be a member of many different moral communities all at the same time.

In Case #3 above, consider that once Karen became a parent, it became appropriate to use moral language about obligations and prohibitions she has relative to her children. These concepts and rules were not applicable to her before she became a parent. This moral language was layered onto the expectations we hold of her just as a person. Had she never become a mother, she would not have had these additional moral obligations and prohibitions. Of course, all of us have certain moral obligations relative to the children in our example. We should not harm or injure them unnecessarily. We should be truthful with them, and so forth. These are moral obligations and prohibitions we have, not because they are our children, but because they are persons and we are persons, and these expectations protect things which all persons want and need in order to flourish, or in some cases, in order just to survive. These are standards of the general moral community. But their mother has a special duty to provide for things such as their shelter and nourishment. This is a duty which is other than what we have. Accordingly, for her to omit or refuse to perform certain actions for her children will make her accountable under the special concepts and rules appropriate to her parental role. Whereas, our omission to perform the same action for her children would not make us appraisable because these concepts and rules have no application to us.

The classic professions of medicine and law have long dealt with the issue of special role standards. Indeed, each of these professions has developed its own code of ethics to publicize the language of these standards. For example, physicians are obligated in a way in which nonphysicians are not to "come to the aid of the sick." The kinds of actions and attempts that they must make differ from those which persons in general must make. Likewise, defense attorneys must represent their clients zealously, within the bounds of the law, with all of the competency they can muster, irrespective of their clients' guilt or innocence. Such lawyers may be appraisable for omitting to perform some act that persons in general might think unnecessary to perform, or even that we do not know how to perform, or do not want to perform. But we would not be appraisable for failing or refusing to perform these actions because the person was not our client. However, the defense attorney who did not do so would certainly be morally accountable. Other professions or sub-communities may also develop codes of conduct, whether formal or informal, which clarify or publicize specific moral standards for their

---

[11]There is a helpful discussion of the relationship between general and special role obligations in Louis G. Lombardi, <u>Moral Analysis: Foundations, Guides, and Application</u> (Albany: State University of New York Press, 1988), pp. 43-65.

members.
     Some special role standards are voluntarily accepted and some are not. Sometimes persons swear allegiance, sign codes of conduct, make pledges or vows. These are examples of voluntarily accepting a set of moral standards which were not applicable before. At other times, some persons have special role standards placed upon them even though they engaged in no deliberate act of acceptance.   Military draftees may be the clearest case of the nonvoluntary imposition of role standards, but even here there can be some voluntary aspects. Draftees do sometimes feel a commitment to their country. Perhaps they might not go so far as to enlist, but if a draft notice comes, they might willingly accept the role of soldier. On the other hand, draftees may express moral reservations about the conduct of war , and receive alternative assignments, thereby refusing some of the role obligations of a soldier.
     The decision to enter a profession, or in most cases, to become a parent, is typically regarded as a voluntary entrance into a special role, and with this comes the willing assumption of special role obligations and prohibitions, morally speaking, even if we do not know the full range of these. There are few parents who know the full range of moral expectations under which they will be held accountable when they have their first child. So, even though there is a language about this difference between voluntarily and involuntarily accepted roles, there are also still times when we are held appraisable under special role rules and concepts, even if we did not voluntarily or knowingly choose them.
     Some unique difficulties arise when one considers the relationship between moral appraisals made of persons just as persons, and those appraisals which are made because a person belongs in some special role. Not all cultural communities seem to handle these difficulties in the same way. The practice varies. So, a description of what we do in ordinary moral language whenever general moral expectations come into contact with our special ones is highly complex.
     1) There are times when general moral standards are compatible with our special role standards and we are appraisable under either or both. Persons should not steal, and neither should parents or soldiers, or such.
     2) There are times when our special roles in life impose obligations or aspirations upon us which are not general moral obligations for the rest of the moral community of human persons, and we are morally accountable under these, even though they are not universally applicable to all persons.
     3) There are times when our special roles in life prohibit us from conduct or label as vices certain character traits which general moral standards would permit, and we are expected to avoid such conduct, even though not everyone is morally expected to do so.
     4) There are times when our special roles in life impose moral standards which conflict with our general moral rules, and we may choose to be appraised under the special role concepts and rules, provided that our conduct is not prohibited by standards which belong to the general moral community of persons as persons.
     To illustrate how this process might work consider the following example which discusses how one's religious beliefs sometimes impose special moral obligations.

A couple of times a week Sue plays tennis with a group of girlfriends at the club. They all usually make a morning of it, playing tennis, and then having lunch. Sue is sitting at the table with three of her girlfriends when the conversation turns to their husbands and marriages. One woman, Kay, says that she believes that the man is the head of the household. He should handle the money and have the final say in family matters. All the other women, including Sue, cannot believe that Kay holds what they consider to be antiquated views. They all hold that marriage is a partnership, share and share alike, make decisions jointly, etc. When they challenge Kay, saying that she must believe in the submissive wife's role because her husband or some other person has brainwashed her, Kay replies, "No, it's not that at all. I do believe I should be submissive. But it's a matter of moral conviction for me. My interpretation of the Bible is that that is what it teaches a wife's role is, and I accept this. I'm not saying you should or that every woman should. You have to decide that for yourself."

This is an example of a self-appraisal which rests on moral concepts or principles derived from one's religious text or tradition. The *choice of* and *participation in* a religious tradition is a special role decision which is usually voluntary, although not always so. The religious tradition and its texts may supplement our set of general moral concepts and rules used as standards in appraisal. If we apply the four categories identified earlier for relating special role obligations to general obligations to the types of examples which could mimic the one provided above, we can see how moral practice proceeds.

1) There are general moral obligations which are also consistent with those derived from religious text and tradition (e.g., You should not steal. Do not commit adultery. Do not lie.)

2) There are standards based on religious tradition or texts which obligate persons who choose that religion to act in a way that general moral standards do not. Kay's use of the moral concept of *submission* is a good example of such an obligation. Another example is the Christian moral imperative: "Love your enemies." A religious person who believes he should love his enemies is certainly free to work as hard as he can at this. He may attend training courses, forgive all manner of wrongs, turn the other cheek, or go the second mile. What is important for us to note is that while there is no general moral standard which obligates such conduct for all persons in general, neither is there a general moral standard which prohibits us from doing so. "Loving your enemies" is within a zone of permission.

If one chooses to follow the teachings of his religion in such conduct, he is permitted to do so. It is important also to acknowledge that those who recognize an obligation to love one's enemies normally understand it to be different from their general moral obligations "to treat others fairly," "not to cause harm unnecessarily," and "to treat others with respect and dignity." Indeed, it seems that a religious believer must say "loving your enemies" requires conduct which goes beyond these general duties, or else he is not marking anything by this standard which is not already addressed by general moral concepts and rules. Religious believers probably do their sub-community a disservice and undercut its uniqueness if they define their special moral concepts and rules in such a way as to be reducible to those already well-established in general moral language. In fact, one of the ways religions enrich human experience is precisely by maintaining their uniqueness, and many religions recognize this in their theological language by stressing the requirement of "conversion," or "catechism," or "induction."

3) There are standards based on religious tradition or texts which prohibit conduct, or label as vicious certain character traits which are morally permitted under general moral standards. Some examples of these prohibitions would be requirements to abstain from conduct such as the use of alcoholic beverages, dancing with a person of the opposite sex, wearing make-up, or adorning oneself with expensive clothes, etc. There are no general moral standards that forbid this kind of conduct, so they are discretionary; and persons may choose whether to abstain or not for reasons of religious preference, or simply because one wishes to do so. Our tastes may certainly be guided by our religious texts or traditions in such areas.   Of course, there might be reasons other than one's religion for a person to avoid such conduct. Someone may refuse to engage in the prohibited conduct simply because of his personal tastes, and for no religious reason at all.

4) Finally, there are standards based on religious tradition or texts which are in conflict with a general moral standard. Consider, for example, the biblical narrative about Abraham's near-sacrifice of Isaac. According to the story, Abraham was directed by God to sacrifice his son, Isaac (Genesis 22: 1-14). Clearly, then, Abraham was commanded by God to perform an action which under general moral standards would be prohibited ("Do not murder" or "Do not kill innocent persons"). In fact, there is a sense in which the Bible presents this command of God in such a way as to stress that it is contrary to ordinary moral expectations in order to point out that this is precisely the way God is testing the amount of faithful submission Abraham possesses.

However, while a claim such as this may have some theological merits, as certain ethical theories have suggested, ordinary moral practice shows that the dangers for harm and injury are too great to be ignored whenever general moral standards are disregarded, or special role obligations or prohibitions are privileged about them. Putting aside general moral considerations destroys the relationships built upon them. In the story of Abraham and his young son Isaac, a relationship of trust and expectation is built upon the moral standards (rules and concepts) which are appropriate for appraising not merely the relationship between two persons, but especially the special role of parent to child. Whenever Abraham takes the religious leap away from these general moral standards, as well as his additional special moral obligations as a parent, and acts according to his belief that the voice of God has directed him to sacrifice his son, his conduct destroys the relationship built upon the other relevant moral standards.

The first time that Abraham asks his son to go and make sacrifice, Isaac goes along dutifully, and in ignorance of his father's plan to sacrifice him. According to the narrative, Abraham ties Isaac to the altar, and is on the downstroke with the knife before God stops him, providing a ram instead. In this case, Isaac is spared. Abraham is praised for being willing to obey God's command to sacrifice his son, even though this action required the suspension of moral standards about how to treat persons, and most especially one's child. Imagine, though, what might happen the next time his father wants young Isaac to go with him to make a sacrifice. It is easy to see that Isaac would be reluctant to go with dear old dad this time! Even if Isaac forgave Abraham for his near-sacrifice, the relationship would never be the same again. Something is fundamentally altered, and the reason is clearly explicable. Morality has been subordinated to religious intuition, and anytime this occurs the tender membrane which guards those relationships we want and need most is jeopardized. In the recent past, the cases of the Ayatollah Khomeni, Jim Jones and Charles Manson illustrate that our ordinary moral practice is to condemn following religious obligations *whenever these conflict* with general moral standards.

What is being said about privileging general moral standards over religious ones whenever they conflict is equally true of conflicts caused by other special roles also; it is not unique to moral standards derived from one's religion that such conflicts sometimes occur. Moral practice shows a disposition to be certain that two things be preserved anytime our general moral concepts and rules come up against the special role moral language we use in the sub-communities to which we belong. 1) With only a few well-established exceptions, special role obligations and prohibitions are binding only for those who voluntarily accept them. They are not binding on all persons. And one of the ways of demonstrating the uniqueness of the role is the manner in which its moral standards define the terrain. In the case of our example of religious obligations, Kay is quite right when she does not insist that her sense of obligation to be a "submissive" wife is to be imposed on every wife. It is a matter of her unique religious commitment. And her willingness to be appraised under this standard defines her as a believer of a certain sort. 2) Whenever general moral standards contradict those derived from special roles in such a way that harm will result from conduct under the special role standard, the general standards are privileged about the special ones. People who sacrifice their children will be blamed. It will not do to say that "God told me to." Or, to take another example, believing that Charles Manson is the messiah is one thing. However, acting according to his messianic command to kill persons in order to show your loyalty to him is something else entirely. Indeed, this latter action will be morally condemned by the general moral community.

Moral and Legal Appraisals

The moral and legal appraisal standards in a community often share many of the same concepts and rules. To do something appraised as illegal, as to do something described as immoral, requires a justification or an excuse. But for all that they have in common, there are some important differences between morality and law which can best be uncovered by watching how we practice moral appraisal in cases in which morality and law come into contact.

> *Suppose that a baby is taken to her family physician and examined because she has fever and diarrhea. Let's say the physician does a routine examination and sends her home, asking that the child be brought in on the following day. On the second day, the doctor prescribes some medication. Then, on the third day, the baby's case worsens. Knowing that the doctor is not in his office , the parents take the baby to the hospital emergency room, where they are told that it is against policy for the hospital staff to treat anyone already under a doctor's care without contacting the doctor. Unable to reach the doctor, and thus denied treatment, let's say the parents return home, where the baby dies.*

There was a time when a hospital had a legal right to refuse to treat whomever it wished. Under such law, the hospital in our example did nothing legally wrong. But was it morally justified in refusing treatment? Well, we might disagree in our answers, but we would not disagree that this is a question which cannot be resolved by appeal to law alone, a question that is very important to notice about the way we practice morality in this context.

Although useful in alerting us to moral issues, our example illustrates that law is not understood in ordinary practice to be coextensive with morality. Law simply is not able to exhaust all the ways we use language to make moral appraisals. Furthermore, sometimes law in general, or any one or more of the many specific laws of a land may itself be appraised morally. We do sometimes say, "I know it's the law, but it's not right," or "It may be the law, but there is a higher requirement on me."

As we have seen with special role issues, relating moral appraisal standards to other practices (e.g., religion) can require a highly complex description. This is true of our understanding about the relationship between morality and law as well. Generalizations about what occurs would include the following. 1) Some conduct is appraised as both morally praiseworthy and legal. In fact, most human conduct may be taken under this description. Examples of such coextensive appraisals would be telling the truth, keeping your promises, and not stealing. 2) Some conduct may be appraised as both morally blameworthy and illegal (e.g., stealing and murder). In this category of judgments it seems that the community has such a vital interest in enforcing its moral appraisals that it will use police power to coerce conformity. Here occurs what some call **the legislation of morality** in the sense that conduct which is considered immoral is also illegal. Criminals may also be morally blameworthy, and this explains why we expect them to show regret and remorse, to feel guilt and shame over their conduct. The wrong they have done is not just an offence against law, but they have also torn the moral membrane which binds the community together.

3) There is some conduct which is not describable under a legal prohibition, but it is still morally blameworthy. For example, there are no laws against breaking promises, except in certain special cases of contracts. However, we do consider it morally wrong to break a promise. If Jill borrows Becky's class notes and promises to return them, she has an obligation to do so. But what kind of obligation does she have? Certainly it is not one of personal taste. Neither is it an obligation of etiquette. But it is not a legal obligation either. If she fails to return the notes, Becky cannot call the police and have Jill arrested. There is no law against failing to return notes, for such conduct is not describable under a legal prohibition. Jill's obligation is moral, yet it is quite real and serious. If Jill fails to return the notes as promised, then Becky will expect her to provide a justification or an excuse for not doing so. Likewise, so will other members in the moral community. Jill's ability to be trusted, to borrow notes in the future, and to continue her special role as Becky's friend may all be affected by her response to this moral appraisal.

4) There is some conduct which we morally praise, but which is not lawful. One thinks immediately of acts of civil disobedience and conscientious demonstration against a morally objectionable law or policy. Refusal to fight in war and acts of nonviolent civil disobedience come to mind as examples of actions which one might describe as morally praiseworthy but illegal.

For Discussion

1) Make a list of 5 intensifying discriminator words which compose part of the vocabulary of moral appraisal as you observe it. Use these in a example describing an action, attempt, or omission in order to recognize the significance of the moral considerations they mark. Avoid using those provided by the author.

2) Make a list of 5 moral concepts which compose part of the vocabulary of moral appraisal as you observe it. Use these in a sentence describing an action, attempt, or omission in order to recognize the significance of the moral considerations they mark. Avoid using those provided by the author.

3) The position taken by the author is that there are no exact synonyms in language, and specifically there are none in moral language. Do you agree with this position? If there are only near-synonyms, but no exact synonyms, what significance would this have for the language of moral appraisal?

4) Choose several moral concepts from those provided in the table given in this chapter and find near-synonyms for them. Try to note the differences between these terms and think about the importance of the difference for moral appraisal.

5) Show how each of the following may be taken under multiple descriptions as a matter of personal taste, a rule of etiquette, a moral appraisal, or a legal judgment. Explain what considerations from this chapter you used in forming your position.

    a) Persons should not go to the beach in the nude.
    b) Persons should not get drunk.
    c) You did the right thing by refusing to attend the meeting.
    d) Persons should not overeat.
    e) You should listen to and heed the advice of your elders.
    f) Do not play in your food.
    g) Do not take pleasure in the misfortunes of others.
    h) Be nice to everyone.
    i) You should tip the waitress 15%.
    j) Do not waste food.

6) Using the traits which seem common to moral rules as they are employed as standards in ordinary language, evaluate the adequacy of the following suggested rules. Explain what considerations from this chapter you used in forming your position.

    a) It is permitted to lie whenever a person thinks it is necessary.
    b) We ought to feed all hungry Americans.
    c) Persons should not force or coerce other persons.
    d) Persons are entitled to enough to eat and drink only if they work for it.
    e) You should keep your promise to kill all those who are immoral.
    f) Treat others as you want them to treat you.
    g) Do not take things which don't belong to you.
    h) Do not deceive others.

7) Relying on our discussion about the relationship between general moral standards used of persons as persons, and those which belong to our special roles in sub-communities, give an example of an action, attempt, or omission which one could commit in the role named which would fit into each of the categories of relationship for the following special roles: a) Compatible with general moral standards; b) Obligates beyond what is required by general moral standards; c) Prohibits in a way not done by general moral standards; d) Contradicts general moral standards.

    a) A Catholic Priest
    b) A dorm or resident hall floor supervisor
    c) A police officer
    d) A public defender
    e) The child of an aging parent

Chapter Two: Determining Morally Appraisable Entities

Introduction

We have been speaking of the group or groups of entities who use moral language as a ***moral community*** .   Observation of moral practice can disclose some of the basic features which determine which entities are members of the moral community. Several of these should be noted now.

1) In order to be considered a member of a moral community an entity must be capable of using moral language. It must make appraisals both of its own conduct and character, as well as that of other entities. At first glance, this observation seems to be of relatively little use since it appears to be somewhat circular.   But this observation is actually quite helpful. It points to the practice of regarding an entity as a member of the moral community only if it can conceive of itself in such a way as to be able to employ moral concepts and considerations in the description of its conduct and character. If it cannot or does not do this, then the entity is not a member of a moral community.

2) In order to be a member of the moral community, an entity must be such that other entities do, in fact, use moral language describing conduct and character. What this manner of practice suggests is that being a member of a moral community is a conferred status, not an inherent one.

3) In this world, there are members of the general moral community, and there are nonmembers. But it is very important not to confuse membership in the general moral community of persons with the actual determination of appraisability in a specific situation. It may appear, at first, that saying that there are members of the moral community and nonmembers of it is another way of saying that there are both appraisable entities (i.e., those which must give an account of their conduct) and nonappraisable entities (i.e., those which need not give an account of their conduct). However, the issue is somewhat more complicated than this in actual practice.

To be **appraisable** simply means *that a member of the moral community has his conduct described under a moral concept, rule, or some special role standard*. Most of the time, a member of the moral community is appraisable (accountable) for his conduct.   However, there are sometimes conditions which make a member of a moral community nonappraisable. A description of moral practice identifies several of these. For example, when the entity has no other choice, or is forced or coerced, or is unavoidably ignorant, mentally deficient, or morally innocent. These conditions for nonappraisability shall be discussed later in this book.

4) Our understanding of the relationship between members of the moral community and their appraisability is sometimes further confused by failing to notice that within the class of entities which are not members of the moral community, there is a language which indicates that some of these entities are given moral consideration, even though they are not appraisable. Put simply, this means that persons often extend the range of moral appraisal to cover their conduct toward some entities which are not capable of moral conduct themselves. Animals represent the most common form of entities extended such moral consideration. Moral practice also reveals that moral appraisals are made about the way persons treat the natural environment as well.   The features of the natural environment are not themselves morally appraised. We do not say that a tree can be *cruel,* or a meadow *kind*, except in "personifying" metaphors. However, we do recognize

that many environmental features, as well as animals, are valuable. And, at least in the case of animals, we acknowledge that they have interests and desires which are to be respected. Such recognition and acknowledgement shows in language whenever we make appraisals of the conduct of members of the moral community toward the environment and animals, and sometimes when we use moral or aesthetic concepts in descriptions of environmental features or life forms. This is what it means to show such entities moral consideration.

Of course, there are also some entities which do not belong to the moral community and which are also not extended moral consideration. Usually, these are nonsentient creatures and objects such as rocks, cans, etc. For example, it would not be cruel to crush a coke can in your hand; but it would be cruel to crush a bird in your hand. Neither the coke can nor the bird is a member of the moral community; but moral practice shows that the bird has been extended moral consideration, although the can has not.

Qualifying as a Member of the Moral Community

We do not use evaluative language, let alone moral appraisal language, about the vast majority of things which make up our world. Moral appraisals are reserved for a relatively minute class of things. For example, you would never hear anyone appraise the character of a rock: "You should be igneous, not metamorphic." The concepts themselves are geologic, not moral. Neither do we address a moral judgment to a tree, "It was wrong of you to drop your leaves here." In fact, if you have ever heard some eccentric geologist or fanatical dendrologist say any such thing, you probably laughed. When it was popular among children a decade or so ago to have "pet rocks", the reason was because everyone knew that using moral language of rocks was a very odd way of treating an entity that was not a member of the moral community. Moral language is simply not used to evaluate the conduct or character of minerals and botanical entities because they are incapable of the conduct we find significant to mark with a moral appraisal.

What moral practice discloses is that we do not make appraisals of entities which have no intentional capacities. An **intentional capacity** *is the ability to form and desire and initiate its satisfaction.* Minerals, for example, have no intentional capacities. They do not desire or seek anything. So, they cannot be faulted, or blamed, or praised for the ways in which they seek to satisfy their desires, or for that matter, for the desires which they have.

Of course, there is sort of grammar that suggests that even such entities as plants have intentions. We do sometimes say things like, "The plant is bent that way because it wants to get to the light." While such language suggests that we may think of plants as having intentions, there is nothing about the way the plant is bent or bends that *requires* us to use this language. We might just as well use some other description. However, in the case of the entities about which we make moral appraisals the practice seems just the opposite. What I mean is that we would have to justify NOT considering them as having intentions or as acting on their intentions.

Of some animals we not only have a language of intention, but they seem to require us to treat them as intentional, even if they do not have language capacities. If Jenny, my German Shepherd, goes to the door and stands, I say "She wants to go outside," or I may ask her, "Do you want to go outside?" This grammar seems to register that I believe that she has intentions. She has desires and interests, and can communicate these to me by her conduct. She even has the ability to require me to treat her as an intentional entity in some senses. If I go to the door and open it asking, "Jenny, do you want to go outside?" she may simply sit or lie at rest, indicating to me, "No, I do not want to."

But let's explore the question of how an entity possesses membership in the moral community a little further. I can say of Jenny, "She knows it is wrong to bite." What I mean by this is that when we play together she often puts her teeth around my arm or hand, but she does not bite down. At first, we might simply say that the force of "wrong" in this appraisal is behavioristic. That is, that I have conditioned her by punishment and reprimand not to bite down on me. However, can we say for certain that the reason she does not bite is because of such conditioning? After all, I remember saying things like, "Ouch, Jenny, that hurts!" when she was a younger pup and would bite. Perhaps she has come to appreciate that I do not wish to be bitten, and that our relationship is on firmer footing if she omits biting. Do we need to know what Jenny is thinking in order to know whether I am making a moral appraisal? Is it insufficient to go simply by her bodily movements alone?

These are deep philosophical waters. Our inability to know what another entity is thinking, the very fact that we cannot get at such information, are both part of what philosophers call the *Other Minds Problem* . The truth is that I cannot know what Jenny is thinking, and so I cannot say for certain whether Jenny knows it is wrong to bite or chooses not to be vicious *because she knows she will be punished if she does*; or *because I have expressed pain and injury when she does, and she does not want to hurt me*. And without this knowledge, I am really not very comfortable saying that she is the kind of entity which can conduct herself morally.

One partial solution to the other minds problem may be found in the view that an entity could communicate to me what it was thinking. I could have access to Jenny's intentions and thoughts if she could communicate with me. But Jenny cannot tell me what she is thinking. Her behavior is all I have to go on, and it is not clear enough to resolve this puzzle for me. An interesting feature of my relationship to my dog is that she does know when she is permitted, even when she *ought* to bite (i.e., when I command her to do so). But, is this because she wants to please me, realizing that I am the kind of being which enjoys being pleased? Or does she do it because I reward her? Or does she do it because she is afraid of punishment if she does not? Or does she do it because she knows that I would not make such a command if I were not in danger, and she does not want to see me hurt? With nonhuman animals such as Jenny, all of this is very difficult, if not impossible, to determine. If such animals could communicate verbally, then some important questions might be answered about whether they are to be regarded as members of the moral community.

My sons can communicate in this manner, as can most other humans. But the matter of knowing what someone intended to do or say is not nearly so simple as just letting him tell us what he was thinking. Persons may sometimes tell us that they intended to do something, when they really had no such intention at all. Or, they may not know what their intentions were, or what they were thinking when they acted. Or, sometimes intentions can be multiple, and so a person may actually be unclear himself about which of his intentions was most prominent.

Suppose, however, that we put aside these additional difficulties with the determination of what one's intentions were and ask a different sort of question. Is intentional capacity the only factor which moral practice shows to be uniquely shared by those within the moral community and absent from all others.

I say of my niece, "She knows it is wrong to bite." or "Kam is not vicious". Do I mean to be using "wrong" in the same sense as when speaking of my dog, or in some other sense? I can appreciate, as you can, that this is arguable. Some psychologists might want to say that the value indicator word "wrong" and the moral concept "vicious" function in exactly the same manner in both descriptions. They might hold that my niece has been conditioned to avoid biting because biting brings punishment.

Yet, I am not at all sure that ordinary moral practice really supports this view. Let me explain wherein I think moral practice shows that there is a difference. The difference between my niece and my dog is not just that my niece can use language. It is also the fact that she can understand certain considerations which I might bring to her attention. For example, one way that I could be instrumental in my niece's decision that it was wrong to bite, or in her choice not to be vicious, would be to take her aside and talk with her. But I am not simply making a point about the practice of using language here. I wish to call attention to how language is being used.

I might ask what reasons Kam had for biting, why she was doing such a thing. I might ask about the outcomes she expected. I could explain to her how others felt when she did this, and ask her how she would feel if she were bitten by someone else. Since my niece is the type of entity who can understand and appreciate the importance of such questions, then this suggests that she is capable of functioning as a member of the moral community. The difference between my dog and my niece lies in my niece's *capacity for appreciating how her conduct affects others*.

My niece may *tell* me that she has stopped biting because she realized that this conduct displeased her parents, whom she has a desire to make happy. Or, she may add that she realized it also caused pain to others, and they did not want to be around her when she would bite. And certainly, if she tells me these kinds of things, then the force of the word "wrong," when used of my niece, means more than just that she would be punished if she bit others.

My niece is capable of responding and acting toward others in certain ways which indicate she appreciates that other entities have rights, desires, and interests, and even that her own interests are connected to those of others. I could certainly say to my niece that she should stop biting or not be vicious because it displeased her parents, and hurt others, and that others will soon not want to be around her if she continues such behavior. Perhaps my niece would change her behavior, or maybe she would continue, indicating that she does not care what others think. But the point is that my conduct indicates that I believe she is able to appreciate such an approach. In all of this, I *appealed to her ability to appreciate the desires, rights, and interests of others,* such as her parents' interest in being proud of their daughter, or the fact that others have a desire not to be bitten. Now can you imagine this little heart-to-heart talk making much sense to my dog? Probably not, and that is very significant. The point is that we simply would not practice conversing with a dog in this manner.

An important by-product of deliberation of this sort is the capacity to *feel regret* . By means of my conversation, I may be able to engender in my niece a feeling of regret for her failure to consider her previous conduct from the point of view of others' rights, desires, and interests. The capacity to regret is an important feature in moral practice, and members of the moral community all show that they possess such ability. Of course, I recognize that feeling regret and making one to feel regret is often misused and abused in moral appraisal. Persons feel regret or guilt who should not. Regret and guilt are used by others as power strategies to get us to do what they want us to. But we are not commenting at this time on the proper conditions which legitimize guilt, we are only noting that moral language reveals that members of the moral community have the capacity to feel regret.

We cannot be sure that most animals have the capacity to appreciate that other entities have rights, desires, and interests and that their conduct may affect these in desirable as well as undesirable ways. In fact, humans are the only animals that we know for certain to have this ability.[12] My being able to speak to my niece in the manner I have described is part of what it means for me to be a member of the moral community, and her capacity to appreciate these considerations is part of what it means for her to be a member of the moral community. To be a member of the moral community, I must also have her ability to appreciate such considerations, and she must have my ability to raise them in regard to the conduct and character of others.

But we are not finished yet. There is something further to uncover. The way I conduct my "heart to heart" with my niece discloses something else about being a member of the moral community. *She can also express her resolve to change* her behavior. She can decide to try to be more attentive to the needs, desires, and interests of others. Or perhaps she may alter her behavior out of self-interest, because she wants to be accepted by others into relationships which she both wants and needs.   The point is not whether she desires to change for the "right" reasons, but only that she has the capacity to weigh this out and plan to change.

This capacity requires that an entity be capable of some highly sophisticated *deliberate reasoning*. It would be nonsense to fault a tree for dropping its leaves in one place rather than another, not only because the tree cannot move, but also because the tree does not decide, or deliberate, or think about whether to drop its leaves in one place rather than another. It cannot take into account the rights, desires, or interests of any other entity which might be affected by where it drops its leaves. It does not weigh its options. It cannot consider whether what adversely affected others in the past should be altered so as to prevent this from occurring in the future. But the language I use with my niece shows that I consider her capable of such deliberation.

Philosophers include this capacity in the concept of self-consciousness. An entity which is a member of the moral community is considered to possess self-consciousness. Any member of the moral community must have the capacity to perform self-evaluation. It must not only be able to be aware of its desires, motives, and reasons for acting, attempting, or omitting. It must also have the capacity to formulate a wish to change its behavior and refine a plan for doing so as the result of deliberative reasoning. It is her capacity for self-consciousness which makes it possible for me to pull my niece aside and begin reasoning with her, suggesting that she stop biting because it displeases her parents and it hurts others,

---

[12]See Daniel Dennett's discussion of the various orders of intentionality in "Conditions of Personhood," in Identities of Persons, edited by Amelie Rorty (Berkeley: University of California Press, 1976), pp. 111ff.

so that others will soon not want to be around her. It makes sense for me to speak this way to my niece. I would not make such suggestions if I did not believe her capable of self-consciousness. It is precisely this lack of self-consciousness, more than any other single factor, which makes it inappropriate for me to try this way of talking with nonhuman entities, even animals.[13]

If we have our account of moral practice substantially right, then there are several interesting issues which emerge now.

1) If an animal could develop a sign language which would enable it to communicate in ways analogous to nonspeaking humans, these considerations might be complicated in the extreme. Perhaps an animal might then display a self-consciousness which heretofore we have been unable to recognize. If it manifested intentional capacity, language, reason, self-consciousness, it could presumably use moral language and thereby become a member of the moral community. While the membership of the moral community is often thought to be confined only to human persons, if an entity replicated the features which are present in moral practice, then it may be a member of the moral community, even though it is nonhuman. Nonhuman animals with a developed sign language of this sort might make moral appraisals of human persons, and of each other.

2) By the account we have developed, some special notice should be taken of what we do in moral practice with entities which are genetically human but which fail to possess all of the features typical of membership in the moral community. In practice, these persons are treated with moral consideration, but not as members of the moral community. We value them; but we do not appraise or judge them.

3) In moral practice there are some entities which seem to possess the features noted but they are not humans. In fact, they may not even be biological life forms. I am referring specifically to the use of moral language in appraising institutions, nations, corporations, and so forth. The language about corporate moral appraisal shows that we believe that some artificial entities like corporations and nations can satisfy the conditions of **moral personhood,** and that they are regarded as members of the moral community capable of being moral agents. We do appraise their conduct.[14]

Benefits of Membership in the Moral Community

Being a member of the general moral community, made up of persons who exemplify the features identified in this chapter, has many implications. The most important of these is that other members of the moral community are willing to form relationships with us, especially those relationships necessary for our survival, but

---

[13]Ibid.

[14]Peter A. French, Collective and Corporate Responsibility (New York: Columbia University Press, 1984), pp. 31-48; 78-94. For different approaches see John R. Danley, "Corporate Moral Agency: The Case for Anthropological Bigotry," in Ethical Issues in Professional Life, edited by Callahan, pp. 269-274. And Manuel G. Velasquez, "Why Corporations are not Morally Responsible for Anything They Do," in Ethical Theory and Business, edited by Tom Beauchamp and Norman Bowie (Englewood Cliffs, N.J.: Prentice Hall, 1988), pp.69-76.

also those which afford us our best opportunities to be happy, to have a sense of fulfilled purposes and achieved goals, and to flourish during our lifetimes. This willingness on the part of others to form such relationships depends greatly on the perception they have of the kind of person we are and how we conduct ourselves morally speaking.

Our recognition of the appropriateness of moral language as a guide for our conduct admits us into the relationships we want and need. If the moral community should come to believe that we no longer recognize moral language as binding on us, then this would mean the disintegration of confidence in us as someone worthy of just those kinds of relationship which we need and want.[15]

Possessing membership in the moral community of persons, therefore, is a benefit. Once we possess moral credit, then our behavior may either enhance or deflate its value. If we conduct ourselves, or appear to behave, in such a way as to be described as a breach of moral expectations, we will be accountable to the moral community. In these circumstances, other persons deserve a justification of our conduct or an excuse and an apology; or some redress for this breach, either because they have chosen to risk relationships with us in various ways, or because they have come to do so through the course of life's events. At the same time, since our moral credit has been called into question, we are entitled to offer a justification, or an excuse, or to ask for forgiveness and to give assurances of better conduct in the future.[16]

On the other hand, if we are unwilling in times of accountability to reveal our thinking, intentions, justifications, and excuses to others in the moral community, or if our description falls short of being one which is acceptable by others, then our moral credit will be damaged. At such times a serious accusation may be cast on our character. We may find difficulty in winning the confidence and trust of others, which means we will be denied the relationships we need and want in order to flourish. Or, at the very least, these relationships may be limited or significantly altered from their previous form.

Qualifying as an Entity Worthy of Moral Consideration

There is a difference between an entity's being such that we use the language of moral appraisal about its conduct and character, and its being deserving of moral consideration, and thereby acknowledged by members of the moral community as having worth. Moral practice reveals, of course, that all entities which are members of the moral community are also worthy of moral consideration. However, practice also reveals that there are entities which have interests and desires recognized by the moral community as worthy of protection and support. The moral community creates such consideration by using moral concepts and rules to guide the conduct of its members toward these other entities. Assignment of moral worth occurs whenever members of the moral community

---

[15]Kenneth Pahel, "The Public Process of Moral Adjudication," Social Theory and Practice 2 (Summer 1985): 191.

[16]Ibid. See also, Elizabeth L. Beardsley, "Moral Worth and Moral Credit," Philosophical Review 66 (1957).

place moral prohibitions and obligations on its own members relative to any entity whatever. There is a moral language about cruelty to animals and respect for trees, rivers. This kind of language reveals that the general moral community recognizes such entities as worthy of moral consideration.

About natural entities such as the redwoods, for example, we have a language which says that they should be left alone, protected, nurtured, loved, and/or admired. Persons express gratitude and appreciation **for** them. We protect them, blame those who abuse them, and such. But we do not make moral appraisals **of** their conduct or character, so they are not members of the moral community itself. This observation may be taken from moral practice in itself. As to whether there are conditions for determining which entities are worthy of moral consideration, this issue is discussed elsewhere. (**Cf. Are There Theoretical Criteria for Determining Which Entities Are Worthy of Moral Consideration? in Ch. 9**)

For Discussion

1) In one sentence, state your understanding of what the author means by "the moral community."

2) Are you a member of only one moral community, or of several? If several, give two or three examples. In those cases in which the standards recognized by general moral community come into conflict with those imposed by the special moral communities to which we choose to belong, which should take preeminence? (Remember our discussion of special roles and the ways in which the general moral community of all persons and our special moral communities are related in language).

3) State your understanding of the author's distinction between being a "member of the moral community" and "being worthy of moral consideration." Agree or disagree with his viewpoint. Give two reasons which support your position.

4) Under the criteria given by the author, should babies be regarded as members of the moral community or as entities worthy of moral consideration? What about human persons in comatose states?

5) Which of the following, if any, are appraisable entities and why? Explain what considerations from this chapter you used in forming your position.

    a) Commander Data in the television show "Star Trek: The Next Generation" (or any other android--such as in the movie D.A.R.Y.L.)

    b) Hal the Computer in the movie, "2001 a Space Odyssey" or Colossus in the movie "Colossus: The Forbin Project"

Chapter Three: Determining Appraisable Events

Introduction

Is everything that a person does morally appraisable? Are there some events which persons cause, or which happen to persons, which are not the proper subjects of moral appraisal? Are there events for which a person is appraisable which are not actions at all? Consider this chart which provides a partial list of event categories.

Events

Actions   Attempts   Omissions   Mistakes   Accidents   Sharings   Happenings

The class of events in our biographies includes more than our actions, as the above continuum shows. Even this exhibit is only meant to illustrate the range of events which are a part of our lives; it is not intended to be exhaustive. What it helps us see is that actions are only one type of event. A totally complete biography of a person would include more than the person's actions. It would also include things he attempted or omitted, as well as some things which just happened to him, or ways in which he shared with other persons in bringing about events.

For example, consider "waking up." This is an event which happens to us everyday, but are we appraisable for it? Probably not. There is some difference between a "waking up" which happens to us and an event for which we are accountable.[17] But there is a difference, and can we get at the difference by a description of when and how we use moral language? Our moral language reveals several kinds of events which are noteworthy.

1) A person may be the direct cause of an event because he has control over its occurrence. In such a case, he is **an agent** and the event is **an action.** He may directly cause a morally praiseworthy action, or he may cause a blameworthy or untoward action. A person may also cooperate with others in causing actions, and this may be done in more than one way. If the act could have occurred because of the action of others, regardless of the agent's cooperation, but he does participate, then he is still acting as an individual agent, along with others. The person is one of several **multiple agents** which are each and every one appraisable. However, if the act could not have occurred unless he acted in concert with others, either in its performance or its planning, and he does so, then the person is a part of a **group,** and the group is appraisable. This is not to say that the agent may not be appraisable as an individual as well, but only to note that appraisals of group conduct are made in ordinary language. So, a person may be appraised individually, along with other agents, as a group member, or in many combinations of these.

2) A person may be appraisable for events other than those he actually causes, whether individually, along with others, or in a group. Moral language is also used of the **attempts** made by persons. Attempts are exercises of effort to cause an event, but which fail to achieve their ends. They are unsuccessful acts or

---

[17]Irving Thalberg, "Verbs, Deeds and What Happens to Us," quoted in Judith Thomson, Acts and Other Events (Ithaca, N.Y.: Cornell, 1977).

omissions. Attempts of persons may be appraised individually or as a multiple agent. Groups may make attempts as well.

3) Sometimes a person may have regulative control, rather than direct control, over an event. He may insure the occurrence of an event by inaction, or he may prevent its occurrence by omitting to do it. In such cases, persons may be appraisable for their **omissions**. Persons may omit individually or as a multiple agent. Groups may omit in appraisable ways too.

4) Another way in which regulative control may be exercised is whenever a person **intervenes** to make it possible for an event to occur, which otherwise would not, or else attempts to do so. Groups too may intervene in such a way as to be appraisable.

Actions

Moral language is often concerned with tracing the **cause** of an event back to a person.[18] If the occurrence of an event required my participation, and without it the event could not have occurred, then I am a cause of the event. Yet, there are many examples of our causing things to happen for which we are not appraisable. I may sneeze, wake up, or outlive Bill. These events are traceable to me, but just because they are traced to me does not mean I am appraisable for them.

So, something else is needed in order to make an event in my biography appraisable as an action, other than simply that it is traceable to me as its cause. Think about sneezing. Is it possible to turn a sneeze into an appraisable act? You can say to me, "You should not have sneezed; it was wrong of you to do that." This is a description which could function as a legitimate value appraisal. The description could be a legitimate value appraisal if I sneezed in order "to frighten someone," or "to warn someone," or "to antagonize someone." If I have some *intention* in what I cause, then I am aware of it. I desire to do it. It is known to me.[19] The intentionally caused event is no longer simply a happening, it is an action. I am no longer just an entity with events happening in my life; I am **an agent**.

If we pay attention to the logic of many moral concepts which we know exemplify appraisability, we will see that they all imply that the person moved

---

[18]I am going to take this opportunity to suggest some fine studies of the concept of *agency* : what it means to do an act and to be appraisable for it. What I have to say on this subject is indebted largely to Donald Davidson, "Agency," in Essays on Actions and Events (New York: Oxford University Press, 1982), pp. 43-61. Another fine work is Jennifer Hornsby, Actions (London: Routledge & Kegan Paul, 1980). A quite technical work already noted is Judith Jarvis Thomson, Acts and Other Events. Robert Sokolowski, Moral Action: A Phenomenological Study (Bloomington: Indiana University Press, 1985) addresses moral action particularly, as does Eric D'arcy, Human Acts: An Essay in Their Moral Evaluation (Oxford: Clarendon Press). Action and Responsibility, ed. by Michael Bradie and Myles Brand (Bowling Green, OH: Bowling Green State University, 1980); Action Theory, ed. by Myles Brand and Douglas Walton (Dordrecht: D. Reidel, 1976); Donald Davidson, Essays on Actions and Events (Oxford: Clarendon Press, 1980; The Nature of Human Action, ed. by Myles Brand (Glenview: Scott, Foresman, 1970).

[19]The importance of this kind of knowing is discussed in Davidson, p. 50. See also, Kurt Baier, "Action and Agent," Monist 49 (1965).

intentionally.[20] He "insulted" her; she "lied" about what happened; Bill "cheated" Mary. These acts must be done intentionally.

One philosopher who has observed the importance of intention to our ordinary language of moral description is J. L. Mackie. Mackie has said that the most basic rule for what is appraisable in a person's biography is "an agent is responsible for all and only his intentional actions."[21] Mackie calls this **the Straight Rule of Responsibility.** However, this guide for appraisability seems to be very useful only until one considers the problem of determining how far we should extend a person's intentions. It is clear that there are some appraisals in language which extend intentions well beyond what a person voices as his conscious intent in acting, attempting, or omitting as he did. Sometimes, it is very difficult to differentiate what one intended to do from the effects of one's action which were not a part of one's intention.

> *Suppose we are at the neighborhood baseball diamond to practice with our team. Let's imagine that you are pitching some balls and various team members are taking batting practice. Up to bat now is Jimmy. Jimmy picks up the bat, takes a few practice swings, and then hits the ball you pitched. The ball is a foul, it curves back behind the third base dugout and crashes right through Big Robbie's windshield!*

Is Jimmy accountable for smashing Big Robbie's windshield? Well, this question does not seem to be easy to answer. We know Jimmy intended to pick up the bat. He intended to swing it. He even intended to hit the ball. We know this because Jimmy's observable behavior was "walking to the plate," "facing the pitcher," "bat in hand," "swinging at the ball," and "hitting the ball." He did not have to say, "I am going to pick up the bat," "I want to hit the ball," etc. It was enough to observe how he moved. Yet, Jimmy might say, "Sure, I intended to hit the ball, but I did not intend to break out the windshield." The long and short of this is that in determining whether he intended to break the windshield, we are left only with what Jimmy says his intentions were. There is no way, based on his overt behavior, to infer his intentions with respect to the windshield. So, he could be saying truly that he did not intend to break out the windshield.

On the other hand, there may be some way of determining that Jimmy did **not** intend to break the windshield simply by describing his overt behavior. If Jimmy had been standing at the plate talking to the catcher, with the bat resting on his shoulder, and you pitched the ball, which in turn struck the bat and flew over to smash Big Robbie's windshield, then that would be an *accident*--perhaps Jimmy's or perhaps the pitcher's. We would say the breaking of the windshield was certainly unintentional. Yet, even under this description Jimmy might still be appraisable. We do typically require responsibility descriptions of persons whose

---

[20]See Hornsby's discussion of bodily movements and actions, pp. 1-33 and Robert Audi, "Intending," Journal of Philosophy 70 (1973).

[21]J.L. Mackie, Ethics: Inventing Right and Wrong (New York: Penguin Books, 1977), p. 208.

accidents cause harm. So, we do sometimes appraise persons even though their actions were unintentional. Something's happening by accident does not exempt the person who caused it from moral appraisability. Indeed, we recognize appeals such as "it happened by accident" as excuses which diminish blame. On the other hand, we might claim that perhaps Jimmy was "careless" or "reckless." "Had he been more careful the accident would not have happened," we might say. The question may arise, "Why did he turn around and start talking to the catcher just as you threw the ball?"

Be that as it may, the original description of the story indicates Jimmy "swung the bat" and "struck the ball" intentionally, and not by accident. Although Jimmy says that it was not his intention to break Big Robbie's windshield, it is possible that we may still use language which holds him accountable [22]

Jimmy's case reminds us that the consequences of actions sometimes stretch out rather far, and that the effects of what we do intentionally may not have been a part of what we are conscious of in doing the act itself.   Joel Feinberg has called this the **accordion effect** of actions.[23] Feinberg points out what we all know: that ordinary moral language shows that we do often hold a person appraisable for his actions, and for all the effects of his actions which he also intends. The reason why we hold a person appraisable for the intended effects of his action, and not just for the movement of his body--which is the act itself--is that acts do in fact unfold like accordions.   Otherwise, a person might protest that he should be appraised for "pulling the trigger of the gun," which he did intend to do, but not for "causing the death" of the person at whom the gun is fired.

But appealing to the concept of the accordion effect of actions really provides us no litmus test for determining how far one's intention extends down the accordion effect.   It does not give us a way of looking into one's psyche to know what our shooter intended or what Jimmy intended, for that matter. Determining appraisability under such conditions is especially complicated when someone is trying to protest that his intentions do not extend across the entire accordion to cover all of the consequences of his action. So, it would help greatly if there were some clue in our ordinary moral practice which would help us understand how far we do, in fact, extend appraisability through the accordion effect.

Let us look at what kind of descriptions and language we might use in the case of Big Robbie's broken windshield. Consider that by "taking the bat" and "striking the ball" with parked cars nearby, Jimmy knew there was some risk, be it ever so slight (depending on his ability as a hitter), that a ball might hit a car. By not asking that cars be moved, he assumed this risk too. He knew "breaking a windshield" was one of the possible outcomes of his action. Indeed, since Big Robbie's car was parked near the fence, he knew "breaking Big Robbie's windshield" was one of the possible outcomes of his action. But he acted anyway. All of this makes perfectly good sense, and could be said to Jimmy with no

---

[22]See Arthur Danto's discussion of the difference between basic actions, such as moving a hand, and other actions that are caused by the basic acts, such as moving a stone. "Basic Actions," American Philosophical Quarterly 2 (1965): 108-125.

[23]Joel Feinberg, Doing and Deserving (Princeton, N.J.: Princeton University Press, 1970), the chapter entitled "Action and Responsibility."

problem. Can we capture this knowledge in a moral description of Jimmy's action?

Peter French has observed that the language of moral appraisal includes in its assessments both what the agent says he intended, and what he was *"willing to have happen as a result or outcome of some act he did intend to do.* " [24] What we find in language is that we do not hesitate to hold an agent accountable for every effect of his action which he is willing to have happen as a consequence of some intended act; whether he actually thought about it and consciously intended the outcome or not. Language shows, then, that an agent is appraisable at least this far down the accordion effect of his actions.

Not having the cars moved means Jimmy was willing to risk, as an outcome of "hitting the ball," that "a windshield could be broken." He should not be surprised, therefore, if Big Robbie holds him appraisable for "breaking the windshield." This conforms well with our ordinary practice. *We will not merely say. "Jimmy hit the ball." but "Jimmy broke the windshield."* **What all of this means is that we do, in fact, hold persons accountable for the effects of their action, which they did not consciously intend, but which they were willing to have happen by intentionally acting as they did.**

At this point, we must make an important distinction. What we have said does not mean that Jimmy really intended to break out the windshield, and that his protests are designed only to cover this up. On the contrary, we should take Jimmy seriously in what he says, unless there is some good reason not to. I mean, if Jimmy were "throwing a brick" at Big Robbie's windshield, rather than "taking batting practice," and then said, "Oh, I didn't intend to break the windshield," then it would certainly be rational to doubt his word. However, under the description of our batting practice case, we may feel safe in accepting Jimmy's plea that he did not intend to break the windshield. But what we **are** saying is that in addition to considering what a person intended to do whenever we decide whether to make a moral appraisal or not, our moral language takes into account as well what the person was "willing to have happen."

There is another way of approaching this same point. It would be interesting to see what Jimmy's action at the plate would be if **his** car were parked alongside the third base line. After all, we are sometimes willing to have many things happen, to take various kinds of risks, provided that only others or their possessions will be affected. But we are much less willing to have something happen if it may effect us. Of course, what is significant about this is the observation that from the moral point of view things should work just the opposite. It is one thing to be willing to accept risks for ourselves, it is something else-- something we must be very cautious about--to impose risks on others by our actions, and what we are willing to have happen.

---

[24] Peter French, The Scope of Morality (Minneapolis: The University of Minnesota Press, 1979), p. 22. French puts the matter more technically than this in stating his *Primary Principle of Accountability:* "a person can be held accountable for only and for all of his (intentional) acts, and for those events that occur that he indirectly or collaterally intended, including those collaterally intended nonoriginal or double effects that involve the actions of other persons." See also, Gerald Dworkin and David Blumenfeld, "Punishment for Intentions," Mind 75 (1966).

We should not overlook Big Robbie's appraisability. The same kinds of things we have been saying of Jimmy's actions might be said of Big Robbie's as well. After all, in parking his car along the third base line, he assumes the risk that an errant ball might be hit foul and into his windshield, even though his action of parking there probably does not involve any intention that a ball should be hit through his windshield.

However, even if Robbie were appraisable under this description, this does not mean that we will not use appraisal language of Jimmy's action too. It only means that Big Robbie may be regarded as accountable also. In the language of a responsibility description we may say, "Well, Robbie you shouldn't have parked there. You knew what might happen. You are partially responsible too."
We could even redescribe another situation.

In fact, Robbie's responsibility might be even more extensive. Imagine that he needed a new windshield, and so he parked there hoping that someone would smash his old one. It is certainly the case that some persons who have car fenders damaged as a result of their own fault, sometimes seek an accident with another car in order to try to make someone else pay for a new fender.

In summary, we can observe that if we were at the baseball diamond when Jimmy knocked out Big Robbie's windshield, we might have heard Jimmy say to Big Robbie, "I am sorry, I didn't mean (i.e., intend) to." What we would not have heard him say is, "I didn't do it" (i.e., "It wasn't my act"). It would be just silly for him to say the latter, but certainly not the former. Even if Jimmy protests that it was "no part of his intention" to "break the windshield," both what we have called the accordion effect of actions, and the "willing to have it happen" consideration explain our use of moral appraisal language in these circumstances. "Breaking the windshield," even "breaking Big Robbie's windshield" was included in the kinds of events Jimmy was "willing to have happen" as a consequence of his intentional act of "hitting the ball." And this description helps us understand why Jimmy might say, "I am sorry."[25] Of course, even if Jimmy's "I am sorry" is the admission of the acceptance of appraisability, that does not mean that Jimmy is thereby indicating that he is willing to accept any or all of the responsibility for paying for restoring the windshield. Responsibility descriptions of this sort are secondary to establishing the matter of appraisability. Big Robbie must share some of the responsibility too. We know, then, by looking at the language of appraisability that we are held accountable whenever an act is traceable to us. We are subject to moral appraisal, not only for the intentional act itself, but also for the effects of the action which we intended, and even for those which we were willing to have happen as one of the possible outcomes of an intentional act.

---

[25]I think this consistent with what Michael Zimmerman means when he talks about indirect freedom generating indirect laudability or culpability. An Essay on Moral Responsibility (Totowa, N.J.: Rowman and Littlefield, 1988), pp. 24-54.

Attempts

> *Suppose Don is jogging by the river when he sees a young girl floundering and drowning. Suppose he is not too tired, since his run has just begun, and that he knows that the water here is only four feet deep, and that he could stand up easily. Besides, let us say, he is an accomplished swimmer, and that he knows CPR as well. Now, imagine he swims vigorously to the girl, snatches her up, and wades back to shore, where he administers CPR, but she dies anyway.*

OR

> *Suppose Fagin sets about as his intention to train a gang of young boys to steal for him in order to support his bizarre and drug-laden lifestyle. Suppose there are five boys in his gang, and all but one, whose name is Oliver, learn their lessons well. For some reason, try as he may, Fagin cannot train Oliver to steal; Oliver remains truly honest and upright.*

Even though the content of these cases is widely different, they have in common something very important. They are both **attempts**. In the first case, Don did not save the girl. He had the skill and the willingness. He even put forth a reasonable effort to do so. But he did not save her. However, he did *attempt* to save her. In fact, it was a convincing attempt to do something morally praiseworthy. On the other hand, in the second example, Fagin's intentions are quite different. He wants to corrupt the youth for his own selfish gain--to do something morally blameworthy. Yet, as resourceful as he is, as much as he knows about stealing, and in spite of the fact that the rest of the boys learn their lessons well, Oliver does not become a thief. Fagin only attempted to corrupt him.

Will these persons be appraised for their attempts, or are persons appraised only if they are successful? Will Don be praised for *trying to* save the little girl, and Fagin blamed for *trying to* corrupt Oliver, even though neither succeeded? I answer plainly, yes. We would certainly find it possible to offer as one responsibility description of these situations: "Don, you did the right thing, you tried to save her, and that's all that anyone could expect of you." On the other hand, we could also say to Fagin, "It doesn't matter that Oliver never did wrong, you tried to get him to, and you were wrong to do that."[26]

It seems that some attempts are "**convincing attempts**" and some are not. What makes the difference in judgment? Well, we usually call an attempt convincing if the agent is performing the sorts of actions which constitute a reasonable effort to be successful, even though what is "reasonable effort" is as open to interpretation as is "convincing attempt".

---

[26]Hornsby seems to support this analysis, pp. 33-44. Other works on attempts are: Charles R. Carr, "Punishing Attempts," <u>Pacific Philosophical Quarterly</u> 62 (1981); Graham Hughes, "Attempting the Impossible," in <u>Responsibility</u>, ed. by Joel Feinberg and Hyman Gross (Encino: Dickenson, 1975).

> *Krista promised her mother that she would stop by the cleaners and pick up her father's shirts because he was taking a business trip the following day. After school, Krista went with Margaret and Jeff to the record store, and then to get a coke. By the time she arrived at the cleaners the store was already closed. When she arrived home, her mother said, "You should have kept your promise to me; now your father does not have the shirts he needs." But Krista replied, "I tried mom, really I did. But I was just so busy that the cleaners was closed by the time I could get there."*

Krista wants her mother to appraise her on the basis of her attempt to pick up her father's shirt, not on whether she was successful or not. However, Krista's attempt is not a very convincing one. Her mother may reply, "Well, you didn't try very hard. If you had, then you would have gone by the cleaners first." In order to make a reasonable attempt to get to the cleaners before it closed, Krista should have performed certain actions in a given order, but she did not. If we ask whether what defines "reasonable effort" is a subjective judgment, the answer is "Yes, of course." However, this judgment may not necessarily be an individual one. In fact, what is a "reasonable effort" may be understood to be *the effort we would expect any other person to exercise to achieve the desired end.* Still, this is not precise. Some persons are "perfectionists" simply because this concept marks their efforts as more than what it is reasonable to expect. But there are no iron-clad ways of drawing these lines. The moral community simply tries on alternative descriptions until agreement is reached; or else, it tolerates some margin of disagreement, until the matter becomes more crucial.

In summary, we may say that ordinary moral language makes appraisals of persons for all actions they do intentionally, and the effects of such actions they either intend, or which they are willing to have happen. Persons are also appraisable for the things they attempt to do, even if they are not successful.

Omissions

Persons may also be held accountable for their omissions. Consider an example taken from Peter van Inwagen's article, "Ability and Responsibility".[27]

> *Suppose Jim witnesses a crime and considers calling the police to report it. But because he does not want to get involved, he decides against calling and does nothing. However, what if, unknown to him, the telephone system is down anyway and every available phone is not working. So, even if he had "dialed", he could not have "called" the police.*

Would we say that Jim is appraisable for "not calling" the police? I agree with the position van Inwagen takes in his article, that we would *not* say so. However, we

---

[27]Peter van Inwagen, "Ability and Responsibility," <u>Philosophical Review</u> 87 (April 1978): 205. I adapted the example by inserting a fictious name and summarizing it very compactly. Not all omissions are negligence, but some are. See Michael Zimmerman, "Negligence and Moral Responsibility," <u>Nous</u> 20 (1986a).

would say Jim was appraisable for "not trying to call" or "not attempting." Another way of saying this is that Jim is accountable for **omitting** to attempt to call the police.

Suppose Jim knew the phones were inoperative. In such a case, he would not be appraisable for omitting to call the police--**provided phone inoperation was the reason he omitted to call.** If he knew the phones were inoperative, and omitted to call the police, but he would not have attempted to do so anyway, because he "did not want to get involved" or "it was too much trouble," then he is appraisable for such an omission, even if the phones did not work.

We can get even clearer on the matter of omissions by studying this example.

> *Suppose Jack knows full well that the belief Mary holds about Sally is false, but Mary thinks her belief is true. Mary is in the position of having to provide a reference for Sally. If Mary tells others of her belief, presenting it as the truth, as she intends to do, this information will ruin Sally's reputation and cost her the promotion she really deserves. Jack omits telling Mary the truth and stopping her from passing along the false belief about Sally because he does not like Sally.*

Jack is not passing along false information. He is not lying. Neither is he conspiring with Mary to ruin Sally. What he is doing is simply *omitting to act.* This does not mean that he is committing an act of omission. Such language iscontradictory. Jack is appraisable simply for his *inaction* . [28]

Suppose we find out about all that transpired in our example. We may challenge Jack by saying,"Why didn't you tell Mary the truth? You could have prevented this whole thing, but you didn't." Or, if Mary found out about what Jack knew, she might say, "You should have stopped me. You knew all along that what I believed about Sally was untrue, but you stood by and let me ruin her."

The language used in these appraisals reveals that we think persons *can be in control of their omissions.* Being in control of one's omissions is the crucial point in deciding accountability. Jack is accountable for his inaction because it was in his power or control to prevent Mary from passing along false information, but he allowed it to occur when he could have prevented it. If it had not been in Jack's power to stop Mary from passing along false information, then he would not be appraisable. In this case, though, since he failed to act, his omission was actually the reason why false information was relayed. Therefore, he is accountable.[29] We

---

[28] I think Judith Thomson has proven that there is no such entity as an act of omission. See her discussion of "Omissions" in <u>Actions and Other Events</u>, pp. 212-218. Other discussions of omissions include the following. Graham Hughes, "Omissions and *Mens Rea*," in <u>Freedom and Responsibility</u>, ed. by Herbert Morris (Stanford: Stanford University Press, 1961); Douglas Husak, "Omissions, Causation and Liability," <u>Philosophical Quarterly</u> 30 (1980); and Elazar Weinryb, "Omissions and Responsibility," <u>Philosophical Quarterly</u> 30 (1980).

[29] John Martin Fischer discusses the relevance of control to appraisability at length in "Responsibility and Failure," <u>Proceedings of the Aristotlean Society</u> (1985-1986): 251-270. See also, Zimmerman, pp. 32-40.

have already uncovered the grounds for appraising omissions in ordinary language much earlier in this chapter. The "willing to have happen" guide, which we have been employing to understand how far down the accordion effect of actions appraisability extends, is founded on the language necessary to establish assessment of omissions. To know if Jack was "willing for it to happen" that Sally be ruined, all we have to ask is, could he have prevented it, but he was unwilling to? Or, was it in his control to regulate whether or not the relay of false information occurred? Since it was in Jack's control to prevent the ruining of Sally, then he is appraisable for his omission to act. The fact is that he could have prevented the ruining of Mary, but he was unwilling to. Jack's omission is called a **refusal** in the language of responsibility description. Refusals are one type of morally appraisable omission. They are omissions made intentionally, deliberately, and for a purpose.

Though refusals are appraisable, not all are blamable. Refusing may be done for a benevolent or desirable purpose. A parent helping her daughter with math homework may reach a point at which she refuses to help further. She may say, "No, I'm not going to show you how to work any more problems. See if you can do them on your own, and then show me your work." This omission is not blameworthy, because the objective of the mother is to provide the risk and stimulus which are required to demonstrate that one has learned. Refusals of this sort might actually be praised in our responsibility description.

What about cases like *"Passing the Buck"*? These are refusals. But are they blameworthy or praiseworthy? The answer depends on the context.   Sometimes refusing to help (or decide) and suggesting that it is some other person's job or position to help (or decide) is actually praiseworthy, and sometimes it is not. If Harvey knows that he is incapable of teaching the soccer players the various strategies of attack at a corner kick, he is appraisable for refusing to do so. But we may praise him for assigning the task (not *passing the buck*) to Joe to teach the players, since Joe is better qualified to instruct them than he is. *Passing the buck* is a moral concept used to blame. Persons who refuse to help or decide in morally appropriate ways are not described under the concept of *passing the buck*.

We may be held appraisable for other types of omissions which are not refusals. Consider this example.

> *Larry is a lifeguard at the local beach swimming area. He has wanted this job for a long time, because he has always believed that girls are really attracted to lifeguards with great tans and such. Well, one afternoon, while Larry is visiting with two great looking girls in bikinis, a surfer falls from his board and is hit in the head. The surfer is disoriented and bleeding. He begins to flail the water and cry for help. Ordinarily, Larry would see the man and use his skill to save him. However, Larry is distracted, talking to the girls.*

We may say of our lifeguard that his is an appraisable omission. He could have acted and at least attempted to save the drowning surfer, but he did not do so. However, notice that his omission is not the same as Jack's. The lifeguard does not look into the ocean and see the drowning surfer, and then decide to talk to the coeds instead. His omission is not a refusal. We may search for the right language to use in responsibility description. We will try different conduct discriminators in order to establish his degree of responsibility. We may say that his omission is *negligence* or *carelessness*.

Intervening Agents and Appraisable Events

If I agree to act, attempt, or omit at your request, I am appraisable. But you are appraisable also, even if you made no bodily movement, and did not participate beyond the making of the request. Let's take a fairly obvious example.

Suppose Irving hires a hit-man to murder his business partner. Irving may never see this man. He may only talk to him by phone. He may learn that the deed is done only by reading about it in the newspapers, but he is nevertheless appraisable for the murder.

Irving's responsibility for this murder may be different than that of the hit-man. We may use different appraisal language about these two men. We may hold the hit-man more blamable for the action since he was the direct cause of the murder. But Irving does not escape appraisability simply by being remote.

Why is it, though, that we would make a moral appraisal of Irving? After all, he did not pull the trigger. He did not cause the person's death; the gunman did.

1) One way of approaching this, based on what we have already uncovered from the language of moral appraisal, is to say that Irving intends (he is not just willing for it to happen) that the hit-man will kill. We know this is his intention because Irving actually makes a contract with the hit-man, paying him to kill.

2) A second way of describing the reason for Irving's appraisability is to point out that this is an act which would not have occurred except by Irving's intervention. The hit-man was not going to do this murder irregardless of what happens. Irving was the connecting link between the hit man and his victim. If Irving does not intervene, then the hit-man goes his way, and Irving's chosen victim is not a victim at all. So, Irving is at least a cause, if not **the** cause of the murder, and he cannot escape appraisal.[30]

Whenever an action would not have occurred, an attempt would not have been made, or an omission would have instead been done, except for an agent's intervention, and the agent chooses to intervene, he is appraisable.

Suppose that Sherlock Holmes is called to investigate a poisoning in Devonshire. When he arrives, police are questioning Lord Shambley's brother, with whom the Lord, who is now dead, had a violent argument just the day before. The brother admits he brought a bottle of wine to Shambley, the very bottle containing the poison, but he denies being the murderer. The police arrest him anyway. Holmes and Watson spend days following the trail of the wine.

---

[30]For further discussion, see Alan Donagan, The Theory of Morality (Chicago: University of Chicago Press, 1977), p. 47 and Zimmerman, Essay on Moral Responsibility, pp. 98-103, and "Intervening agents and Moral Responsibility," Philosophical Quarterly 35 (1985a).

They learn that the wine arrived by special delivery the day of the murder, and so they interview the driver of the delivery carriage. He identifies the seller which sent the wine, but the wine bottle came not from the store, but from the personal stock of a friend of the Lord's. Upon query, they find that this friend had been forced to sell everything he owned because of debts to the Lord, but that the man bore no grudge. However, the man's son, forced to work for Lord Shambley as his butler, did hold a grudge against the Lord for abuses of days gone by. Holmes finds that the butler, knowing Shambley had bought the wine, poisoned it before it was ever taken from the cellar to be sent to the store.

Who is appraisable in this account? Consider the intervening agents: the brother, who brought the wine to Shambley; the delivery boy, who carried the wine from the store; the seller who bought it from Shambley's friend; the Lord's friend, who was forced to sell it to meet debts to Shambley; and the butler, who poisoned it. Is it not the case that each of these persons made it possible for the poisoned wine to be in Shambley's hand? Couldn't we say, "if the delivery boy had not brought it..." or "if the brother had refused to pour it..."? The butler could have put the poison in the wine, and yet, had it never been delivered or poured, it could not have caused its deadly effect.

The difference in this case and the hit-man example is clear enough to you, I am sure. The intervening agents in the Holmes case are not consenting or knowing agents. They are not intentional or willing parties to the poisoning. They will probably claim unavoidable ignorance, saying "they could not have known" the wine was poisoned. So, they are not appraisable even though they are intervening agents. Conditions such as "unavoidable ignorance" which make agents nonappraisable are discussed in another chapter.

Multiple Agents and Appraisable Events

Here I do not mean to discuss how appraisability is divided between ourselves and others. Appraisability is not divisible. To be appraisable just means one has met the conditions for moral accountability. The fact of one's accountability cannot be shared. That a person is appraisable is not a function of how many people are involved. If we are appraisable, then it is ours, regardless of whether, and how many, other people may also be appraisable. However, moral language does indicate that we apportion the responsibility or the degree of blame or praise which is assigned to two or more agents who share in an appraisable event. We can share responsibility or speak about degrees of responsibility, blame, or praise. But we do not share appraisability. Some relevant factors in considering one's share of blame or praise include such things as what role one played in bringing about the event; that is, whether the occurrence of an appraisable event required my participation, and whether it could not have occurred except for my intervention. If my involvement was determinative, then I am more responsible, but not any more appraisable.

If I, along with you, act, or am willing to have an effect result from my action; or if I, along with you, make an attempt; or, if I, along with you, omit to act then we are both appraisable, *but not as a group, only as individuals.* For example, suppose we are siblings and by coincidence, rather than by plan, we both intend to have our widowed mother's house painted. We may hire painters, and even send them over to the house on the same day. They may drive up on opposite sides of the house and each be painting one side of the house when mom walks out. Our surprised mother will say to us, "Oh, you two, when will you ever learn to talk to each other?"--meaning that she recognizes that it was not a joint effort--but each one is doing the act individually.

If I, along with you, try to perform an act, but we fail, we are still appraisable for the attempt, but individually. If the attempt is to do something which would be laudable, then we should both get trophies. What kind of trophy or ribbon goes to whom, is left to the responsibility description of how much effort each put forth relative to the other. We may get the same, or one of us may have tried harder than the other did to make the event occur, thereby deserving greater honor.

If I, along with others, could have prevented an event, it was within the control of any of us to do so, but we all omit to act, then we are each appraisable, as individuals. For example, if four persons are standing around and any one of them could lift a piece of furniture off of a child's foot, but none of them does, they are all appraisable, but one at a time, not as a group. Of course, some may be more to blame than others, depending on the context.

Groups of Persons and Appraisable Events

There is a language about groups which makes moral appraisals of group conduct and character. "The team won the game." "The people elected a President." "The Congress passed an amendment." It might be perfectly appropriate to say "The team won the game," without saying that any individual player on the team won the game. Yet, not all groups are of the same type. It would be difficult to say that "the gang raped her" without also meaning that some one of the gang members raped her; or "the group standing on the corner crossed the street," without also meaning that some of the members of the group crossed the street."

Some groups are simply **numerical or random collectivites**. Take, for example, "the group on the street corner." This group is not gathered for any purpose. The persons do not consult, plan, and execute conduct. One could say that there was a group of four of us standing around the child with the furniture on his foot. However, this is merely a random or numerical group. It is more like what we would call a *grouping,* that is, the grouping of people who were standing by the child with furniture on his foot. These individuals simply all happened to be standing by the child. Furthermore, removing the furniture from the child's foot does not require that they act in concert, by a plan, or after agreement. Any one of them could remove it. We appraise the members of such random collectivites individually, and we may attach different weightings of blame and/or praise to the various members of the random group. Other examples of such collectivities would be "the people on the corner" or "those in the bank." Appraisability in grouping instances occurs in ordinary language just as we have seen it practiced in multiple agent appraisals, where each person is appraised individually, and responsibility can be greater or lesser, depending on relevant factors raised in the description of the event.

However, sometimes we appraise the group **holistically**. There is a language of appraisal about groups which is not reducible to language about individuals. "The team won the game" is a good example of such language. "You are true champions," we may say to the entire team.   There are times when groups are appraisable and individuals are not. Mega Oil may be appraisable for driving the small independent gas stations out of business, but that does not mean every individual, or even any one specific individual associated with Mega Oil is appraisable for such action. "Driving out the independents" may not be any **one** person's intention in the corporation.[31] If we take note of the groups about which we make moral appraisals, our practice shows that each has an **internal decision procedure which determines the action, attempt, or omission of the group.** If the group is acting in concert, or according to a plan, or after following certain procedures of decision, then the group is appraisable.

There are times when we may appraise a group as well as--**or** even instead of--the individuals which make it up.

Suppose that four persons are standing by a child with a piece of furniture on his foot. Imagine that any one of them could remove the furniture,but no one does. Then they are appraisable individually. But suppose that they see the child's situation and then discuss among themselves the action of removing the furniture. After consideration of the alternatives, they decide mutually not to remove the furniture.

In this case they are appraisable as a group, even though they may also be appraised as individuals.

Even in group actions, attempts, or omissions, individuals may also be appraisable. Furthermore, the responsibility for blame or praise may not be equally distributed. Some individuals may bear more blame or praise than others do. Still, the point is that ordinary language shows that there are times when we want to reserve the prerogative of blaming and praising both individuals and groups. The intuition which seems to lie behind our language is that something like consulting and agreeing with others to do something like drive out the independent gas stations owners is an action that a corporation, with its extensive assets and resources, should be held appraisable for, and not something for which only the individuals who manage it are appraisable. We seem to want to be protected from groups and not just individuals. Likewise, we want to encourage praiseworthy conduct on the part of groups, and not merely individuals, because groups typically wield more power. Of course, we may wish to hold an individual appraisable as well as the corporation. We may even wish to hold some individuals within the corporation more responsible than others. The same conduct is capable of many descriptions, and moral language is rich enough to accommodate them all.

In the case of a soccer team, we might say truly, "You are all champions. It

---

[31]The discussion of collective responsibility is quite technical. The following works are very helpful. Stanley Bates, "The Responsibility of 'Random Collections,'" Ethics 81 (1970-71); D.E. Cooper, "Collective Responsibility," Philosophy 43 (1968) and "Collective Responsibility-- Again," Philosophy 44 (1969); R. S. Downie, "Collective Responsibility," Philosophy 44 (1969); Virginia Held, "Moral Responsibility and Collective Action," in Individual and Collective Responsibility, ed. by Peter A. French (Cambridge: Schenkman, 1972).   For an excellent introduction to corporate appraisability see French, Collective and Corporate, pp. 31-66.

was a team effort today." But we may also recognize that some players contributed more than others. The midfielder who was injured in the first half made a contribution, but perhaps the striker who scored the winning goal or the goalie who stopped the opponent's penalty shot played a more significant role in the victory. They may receive MVP awards, but the team will receive a trophy, too. Ordinary language makes all such descriptions possible, and the fact that it shows such versatility indicates that we regard all such appraisals as necessary.

Before we close this discussion, we should observe that it hardly seems very useful to hold a group appraisable for an action, attempt, or omission, unless there is some reason to believe that doing so would serve a constructive purpose in the moral community. We want to consider whether the group could make reparation in a way that the individuals could not do so (e.g., corporate assets are usually more extensive than individual ones). Or, we might want to consider whether holding a group appraisable might change the decision structure in the future, or make the policies according to which decisions are made more reflective of the kinds of things the general moral community find worth protecting or praising.

For Discussion

Take a position on the appraisability of the agents in the examples below. If a person is appraisable, explain why, using the concepts discussed in this chapter. In some examples, many or all agents may be appraisable. Do not involve yourself too deeply in thinking about the responsibility description (i.e., how much blame or praise to assign). These issues will be considered later.

1) Jamie borrowed her sister's new skirt to go to a sorority party, knowing that the evening plans included a hay ride and all night scavenger hunt around a farm. During the evening the skirt became soiled and torn. When Jamie returned home the next morning, and her sister saw the skirt, Jamie said, "Don't blame me. I didn't intend to tear the dress." Is Jamie appraisable? Explain what considerations from this chapter you used in forming your position.

2) The Board of Directors of a local hospital decide not to treat an emergency room patient because he is indigent and cannot pay for his care. The patient dies. Is anyone appraisable? If so, whom? Explain what considerations from this chapter you used in forming your position.

3) Paul and Mandy are newly married. They are both still in college and struggling to make ends meet, but they are very happy. The brakes on Mandy's 1983 Honda Civic are worn out, and the estimated cost to repair them is quite expensive. Jim decides to fix them himself, even though he has never done this kind of work before. So, he works on the car on Saturday morning. Later that day, Mandy drives across town to do some shopping at the mall. While on the expressway, her brakes fail and she speeds out of control under an eighteen-wheeler. The truck smashes into several cars. In total, four cars and the truck are damaged. Several people are injured, and Mandy is killed. Is Jim appraisable? If so, for what? Explain what considerations from this chapter you used in forming your position.

4) In the movie, "The Accused," several men in a bar watch while a female customer is beaten and raped by three other men. The "watchers" do not participate in the beating or rape themselves, but they do nothing to stop it. Are they appraisable? If so, for what? Explain what considerations from this chapter you used in forming your position.

5) Bill is really in need of some money. He has a motorcycle which he bought a few years ago before he bought his car. The motorcycle is heavily insured. Lately, several robberies have occurred in his neighborhood. Usually, Bill brings his motorcycle inside the house at night because he does not want it stolen. But one night he chooses to leave the cycle on his front porch, hoping that it will be stolen and he can collect the insurance and pay his bills. Is Bill appraisable if the cycle is stolen? If so, for what? Is he an intervening agent? If so, in what? Explain what considerations from this chapter you used in forming your position.

6) Suppose that Dr. Bryan asks his nurse to prepare an inoculation for one of his patients. She does so, but puts in the wrong dosage. Dr. Bryan gives the shot, and in a very short time the patient has a severe reaction. Is Dr. Bryan appraisable? If so, for what? Explain what considerations from this chapter you used in forming your position.

7) Five high school students who are angry at their math teacher decide to vandalize her home. One of them throws eggs at the siding on the house. Another pours paint on the front porch. The other two pull up shrubs from the flower beds. The last student stands watch. Are these students all appraisable? Are they appraisable as a group, or as multiple agents, or as both? Explain what considerations from this chapter you used in forming your position.

8) Paul parks his car in a fire lane of the dry cleaning shop next door, in order to go into the grocery store to buy food for his pool side barbecue party later in the evening. The grocery store parking lot is full, and he intends to be in the store for only a few quick minutes. While he is in the store, the dry cleaning shop has an explosion, and a fire erupts. The nearby fire trucks arrive, but cannot get to the building because Paul's car is blocking the lane. The cleaners burns to the ground and two persons are severely injured. Is Paul appraisable? For what is he appraisable, if he is? Why is he appraisable, if he is? Explain what considerations from this chapter you used in forming your position.

9) The decision to hire a new executive director for the Human Services Referral and Information Bureau is to be made by the search committee. A unanimous vote is not required by the rules established by the committee. One of the two final candidates, who is the best qualified and had a fine interview, is a black woman. In the final discussions about whom to hire, it becomes clear that all but one member of the committee do not want a woman for this position. A black man who does not have the same qualifications as the woman is hired, with only one dissenting vote. If the woman feels she has been discriminated against, whom should she appraise? Is the committee appraisable as a group, or as multiple agents, or both? Explain what considerations from this chapter you used in forming your position.

10) In an elementary school P.E. class in which he is a student teacher, John sees Randy's back and side while Randy is showering. The bruises and abrasions on Randy's back are clear evidences of abuse, but John says nothing about it to his supervising teacher, to the principal, or to Randy. A few weeks later, Randy is nearly killed by his father as the result of a severe beating. Is John appraisable? If so, for what? Explain what considerations from this chapter you used in forming your position.

11) One of your neighbors, who is retired, has organized a neighborhood watch program because there has been a rash of home robberies in your area. On Tuesday afternoon, he sees some persons enter your house and begin moving out your stereo, T.V., and such. He calls the police, but they do not respond. Is your neighbor appraisable? If so, for what? Explain what considerations from this chapter you used in forming your position.

12) Janie and her friends attend an all-girls prep school in a small New England town. Late one night they decide to go swimming in a nearby lake. They break the school rules by being out after curfew, and they skinny-dip in the lake. Are they appraisable as a group, or as multiple agents? Which strategy would be most appropriate? Explain what considerations from this chapter you used in forming your position.

13) Three teenage neighborhood boys are shooting their BB guns at cans and other targets. As they walk on the crossway over the expressway going downtown, one boy shoots at a car passing beneath them. The BB hits the windshield, and a horrific accident occurs when the driver of the car swerves. A witness has seen the boy fire at the car. When the boy is caught and questioned, he says, "Sure, I fired at the car, but I did not mean to cause the wreck." Is the boy appraisable? If so, for what? Explain what considerations from this chapter you used in forming your position.

14) A manufacturer of automatic and semi-automatic weapons has sold these guns to the general public. Drug users and pushers have committed several murders using these weapons. Since the guns are readily available, and because they fire bullets so rapidly, the shooting victims are usually killed from multiple wounds. Some innocent bystanders have also lost their lives. Is the company appraisable for making and selling such weapons as these, knowing what the accordion effect of its action is? Are they willing to have this kind of thing happen? Explain what considerations from this chapter you used in forming your position.

15) The NAPCO aluminum smelter in a rural city routinely dumps chemicals from its refining process into a small lake by the plant. Fishermen begin to notice large numbers of dead fish and trees along the banks of the lake. When the company officials are approached they say, "But we did not intend to poison the fish or environment." Is the company appraisable? What about the supervisor who ordered the dumping? Explain what considerations from this chapter you used in forming your position.

16)   A student steals an in-house admission exam for the School of Nursing. Five other students use it too. Are these students appraisable as a group, or as multiple agents? Which strategy would be most appropriate? Explain what considerations from this chapter you used in forming your position.

17)   You are with a group of college students traveling in France for three weeks. While you are eating in one of the sidewalk cafes, Kelly is using her new camera to take pictures. After you leave, Kelly discovers she left her camera back at the cafe. You return with her, but the camera is gone. When you ask the waiter about it, he says, "Yes, I saw one of the neighborhood children take the camera, but I did not say anything. It was none of my business." Is the waiter appraisable? If so, for what? Explain what considerations from this chapter you used in forming your position.

Chapter Four :   Conditions Which Remove Persons From Moral Appraisability

Introduction

Moral practice reveals that members of the moral community may be categorized in various ways. Here are three of the more important categories.

• There are situations in which we decline to use moral language of a person or his conduct. The person is **not accountable** or **nonappraisable** for his conduct or character. We do not expect such a person to offer a justification or an excuse for an action, attempt, or omission. Sometimes a person, who is a member of the moral community, may be nonappraisable because of the specific situation. Our practice shows that this occurs when they were forced or coerced, when they had no other alternative conduct available to them, or when the situation restricts their knowledge in ways which it is unreasonable to expect them to remedy. At other times ordinary practice exempts persons from moral accountability because they have a mental or cognitive deficiency which removes them from appraisability, either temporarily (moral innocence) or permanently (mental incapacity). However, in all cases, to say that someone is not appraisable does not necessarily mean that they are unworthy of moral consideration. Indeed, certain disabilities may actually require that special moral consideration be given to them. Our moral grammar has special provisions for the mentally ill.

• There are cases in which a person has no conditions either situationally or internally which remove him from moral accountability for his conduct or character, and he can defend himself or his behavior when challenged. The practice is to make an appraisal of him, and when we assess his responsibility, we can see that what he did was morally right because he can offer a **justification** for his conduct.

• There are examples in which a person has no conditions either situationally or internally which remove him from moral accountability for his conduct or character, and he admits wrongdoing, but he has an **excuse** which will diminish the degree of moral blame for which we say he is responsible.

The remainder of this chapter will discuss the various language strategies employed to support the non accountability or the **nonappraisability** of persons.

1.   Having No Other Choice

We sometimes hear, "Don't hold me accountable; I had no other choice." This language expresses a sense that unless there are alternative possibilities, we should not appraise a person's conduct morally. At first sight, this certainly seems true. How can we be accountable for our conduct if we had no options available? If we had to act or omit as we did, then we really had no choice. If we did not have a choice, then we should not be blamed or praised for our conduct. Praise and blame seem to be reserved for things which we choose to do, or attempt, or omit. A deep-seated moral intuition seems to be captured in the plea "Don't hold me accountable; I had no other choice."

But is it really our moral practice that **unless** we have more than one alternative from which to choose, then we are not morally accountable? This may seem to be a theoretical question, but before treating it in this manner, perhaps some clarification may be achieved by describing moral practice.

> *Suppose Jean Paul is mountain climbing with six other persons.*
> *Among his fellow climbers is a married couple, Bridgette and Alf.*
> *Jean Paul is madly in love with Bridgette, and she with him.*
> *However, she feels a loyalty to Alf who is many years older than*
> *she. Jean Paul has thought many times that he would like to be able*
> *to get rid of Alf. As they are going up the North face of the*
> *mountain, Jean Paul is next to last in line, and Alf is last. Suddenly,*
> *Alf slips and falls. He bangs against the rock and is knocked*
> *unconscious. Alf is tied to Jean Paul and the others by safety ropes,*
> *but the impact of this fall pulls everyone away from the wall ,*
> *except the lead man.   With the wind whipping poor Alf around*
> *terrifically, the only way to save the others is to cut him loose. Jean*
> *Paul has no other choice, and is told so by the others who are*
> *frantically trying to regain their holds.*

Now, our first inclination is to release Jean Paul from appraisability. We may say he has no alternative, and there should be no moral appraisal whenever a person has no alternative to acting as he did. However, we should be careful here. There is something else to mention. Our actual practice certainly recognizes the difference between "having no other **numerical** alternative" and "having no other **moral** alternative." The difference is very important.

Actual cases of having no other numerical alternative are rarely recognized in ordinary moral practice. Just try to imagine instances when a person has one and only one alternative, numerically speaking. In almost any example which can be suggested, we can still say, "Well, there is always something else you could have done."   Our   example   of   Jean   Paul's   dilemma   is   not   a   "having no other **numerical** alternative" case. Jean Paul could have done otherwise than he did. But it is fair to say that we would probably recognize his action as one which fits under the description, "having no other **moral** alternative." This is an important point to note because we cannot really consider "having no other **moral** alternative" to be a grounds for nonappraisability. In fact, once we interject the modifier **moral,** then we are making an appraisal of what Jean Paul did. "Having no other **moral** alternative" is usually a responsibility description which means that one has done "the lesser of two evils," and such cases are best treated under a discussion of excuses. So, Jean Paul is appraised by saying he had no other moral alternative, even though his blame is clearly diminished, perhaps even to the point of being virtually nonexistent. Still, though, we have recognized that he should give an account or description of why he did what he did.

However, suppose that we say for the sake of argument that Jean Paul had no other **numerical** alternative. Would this description exempt him from appraisability? And more broadly, would it always and every time exclude anyone from appraisability? Our practice yields the reply, **not necessarily**. Consider this expansion of our example as a redescription of a case in which Jean Paul would still be appraisable, even though he had no other **numerical** choice.

> *As Jean Paul cuts the rope and watches Alf's body fly down the*
> *deep gorge to the rocks below, he thinks "Finally, I'm rid of him,*
> *and I have my beloved Bridgette."*

Let us put aside for the moment the objection that we could hardly know of Jean Paul's inner thoughts and motives unless he tells us (this is the *other minds problem* again), and pretend that we know his thoughts. Under this description of the case, we would refuse to exempt Jean Paul from moral appraisability, even if he had no other numerical alternative. It is fairly easy to see why this is our practice, and we can explain why by looking at the types of interrogatives we could raise. Among the many questions we could ask would be the following: "Did you cut Alf loose **because you had no other choice?**", or "Did you cut Alf loose **because you wanted to be rid of him in order to marry Bridgette?**" Jean Paul's answer would be very important to the moral community and to our decision about his appraisability. "Having no other numerical alternative" may *not be the reason* for his cutting Alf loose. He may have another reason, such as "wanting to get rid of Alf" or "having his beloved Bridgette." If he acts from one of these other reasons instead of the reason that he "has no other numerical alternative," then he will be appraisable morally, **even if** he, in fact, has no other numerical alternative.

Harry Frankfurt explains this observation about moral practice very well.

> The fact that a person lacks alternatives does preclude his being morally responsible when it alone counts for his behavior. But a lack of alternatives is not inconsistent with moral responsibility when someone acts as he does for reasons of his own, rather than simply because no other alternative is open to him.[32]

It is certainly a better description of how we actually proceed in the use of moral language to say moral appraisal is not used "if a person has no other numerical alternatives **and** if absence of alternatives was the reason why he acted, attempted, or omitted."

Another way of putting this is suggested by John Martin Fischer. He holds that in moral practice one is sometimes held morally accountable for his conduct, even though he *could not have avoided* performing it.[33] The point is that unless absence of alternatives **is the reason** why a person acted, attempted, or failed to act as he did, then we still hold him appraisable morally. Strictly speaking, an agent is nonappraisable under the description of having no other alternative, only if he has no other **numerical** alternative, **and having no other numerical alternative is the reason why he acted, attempted, or omitted.**

---

[32]Harry G. Frankfurt, "What are We Morally Responsible for?" in How Many Questions, edited by H. Cauman (Hackett Publishing Co., 1988), p. 321.

[33]John Martin Fischer, "Responsibility and Failure," Proceedings of the Aristotlean Society (1985-1986): 251. Other works which discuss "Having No Other Choice" are: David Blumenfeld, "The Principle of Alternate Possibilities," Journal of Philosophy 68 (1971); Robert Cummins, "Could Have Done Otherwise," Personalist 60 (1979); Harry Frankfurt, "Alternate Possibilities and Moral Responsibility," Journal of Philosophy 66 (1969); Winston Nesbitt, and Candlish Stewart, "On Not Being Able to Do Otherwise," Mind 82 (1973); and Michael Zimmerman, "Moral Responsibility, Freedom and Alternate Possibilities," Pacific Philosophical Quarterly 63 (1982).

> *Suppose we alter our case of Jean Paul's dilemma one more time.*
> *Alf is swinging and everyone is yelling,"Cut the rope, cut it!!"*
> *Jean Paul yells up, "I just can't! I'm in love with Bridgette, and if I*
> *do, I'll feel like I murdered him."*

How would such an alteration effect your assessment of Jean Paul's appraisability? How would it change your evaluation of the degree of blame he should bear? Would it effect your appraisal of his character? If so, how?

2. Being Coerced or Having No Control

Cases in which we consider a person nonappraisable because he was coerced into conduct he would otherwise not do, or he was forcibly prevented from acting as he would like to do are in some ways similar to the "I had no other alternative" or "I had no other choice" issues discussed above. However, they still merit some separate consideration for purposes of clarifying our understanding about how these are handled in moral practice. Consider this example.

> *Bill and Russell were on a wilderness back-packing trip. During the*
> *night, a group of bikers stormed into their camp and tied them both*
> *to trees. The bikers stole their equipment and destroyed their*
> *possessions. Because Russell protested, they cut him loose from the*
> *tree. Then, they beat and killed him. During his agony, he called*
> *out, pleading for Bill to help him. The following morning Bill and*
> *Russell were discovered by Park Rangers. After he was given some*
> *time to compose himself, Bill told his story, providing a description*
> *of his omission to help.*

If we were Park Rangers who arrived late on the scene, after Bill had been untied, we might test to see whether Bill's omission was morally appraisable. We might ask, "Did you try to help your friend?" or "Where were you when your friend was being killed?" We might use these questions because we think a moral standard like "We should help those who will suffer (be injured, killed, harmed) unless aided" is applicable to the Bill and Russell example. "Giving help" was not an action alternative available to Bill. Giving aid was not under his control. He was coercively and involuntarily prevented from helping. Accordingly, our practice is such that Bill will not be morally appraisable for omitting to help Russell. Persons are not appraised for their conduct when it is not in their control to move in the morally relevant ways. In fact, if someone tried to hold Bill accountable for his failure to help, we would think that this person did not understand Bill's situation, and we would go to some lengths to redescribe it.

Immanuel Kant, an 18th century philosopher, captured the instinct which lies behind our choice not to use moral language in these cases in his famous dictum: **"ought implies can."** What this means is that a person must be *able* to perform as required, in order for a moral obligation or responsibility to exist. Unless the agent is *able* to do what is morally expected, then he will not be appraised under the obligation. Absence of control, a deed's not "being up to us," means that we are not appraisable for what happens.

But, of course, we should make the same point here that we made when dealing with "having no other numerical alternative" cases. Absence of control or coercion is grounds for nonappraisability, only if it **is the reason why the act or attempt occurs, or why one omits.** In order to exempt one from appraisability on the grounds of not being in control of one's conduct, we will want to be sure that the appeal to "having no control over one's conduct" is not being used to shield another morally significant consideration. We can illustrate this by altering our example of Bill and Russell's fateful night.

Imagine that all the while on the hike, old Bill has been plotting to kill Russell because Russell is the only person who knows that Bill is involved in buying and selling cocaine.When the bikers begin to beat Russell and Bill is tied to the tree, Bill thinks, "Good, now I'll not have to worry about how to get rid of Russell anymore."

This slight alteration in our example would change our evaluation of Bill's moral appraisability, provided, of course, that we had access to these thoughts.

Consider another alteration that is relevant to Bill's appraisability.

Suppose Bill was not tied up but hiding in the bushes, yet because he was afraid , he did not help Russell.

It is certainly possible that we can understand and empathize with this fear. Virtually anyone in such a situation would be afraid. Yet we recognize that under this description Bill is not externally restrained. He does have control over his movements. Bill may describe his feelings by saying, "The fear was like a rope binding me to my station." But this is a psychological description of internal restraint. Moral practice recognizes the difference between external and internal forces and these are treated differently. In this redescription of our example, Bill is saying that he had no control over what happened because he was internally restrained by fear. Our practice in cases of such internal restraint shows that appeals to fear are usually excusing strategies, not nonappraisability ones. We do often regard fear as an excuse which diminishes blame, especially if it is fear for one's life. In a situation such as Bill's, the fear excuse may virtually eliminate blame. In Bill's appeal to fear, though, we would not just say, "Yeah, whenever I am afraid, I don't consider myself accountable either." So, he is probably appraisable, even though we recognize that fear may inhibit conduct. Our appraisal of Bill is altered, even if slightly so. We want to know if Bill was afraid for his life, in which case he seems to have a good excuse, and maybe even a justification, for not aiding Russell. But, perhaps Bill was just scared and did not even thinkabout self-defense, or the odds against him, in which case we may be more inclined to blame him for not making an attempt to help. There are some circumstances in which the moral community expects us to fulfill our obligations, even if we are scared. It is perfectly ordinary to hear, "Sure, I was afraid, but I knew I should help."

In our original telling of the story of Bill and Russell, Bill is cleared of appraisability because of external coercion. It is not in his power or control to help Russell. He could not help, no matter how badly he wanted to. Whereas, in this retelling of the story, Bill's appraisability position is more like what Aristotle called a mixed case in the <u>Nicomachean Ethics</u>.[34] In the redescription, Bill's fear will be treated as an excuse for his omission, but not as grounds for his nonappraisability.

One can find many examples of the "I had no control over my conduct" claim for nonappraisability in moral practice. Persons sometimes claim exemption from appraisal because they were drunk or drugged at the time of wrongdoing. These are often presented as "I was not in control" cases. In such instances, persons claim that the drug was the reason why the conduct occurred. Should we, then, exempt such persons from accountability?

A look at ordinary moral practice shows that if such persons were drugged *against their will, or unknowingly,* as when the punch at a party is spiked without the guests' knowledge or consent, or if a drug is administered to a person unknowingly, then we are usually prepared to exempt persons from appraisal. Instead,we will appraise those who gave them the drug. However, if persons become drunk, drugged, or otherwise out of control by their own choice, then we hold them accountable, not merely for their conduct in that state, but *for getting in such a state to begin with* . Remember that Bill has a strong ground for nonappraisability because he did not volunteer to be tied to the tree. It would change our judgment about his appraisability if he had chosen to be tied to the tree, thereby deliberately placing himself in a position where he knew that one of the possible outcomes is that he would not be in control of his subsequent conduct.

The more difficult types of cases have to do with absence of control over one's conduct because of internal coercion: claims made about **internal obsessions** or **irresistible impulses**. A sex offender may say he is nonappraisable because he is *driven* to do what he does. He may say he is not in control of his conduct. Gamblers, drug addicts, and/or alcoholics may make similar appeals. Moral appraisals are sometimes made of such persons, and sometimes not. What makes the difference? Generally, the moral community does not appraise persons with such internal coercions *if these drives did not arise as a result of their past choices and/or developed habits* . That is, if these internal drives or impulses are not describable as voluntarily derived. Determining the degree of voluntary derivation of such a drive seems to be a matter of community decision.

We can know when the moral community has judged a person to be nonappraisable on the grounds of such internal coercions because there will be a shift in linguistic concepts and discriminators. Instead of moral concepts and discriminators, the moral community will use clinical language. The practice is to speak of exempted persons as "sick," not as "wicked," or "immoral." Of course, we may still want to protect ourselves and others from those who are "sick" in this

---

[34]Aristotle, <u>Nicomachean Ethics</u>, Book III, Ch. 1, 1110 in <u>Introduction to Aristotle</u>, edited by McKeon. The subject of coercion and its relationship to moral appraisal has continued to interest contemporary philosophers as well. Robert Audi, "Moral Responsibility, Freedom, and Compulsion," <u>American Philosophical Quarterly</u> 11 (1974); <u>Coercion</u>, edited by J.Roland Pennock and John W. Chapman (Chicago: Aldine and Atherton, 1972); John Martin Fischer, "Responsibility and Control," <u>Journal of Philosophy</u> 79 (1982); William K. Frankena, "Obligation and Ability," in <u>Philosophical Analysis</u>, edited by Max Black (Englewood Cliffs, NJ: Prentice-Hall, 1963); Harry Frankfurt, "Coercion and Moral Responsibility," in <u>Essays on Freedom of Action</u>, edited by Ted Honderich (London: Routledge and Kegan Paul, 1973); and Robert Nozick, "Coercion," in <u>Freewill</u>, edited by S. Morgenbesser, P. Suppes, and M. White (New York: St. Martin's Press, 1979).

way. We cannot simply allow them to conduct themselves freely as they do. However, if these internal drives are judged to be the result of the person's voluntary choices and decisions, then not only will we hold such persons appraisable, but we will refuse to use clinical language of them, and employ moral concepts when appraising their conduct and character.

In a straightforward sense, cases of persons "not having control" or "being coerced" are very difficult to describe. We remember that we could usually find an alternative to dispute the "I had no other alternative claim." This is true of "not having control" claims also. In fact, we think mostly of contrived illustrations such as this one.

> *To frame Gwen for murder, a man forces her to hold a gun. When the intended victim enters the room,the man, holding Gwen's hand, which holds the gun, forces Gwen's finger to pull the trigger.*

We can imagine other things Gwen had it in her power to do. There are many other things that were in her power to do besides allowing her finger to be used to pull the trigger. Acting in many of these ways could have been risky, but sometimes doing what is morally right is dangerous. The point is, even in this extreme example, that the agent has some control over what she does. Our conclusion is that ordinary moral practice does not have a wide space for these types of cases. More characteristically, these are treated by the moral community as accounts which are excuses at best, or more often as evasions and rationalizations, than as genuine descriptions of nonappraisability.

In summary, then, we might observe that internal coercions, impulses, and obsessions, all of which may be conceived of as "I had no control over my conduct" strategies are mixed cases, and determining appraisability is largely a function of how such a person came to be in such a state. Whereas, external coercion, which removes control of one's conduct, especially when this is the direct result of another person's doing, exempts one from appraisability, if such lack of control is the reason for the conduct. Finally, we noted that the fact that doing what is moral may be risky is not a reason for exemption from appraisability.

3. Being Unavoidably Ignorant

Moral practice shows that we allow multiple nonappraisable conditions related to the ways a person may be unavoidably ignorant.

a) "There's No Way I Could Have Known"

Generally speaking, moral practice discloses that a person is appraised if his ignorance about an event or its consequences could have been remedied or avoided, even if this would have been relatively difficult for him to do. Sometimes a person is even appraised for omitting to remedy his ignorance, as well as for the event under evaluation. If someone wishes to exempt himself from appraisal for leaving the keys in your car in the parking lot, by saying "I did not know that someone would see the keys and take the car," it would be perfectly ordinary to reply, "You should have known not to leave the keys in the car." It is reasonable to expect that a person who drives a car, whether that car belongs to another or not, has enough experience and knowledge about car theft to know that the probability of a car's being stolen is certainly increased if the keys are left in it. This person's ignorance was not unavoidable. But was it reasonable enough to function as an excuse? In the section on excuses, we will show how the language of moral responsibility descriptions employs avoidable ignorance to diminish blame. At that point, we shall see that not all avoidable or remedial ignorance is blameworthy to the same degree. However, in our present discussion we wish to see what moral practice reveals to us about the times when an otherwise competent and knowledgeable agent may be considered nonappraisable because he simply could not have known what he was doing, or what the outcomes of his conduct might be.

John Hospers says that an example of unavoidable ignorance occurred when the American Indians first drank the Europeans' alcohol. According to Hospers, the Indians could not possibly have known that drinking it would make them drunk, and thus they were not accountable for becoming drunk, at least for the first time.[35]   If Hospers is correct, then it seems that ordinary practice **does not require** that unavoidable ignorance be such that it is **logically impossible to know** what one was doing or what the possible results of one's conduct might be in order to be nonappraisable. Consider that the Indians in Hospers' example could have experimented with the drink the Europeans gave them. They could have asked questions about its intoxicating powers, since they did have experience with natural intoxicants. It was not logically impossible for them to remedy their ignorance. But Hospers' point is that their's was **unavoidable ignorance because it lay beyond what it was reasonable to expect them to remedy.**

Let's imagine that we could put our range of knowledge on a sort of continuum. The range is roughly from **"logically impossible to know what one is doing or what the effects of the conduct will be"** at one end, to **"anyone should know what he is doing and what effects result from this sort of conduct"** at the other. Somewhere on this continuum short of **"logically impossible to know what one is doing or what the effects of the conduct will be"** is **"unavoidable ignorance which lies beyond what it is reasonable to expect one to remedy."**

> *Suppose that Marshall is taking care of his neighbor's house while the neighbor is on vacation. Just after dark one evening he goes over to the house and finds everything O.K. Then, he decides to go and check in the garage to be sure everything is fine in there, too. When Marshall walks into the dark garage, he flips on the light switch. Just then, the bulb pops. The small spark from the bulb ignites gas fumes which accumulated in the garage as a result of a gas leak which developed after the owner had left. A horrific explosion results. The garage is destroyed and Marshall is killed.*

Is the owner of the home appraisable? If so, for what? Is Marshall accountable for his own death and/or the destruction of the neighbor's garage? If not, why not?

Let us assume that the owner kept his garage in a reasonable state of repair, and had no knowledge of a gas leak prior to leaving. Does this mean his ignorance about the gas leak was unavoidable? According to the description above, the gas

---

[35]John Hospers, Human Conduct: Problems in Ethics (New York: Harcourt, Brace, Jovanovich, Inc., 1982), p. 362.

leak developed after the owner left. So, it seems unreasonable to expect the owner to know about it, although it is not logically impossible for him to have known about it. He could have had measuring and warning devices installed in his garage, just in anticipation that a leak might occur. But it is just too farfetched to expect such precautions. If we stretch the limit of "what it is reasonable to expect one to know" to lengths such as this, we may take up all the space for any appeal to ignorance. Perhaps we could say that the neighbor is appraisable for Marshall's death, but excused because it is just not reasonable to expect him to have taken additional steps to insure that his garage pipes were safe. Yet this hardly seems advisable. It may be better simply to say he is not accountable. Is it necessary that his ignorance be logically impossible to remedy in order for him to be exempt from giving an account of his action? Or, is it sufficient to declare him nonappraisable because his ignorance was unavoidable; meaning that even though it was not logically impossible for him to know about the gas leak, still it was unreasonable to expect that he should know or should have found out whether there was one or not?

On the other hand, is Marshall's ignorance of the gas leak remedial or unavoidable, and how does our decision about this matter reflect on his appraisability for destroying the garage, and even his own death? If we say Marshall was careless, or negligent, or suicidal, then we make a moral appraisal of his action. Each of these concepts reveals what we think about the range and nature of his ignorance. The very fact that we use this language shows that we believe that he was appraisable. On the other hand, if we speak of him as a "victim", then we are not holding him appraisable. We may call this a "freak accident" or use some other grammar to indicate that Marshall is not being appraised at all, but we will not hold him morally to blame.

b) Mental Deficiency of the Agent

Mental deficiency in which the subject *is not able to understand or appreciate the gravity of his conduct* is commonly recognized in moral practice as sufficient grounds to remove a person from moral appraisability because it creates a type of unavoidable ignorance. Descriptions of mental deficiency are of two basic types: **insanity** and **defect of reason**. A person may have some defect of reason sufficient to render him nonappraisable, and yet not be insane. The defect of reason may be some form of retardation, perhaps physically induced; or else it may be some form of psychological impairment or mental illness.

We should also distinguish defect of reason caused by mental illness, defect, or retardation, as well as insanity, from the types of internal coercion discussed earlier. Obsession, compulsion, addiction, and such are considerations which have to do with the degree of control a person has over his actions, attempts, or omissions, not whether he is unavoidably ignorant. The obsessed or addicted can understand an appraisal of their conduct as morally blameworthy. They may even realize the gravity of the conduct, but they are "unable to control themselves." Whereas, those we classify as mentally ill or defective, retarded, or insane cannot understand an appraisal of their conduct as morally blameworthy or appreciate the gravity of such.

Defects of reason often take the form of simply not knowing right from wrong, or being unable to appreciate moral distinctions because one cannot deliberate properly, or realize the impact of one's conduct either on the interests and desires of others or on oneself. Such inability raises a related consideration which is also helpful in distinguishing those who cannot control themselves from those who are unavoidably ignorant because of mental deficiency or insanity. Notice that the obsessed or addicted may feel guilt and regret, but not be able to stop. However, those who are mentally defective or insane do not know how to use a language of guilt, shame, and regret. They may not know that they should use such a language, because they cannot appreciate the moral nature of their conduct.

Moral practice reveals something very interesting here. If someone habitually steps on the interests of others, we may try out the description that he is very wicked ("without principles"), thereby holding him appraisable. But if blame and remediation fail to alter his conduct, and we cannot call forth guilt, shame, and regret, then we will typically resort to clinical language. The inference from this practice seems to be that we believe that no one could do this and not know it was immoral unless something was mentally wrong with him.

Another way of conceiving this is to point to the difference we make between *the criminally insane* and *the hardened criminal.* The criminally insane are those believed not to be able to appreciate the gravity of their conduct, whereas hardened criminals are believed to be fully aware of the significance and malignancy of their conduct; we have simply concluded that they do not care. Of course, we wish to protect ourselves and others from both types of these people. The fact that the criminally insane are not morally appraisable does not make them any less dangerous. In fact, it may make them more dangerous, because the human community has lost a significant vocabulary for guiding and restraining their actions, attempts, and omissions.

It is doubtful that there is any completely adequate set of criteria which can be formed theoretically to make the judgment that one is insane. The McNaghten Rules designed to perform the function of determining insanity under law are extremely vague and debatable.[36] They state, "To establish a defense on the ground of insanity, it must be clearly proved that, at the time of committing the act, the accused was laboring under such a defect of reason, from disease of the mind, as not to know the nature and quality of the act he was doing, or, if he did know it, that he did not know he was doing what was wrong."

Of course, we have very complete descriptions of mental disorders in the psychological literature. But it is sometimes not clear whether these apply in an individual case, or to what degree these are morally significant. A person could exhibit classically bizarre psychological behavior, but still know how to use moral language and appreciate the effects of his conduct on others. In fact, some clinical labels may carry moral weight as well.

So, what we are left with is the process of trying alternative descriptions of the conduct of such persons, in order to see whether they are incapable of

---

[36]Ibid., pp. 382-383. For further discussion of moral and legal appraisability and mental deficiency consult the following. Robert Cummins, "Culpability and Mental Disorder," Canadian Journal of Philosophy 10 (1980); Antony Duff, "Psychopathy and Moral Understanding," American Philosophical Quarterly 14 (1977); Herbert Fingarette, The Meaning of Criminal Insanity (Berkeley: University of California Press, 1972); Antony Flew, Crime or Disease? (London: Macmillan, 1973); Vinit Haksar, "The Responsibility of Psychopaths," Philosophical Quarterly 15 (1965); and Jeffrie Murphy, "Moral Death: A Kantian Essay on Psychopathy," Ethics 82 (1972).

preventing themselves (internal coercions and impulses), or if they are unable to appreciate the moral appraisals made of their conduct and/or character (unavoidably ignorant because of mental deficiency, or insanity), or if they are simply morally reprobate (hardened criminals).

c) Moral Innocence of the Agent

Moral Innocence is the state in which the subject *is not yet able to understand the effects of his actions, attempts, or omissions, or appreciate the gravity of these*. The category of the morally innocent is separated from that of mental deficiency, because common moral practice takes note of the development of human persons by creating a stage for every person during which one is considered morally innocent, meaning that moral appraisal is not appropriate. But this stage is temporary. The ignorance of such persons, though unavoidable, will pass.

In practice, the same person may be considered innocent about some areas of moral concern, and yet not innocent about others. Here it is difficult to separate the concept of *naivety* from *innocence*. The naive are inexperienced or unacquainted with certain relationships persons have to each other and to entities worthy of moral consideration. But the morally innocent may be well acquainted or experienced with an arena which has an applicable moral language, but not appreciate how this language is to be applied to them or others. A person could be well educated about human sexuality and psychology--certainly not naive about it. However, he might not grasp the possible effects of such activity and the manner in which its attendant relationships may cause harm or bring joy. We should likewise notice the distinction between moral innocence and wickedness. Moral innocence is not equivalent to "intentionally ignoring the moral significance of one's conduct." Appreciating the gravity of one's conduct, but ignoring it, may mean simply that one is wicked.

Consider the description of moral innocence in this example.

> *Little Timmy is eight years old. He loves cars. He likes to go out and sit in his father's car and play with the steering wheel, blinkers, and pedals. He strains to reach the pedals and pretends to give the car gas and shift the gears. Timmy has been told not to play in the car, that it is a dangerous thing to do. He knows the car is huge, heavy, capable of great speed and impact. He has seen car crashes on T.V. and persons hit by cars, too. He knows all of this, but he plays in the car anyway. One day, while playing in the car, Timmy moves the gear shift at the same time he is pressing on the clutch and the car rolls down the driveway. The car builds up speed and flies across the street, jumps the curb ,and runs over two neighborhood girls playing with their Barbie dolls on the sidewalk.*

Is little Timmy appraisable for his conduct? After all, someone might say to Timmy, "That's what happens when you play in the car and you knew it could happen, but you played in the car anyway."

Timmy certainly knew some important facts about cars. He even knew it was wrong for him to play in the car. He is not mentally impaired in such a way as not to know right and wrong. But did he appreciate the gravity of this action?

Was he aware of the potential for harm in what he was doing?   I suggest that he probably was not. And while this is a gruesome event, which may be the incident of little Timmy's loss of innocence, he is not morally appraisable for it.[37] In fact, we sometimes reserve the concept *tragedy* for such an event.

Moral innocents lack certain capacities which are fundamental to being a member of the moral community. These particularly relate to their level of self-consciousness, but they may also be noticeably absent abilities relevant to the ways in which the subject is able to respond and act toward others as persons who have rights and interests protected by moral norms and concepts. To be clearer, our use of the concept of moral innocence is reserved for persons who look at the same facts and conduct as everyone else, but then something escapes their notice or appreciation. Specifically, what escapes their notice is the way a moral description may be made using these facts. In our example, Timmy has failed to catch on to the potential for harm that accompanies his conduct.

But children are not the only moral innocents. Adolescents, and even adults, may be morally innocent, at least in some respects. A teenager, for example, may learn to drive a car; she may know how to work on it, even being able to repair all kinds of mechanical problems. She may know about the relative risks of inexperienced drivers because she watches T.V., reads the paper, and has been warned by seeing films and hearing stories of young drivers who have wrecks. However, she still may not appreciate the moral significance to herself and others of taking her car out for a drive. About this she may be innocent.

Herbert Morris has examined our moral practice about the use of the concept of innocence and specifically the loss of innocence. He recognizes that a morally innocent person is absent a certain kind of knowledge.   It may be that the person does not know how to anticipate that actions often have many possible results; or the person may not know enough about causal connections to appreciate that doing one thing will produce an effect that may be morally blameworthy.

"When one loses innocence one has, then, an awareness of others and oneself and of possible relations between persons that one did not before possess."[38] One experiences himself as capable of inflicting moral evil; and one becomes aware of having had moral evil inflicted upon him. Until such a realization occurs, one remains, to that extent, morally innocent, according to Morris.

For Discussion

Consider the following examples and take a position of the question of the appraisability of the agent involved. Is the agent appraisable? If so, for what?

1) Suppose a cashier at a fast food restaurant sells a hamburger to a customer. The hamburger has been tainted by another employee, because she sees

---

[37]Of course, I am not considering the shared responsibility that his parents may have for his supervision; nor am I concerned with the legal ramifications of all of this. I am only suggesting what we might say morally about his innocence.

[38]Herbert Morris, On Guilt and Innocence (Berkeley: University of California Press, 1976), p. 149.

the customer and wants to do something spiteful to him. Is the cashier appraisable? If so, for what? Explain what considerations from this chapter you used in forming your position.

2) Uncle Billy had a stroke six weeks ago and has finally been released into the care of a nursing home. The stoke has effected his thinking powers and his memory. Sometimes he wanders out into the halls in the nude after his bath. Is he appraisable for walking the halls in his birthday suit? Explain what considerations from this chapter you used in forming your position.

3) Jim Bob is driving his new Toyota pick-up in front of the elementary school where he is supposed to meet his younger sister. As he is stopped at the crossing in order to let children walk across the street, a car hits his pick-up from behind. The car lunges forward and several children are injured severely. Is Jim Bob appraisable? If so, for what? Explain what considerations from this chapter you used in forming your position.

4) Ken and Dave are fishing on the city lake when a storm arises suddenly. The boat is tossed about and eventually capsizes. Both men cling to the underside of the boat, but Dave, having been injured in the accident, becomes groggy. Just before he passes out, Ken grabs Dave's hands and holds on. As the hours pass, Ken begins to loses his grip in the cold water and Dave slips into a watery death. Is Ken appraisable? If so, for what? Explain what considerations from this chapter you used in forming your position.

5) Sarah and Liz share an apartment in the upstairs of an old house near the campus. One night they are awakened by the smell of smoke. As Sarah comes into the hall to inspect what is happening, she sees a raging fire outside Liz's bedroom at the end of the hall. She hears Liz screaming, but she cannot get through the fire and debris to get into Liz's room. Finally, she flees. Is Sarah appraisable for not saving Liz? Explain what considerations from this chapter you used in formingyour position.

6) Joey and Rebecca are residents at a half-way house. They are ages 28 and 23 respectively. Both are mentally retarded and require constant supervision. After a swimming party, they return to the house and Joey sneaks into Rebecca's room. They have sex together, and are caught in the act by one of the attendants. Are they appraisable? Is the attendant appraisable? If so, for what? Explain what considerations from this chapter you used in forming your position.

7) Twin five-year-olds each receive a kitten on their birthday. They love playing in the basement with the kittens. One day when the kittens got particularly dirty, the children washed them in the bathtub, and then put them in the clothes dryer. The kittens were killed. Are the children appraisable? Explain what considerations from this chapter you used in forming your position.

8) What is you response to Fyodor Dostoyevsky's story in <u>The Gambler</u>. He gives a memorable portrait of the compulsive gambler who knows that he will end up penniless, but cannot stop himself. He cannot stop while winning, because he believes that he will continue to win. He cannot stop while he is losing, because

he must recover his loses. The gambler is aware of this pattern, yet he is driven by an overwhelming impulse to gamble. Is the gambler appraisable? If so, for what? Explain what considerations from this chapter you used in forming your position.

9) Provide an illustration or example of lost moral innocence. You might consider a movie such as "Born on the Fourth of July," or "The Lord of the Flies." Or, you might examine a religious text, such as Genesis, Chapter 3. You might even focus on a historical example in which it is said that a people or a nation may lose its moral innocence--such as Vietnam or Watergate. Ask yourself these

a) When someone loses moral innocence, what have they lost?
b) Is it necessary to lose one's moral innocence in order to be fully a person? Or, is the loss of innocence always a "fall"?
c) Is moral innocence lost instantaneously or gradually?
d) What is the difference between losing one's innocence and having it taken from you?
e) Can a person lose moral innocence and not become a cynic or bitter person?
f) Does moral language disclose that we feel guilt or shame over the loss of innocence?
g) Once innocence is lost, can a person ever return to that state?

Chapter Five: Assigning the Degree of Responsibility in Moral Appraisal-- Justifications

Introduction

Moral appraisal should not be likened to the assembling of a bicycle. Our moral practice is too messy to be reduced to a step-by-step set of instructions. Making a moral appraisal is probably more like riding a bike than it is like assembling it. When learning to ride a bike, a person experiences a certain amount of trial and error. Correction and help from others is necessary. And, in the final analysis, there is a kind of nuance and feel which must be acquired by the rider alone, while actually on the bike. After all, learning to ride a bike is not some instinct that we possess in the same way that frogs know how to catch flies. Likewise, neither is *learning* to do a moral appraisal something we know by instinct.

So, what follows in the next three chapters should not be read as a set of instructions to follow in order to establish the degree of moral blame or praise a person is to receive. At the same time, though, a number of cases and examples are given to illustrate some of the characteristic ways we proceed in the moral practice of establishing an agent's moral responsibility. In working with these cases, we will learn something about how moral evaluation works, and thus we will perhaps become better at this important human activity.

Let us return to our bike-riding analogy for a moment. One can instruct another person in this activity, providing procedural suggestions based on having watched others ride bikes, or on riding one oneself. There are some recurring patterns and considerations which characterize this skill. So, also, certain patterns and considerations turn up again and again in the practice of moral appraisal, and these can be captured by a careful description of the way we proceed.

These recurring patterns and considerations should not be understood as component parts of some theory about how moral appraisal **should** be done. We are not offering what ethicists sometimes call a normative theory. That is, we are not trying to correct actual moral practice by reflection and criticism. We are simply trying to describe it. What we have done is somewhat analogous to a person who watches someone riding a bike and then makes observations about the rules, exceptions, and procedures which are exhibited by riders. Such an observer can see what works and maybe why it works; he can also see what does not succeed. If we were to hold to our analogy, then we might say that what follows in these chapters is not to be regarded as something which is fixed or required. It is rather "our way of proceeding" when we engage in the practice of moral appraisal. By paying attention to the practice of appraisal, we can discover the implicit structure of accepting or avoiding blame, including how persons offer justifications or excuses. We can uncover some procedural patterns which occur, and we can learn about rationalizations of conduct, which we reject in ordinary moral practice.

An appraisable agent is **responsible** for what he has done or become. This means that his character and conduct can be accepted, blamed, or praised to some degree. The degree of responsibility assigned is expressed in the language we use. Our choice of intensifying discriminators and moral concepts shows how we evaluate the person's conduct. To help us separate a distinction made in ordinary practice, we shall understand that responsibility comes in degrees, whereas appraisability does not. One either is or is not appraisable; it is an all or nothing thing. But how responsible we shall hold one for something he did varies in degree. Once we decide that it is appropriate to hold a person accountable, we must then decide in what way and to what extent the person is responsible. For ease of communication we will use the name **"responsibility description"** for the account given of an agent's conduct or character according to which some degree of blame or praise is assigned in one of the following ways:

1) under a moral concept;
2) under a general moral rule;
3) under a special moral obligation or prohibition, which is appropriate to the agent.

Responsibility descriptions may be offered by the agent himself, or by any of those in a position to appraise him within the moral community. Usually, responsibility descriptions are provided by both the agent and others. The assignment of moral responsibility is a kind of playing back and forth. You may blame me for an action. I then reply by offering justifications or excuses, usually doing everything I can to minimize any degree of blame. You then counter by examining my justifications or excuses. The goal seems to be to reach consensus on some responsibility description to which you will agree, and which I will accept as descriptive of what I did.[39] Of course, consensus is not the only option. Those making the appraisal may sometimes act violently against those who will not accept responsibility for their conduct, or they may simply withdraw from the agent and ostracize him. The agent who finds his responsibility descriptions are not accepted may offer an alternate description. Or, he may try to attack the appraisal process by denying the moral standards used or impugning the credibility of the moral community itself. Some of these strategies are more fully described in the following paragraphs.

Whenever a person defends his conduct or character as the morally right thing, he offers a **justification.** In this chapter we will make some observations about two patterns of justification which occur frequently in moral practice. One way of justifying is to claim that blaming descriptions of one's conduct have misdescribed what took place. In this way a person offers alternative moral concepts or rules instead of those which other persons are using. We say in effect, "You haven't got it right, that's not what I did." Or, "You haven't got it right, that's not what I am like." Another way of justifying is to try to show that our conduct was consistent with all moral standards for the situation. These descriptions are used when one is being blamed for not having done one's best. In

---

[39]This process is not unlike what John Rawls calls reaching a reflective equilibrium in A Theory of Justice, (Cambridge, MA: Harvard University Pess, 1971), pp. 20, 48-51. There are some very excellent works on responsibility description. Herbert Fingarette, On Responsibility (New York: Basic Books, 1967); Jonathan Glover, Responsibility (London: Routledge and Kegan Paul, 1970); Moral Responsibility, edited by John Martin Fischer (Ithaca: Cornell University Press, 1986), and Responsibility, edited by Feinberg and Gross. An interesting approach to this issue is Edmund Pincoffs, "Are Questions of Desert Decidable?" in Justice and Punishment, edited by J.B. Cederblom and William L. Blizek (Cambridge: Ballinger, 1977).

these cases we are saying, "I did what I was supposed to do," or "I did my duty."

Those responsibility descriptions which do not deny moral wrongdoing but by citing extenuating considerations attempt to diminish the blame which should be assigned to the moral agent are **excuses.** Some excuses have to do with the intentions of the agent. Others have to do with the nature, extent, and type of deliberation under which the event occurred. Still others relate to the agent's purpose; that is, his understanding of the consequences or outcomes expected from his conduct, and what he wanted to achieve.

One of the most basic ways of thinking about the difference between justification and excuse is to consider that a justification says, "Yes, I did it, and it was the right thing to do," whereas an excuse says, "Yes, I did it, and it was wrong, but in this case there were extenuating circumstances which should diminish my blame."[40]

Justifications and excuses which are rejected by the moral community are called **rationalizations**. We will try to notice how a description of some common rationalizations reveals why some justifications and excuses fail all the time and why some work some of the time.

1.   Redescription as Justification

This approach to justification defends a person's conduct or character by holding that those who wish to blame him have not accurately described what he has done or what he is like. So, the person offers a redescription of his conduct or character under a different moral concept or rule in order to defend himself.

A fairly common example of the way this strategy works is seen in the contemporary debate about the act of abortion. Many persons believe that the moral appraisal of abortion depends greatly on how one answers the question: Is abortion murder? A person may attempt to justify an abortion on the grounds that the act of "killing a fetus" is not equivalent to "murdering a person." Practically speaking, what this amounts to is that one is attempting to justify abortion by saying that blaming this action under the concept of "murder" is based on a misdescription. The idea is that we cannot ensnare the act of abortion under the moral concept of murder, unless the action is something approximating "an intentional killing of an innocent person for personal interests, not for self defense." If we try to call abortion "murder", and it is not an intentional act; or the fetus is not a person; or it is done for self-defense, then the act cannot be ensnared under the concept of murder and we have misdescribed it.

Consider another, less controversial, example.

Suppose Steve sits down to study his history and finds that his textbook is missing. Someone else has it. Just then Steve sees

---

[40]This way of thinking about the difference between justification and excuse shows that the use of justification in moral appraisal informs its use in law. In legal theory, the idea of justification communicates that one can make a successful defense against accusation. To be appraisable is simply to be in a position to have to provide an account of one's conduct. Jonathan Bennett, "Accountability," in Philosophical Subjects, edited by Zak vanStraaten (Oxford: Clarendon Pres, 1980).

Ken, who lives across the hall, carrying the book with him to the study room.

Steve might try a responsibility description like, "Ken, you took my book without asking, and that's **stealing**." Steve would be right in recognizing that "taking things without permission" is a part of the moral concept of "stealing." However, there is more to the concept of stealing than just this. For example, normally when we use the concept of stealing, we mean to describe a situation in which "a person has taken something that does not belong to him, and is treating it as though it were his own, to use or dispose of as he wishes, and with no intention of returning it." So, there are features of Ken's "taking the book" which must be present in order for it to fall under the concept of "stealing," other than merely that he "took it without permission."

Ken may reply to Steve, "I didn't steal it. I have no intention of keeping your book. I only **borrowed** it." Then, Ken is offering a substitute moral concept under which he is willing to take responsibility for his action. Ken does not accept "stealing" as a correct description of his action; its blame is too intense. Instead, he offers the concept of "borrowing" as a redescription of his conduct. Suppose Steve then replies, "I don't remember your asking to borrow the book." Steve is here reminding Ken that the moral concept of "borrowing" includes the idea that a thing is "taken by permission of its owner."

Now we can see that Steve is no longer disputing the application of the concept of stealing. In effect, he has accepted the fact that Ken's action is not to be described as stealing. But there is some moral concern he still wishes to consider. He is now questioning Ken's use of "borrowing" as the proper description of what happened. He may believe that Ken has done something blamable even under the concept of "borrowing." Steve may think that Ken is responsible for "omitting to receive permission" to borrow the book. Ken will have a justification for his omission only if "borrowing" may sometimes be done without permission (implied or explicit). If Ken and Steve have used the concept of borrowing to allow "taking without permission"--such as borrowing clothes, notebook paper, books, etc-- then Ken may be justified under the concept of "borrowing" as used here; and Steve has no real moral complaint. He may reply, "We never asked to borrow things from each other before." Of course, Steve may use this incident as an opportunity to redefine the moral ground of borrowing activity between himself and Ken. He may say, "Well, from now on, ask when you want something." However, if Steve and Ken have no explicit or implicit use of the concept of "borrowing" which allowed the "taking of things without permission," then Ken's omission will not be justified, and he will deserve some blame. The best he will be able to do is to offer some excuse for "omitting to receive permission to borrow the book." When he does so, the process may continue further. If he says, "You're right. I should have received permission. I'm sorry. But you were not in the room at the time I needed the book," then Steve will still have other responses to make before the appraisal is complete.

The same kinds of misdescription using moral concepts may occur when speaking of a person's character. For example, we may reproach a father who forces his teenager to stay home and clean his room, rather than allow him to go to the big football game at the high school. "You are *cruel* to make him do that" he may say. But the father may reply, "I must sometimes be a *disciplinarian* ." The father may go on to explain the varied attempts he has made in order to get his son to clean his room, and he may explain to us that this restriction is not very severe. He may enlighten us as to the educational intention of his decision and show us how his son has had opportunity to avoid the restriction. Perhaps we will withdraw the use of the moral concept "cruel" because of this redescription, or perhaps we will offer some other alternative concept.

Our original description of the incident between Steve and Ken can be altered to show another interesting feature of moral practice, this time having to do with rules. Suppose Steve crosses the hall and confronts Ken by saying, "I see you have my book. You really should have returned it by now because you promised that you would; and persons should keep their promises." In this example, we have good reason to suppose that the rule **"Persons should keep their promises"** is the one which determines the responsibility description to be offered, **if** one true description of what Ken did is that he "made a promise." The rule "Persons should keep their promises" is a *reminder* that the moral concept of promising includes the notion of "an agreement between persons which one must keep."

Of course, if Ken merely took the book without making a promise, then the moral rule about promise-keeping would not apply. Any attempt to use it in affixing responsibility would be properly met with some type of redescription justification. Ken may simply say, "I never promised to return the book." If this is a true description, then Ken broke no promise, and Steve could not hold him responsible for breaking a promise which was never made. Ken may be responsible for something else, but not for breaking promises.

Throughout this discussion we have been uncovering several important points which arise out of our description of moral practice. We can notice that moral concepts do not come complete with a key to knowing exactly when they are applicable, even with fairly well-defined and hardened concepts such as "murder" or "stealing." The problem is not so much that we do not know what the concept means, but that we sometimes are unsure of whether it applies or not. That is to say that the point we are making is not like trying to determine when we should use the concept "town" instead of "village" to describe a place. We are much less clear about what must obtain for a "village" to become a "town;" or for a "town" to become a "city," than we are about knowing when "a killing" becomes a "murder" or "the taking of something" a "stealing." In the case of moral concepts such as "murder" or "stealing" some central features can be identified. But even after this is done, we may no more know whether an event is describable under one of these concepts than that a village has become a town. Our description of moral practice has erupted an important point of contact between moral appraisal and what philosophers call **epistemology.** Epistemology, or "the theory of knowledge," is concerned with what is the true description of an event--or with what actually happened. What our description of moral language has uncovered is particularly relevant to the theory of knowledge, and specifically, to the whole idea of what it means to determine "what actually happened." Our account of justification as redescription reveals that determining "what actually took place" is mostly a matter of finding out what responsibility description we can make stick. What we have in ordinary moral practice is the trying on of alternative responsibility descriptions of an agent's conduct or character to see what language is accepted. The description which sticks becomes "what actually happened."

This may be very disturbing when it is first considered. We may want to protest that sometimes "what actually happened" can be determined with much greater objectivity and accuracy than just deciding on what responsibility description we will accept. Persons who make this protest are right to do so. We would claim too much if we ignored this fact. What we have said about the significance of responsibility descriptions to epistemology does not necessarily require us to conclude that just any description of what happened will do, provided that it is agreed to. Consider that in our case involving Ken and Steve, someone standing nearby at the time the book was taken can tell whether Ken made a promise to return the book, or whether he received permission to take the book. Such eyewitness testimony is certainly recognized as relevant to determining what actually happened. Or, if Ken's conversation with Steve was recorded, then the standard rules of evidence would be satisfied; and no matter how much Ken protested to the contrary, we could know whether he made a promise, or whether he received permission to take the book. His blame would only be compounded by deceitfulness, if he insisted that promising not be included in the responsibility description of his action in the face of evidence to the contrary.

Determining "what actually took place," though made somewhat more objective by the addition of empirical data such as an eyewitness or a tape recorder, may still be seen as a function of what one will take responsibility for. What has happened is just that it becomes much more difficult to alter or change the responsibility description in the face of such evidence.

It may be helpful to make one final observation. It is probably a common assumption that persons "know truly" what they did when they acted. So, if a person would simply be honest about what he did, then we could establish his moral responsibility without any problem. But careful attention to moral practice suggests that the matter is not so simple as this. What we learn is that we need others to tell us what we did! We are actually dependent on others, to some extent at least, to help us understand, define, and describe our own conduct. There is no account of "what actually happened" which is inseparable from the dialogue between our own self-description and that of others.

2.   "Doing One's Duty" as Justification

Responsibility descriptions are often hard to form when persons find themselves in situations having multiple moral appraisal standards for guiding conduct, and two or more of these appear to be in conflict. But these cases seem to be very common in moral practice. Such instances are called *dilemmas* . In ordinary moral practice, when one says "I am in a dilemma," he means that he is aware of two conflicting moral requirements, expectations, or values which both seem applicable in the same situation. Persons in dilemmas often say they are in a "no-win" situation. What they mean is that no matter what alternative they choose, they can be blamed for the choice, since every alternative will transgress some moral obligation or detract from some moral value.

Despite the seeming frequency of dilemmas in actual practice, not all persons agree that there are any such things as moral dilemmas. One of the classic theoretical ways of understanding this issue is called moral absolutism. **Moral absolutism** *is a responsibility description which holds that it is always possible for a person to choose at least one alternative which is consistent with all the moral standards which apply to a specific case, and that anything short of this is blameworthy.* Since an absolutist says there is always at least one right thing to do in any moral situation, there are never any "no-win" moral dilemmas according to moral absolutism. Most philosophers believe that Immanuel Kant's decision theory was absolutist: we never face situations in which there is a fundamental irreconcilability between our moral standards. This is an important and controversial view, which has been widely explored in the more technical philosophical literature.[41]

In giving an account of moral absolutism, we must be careful to call attention to the difference between absolutism as a theory, and the descriptive observation that some moral concepts and rules are universal in scope. These two categories are very often confused. But the distinction seems to amount to this. An absolutist claims that there is always a morally defensible alternative in every decision a person faces. However, to say that a moral concept or rule is universal in scope means that the concept or rule, as an appraisal standard, may be applied to all members of the moral community. To hold to the universalizability of moral concepts or rules is, in itself, to say nothing about the decision alternatives themselves or whether there is always at least one alternative which satisfies any set of moral standards. It is quite possible that persons may utilize universal concepts or rules, while holding that there are times when these come into conflict in such a way that one has no decision alternative which meets all the relevant appraisal standards.

In any case, whether it is theoretically true that we *always* have an action alternative which is consistent with all our moral standards in every situation or not, we shall content ourselves with the more modest acknowledgement that it does seem true, simply on a description of moral practice, that there are *some* situations we face in which it is possible to conduct ourselves according to all of the applicable moral appraisal standards. In such cases, the "I did what I was supposed to" or "I did my duty" justification is appropriate.

There is something else lurking in the shadows of moral practice though. Frequently, there is a kind of blaming description which is offered even of those who "did their duty." The appraisal is based on the idea that doing one's duty is not necessarily doing the *best* thing morally speaking. This appraisal has a certain intuitive appeal. For example, while a wife might want her husband to remain faithful to her out of a sense of obligation to the vows he has made, she certainly would prefer that he remain faithful because he loves her. What should we make of situations in which a person's conduct is not describable under any blaming concept, but it is still not "the best he could do"?

Consider the following example.

> *Michael, a young private in the army, has been sent into the field of battle. His best friend Kevin, assigned to the same unit, has just been shot and is seriously wounded. They both know that medical assistance is some ime away and that the enemy is known for its extremely cruel torture of captives. Their unit is withdrawing in a hurry, but Michael does not know how close the enemy is or whether they will overrun the position he is now occupying along*

---

[41]Ornora Neil, Acting on Principle: An Essay on Kantian Ethics, (New York: Columbia University Press, 1975), pp. 132-137. There are various logical issues at stake in offering justifications. Lawrence Heintz, "The Logic of Defenses," American Philosophical Quarterly 18 (1981).

with Kevin. Kevin asks Michael to kill him and then rejoin the unit.
Kevin is in pain, and fears that the enemy might get to him if
Michael leaves him. What should Michael do?

In order to expose some of the important considerations raised by this example, we can first identify the possible moral appraisal standards which may be applicable, and then exhibit some of the available conduct alternatives which Michael might consider.

Possible Moral Appraisal Standards

- Persons should treat others as valuable in themselves, and not as objects to some other purpose (treat others with respect).
- Do not kill innocent persons.
- Do not cause unnecessary harm or injury to another person.
- Prevent suffering, harm and injury whenever you are able, and it does not require a sacrifice of comparable worth.

Some Possible Conduct Alternatives

Kill Kevin and flee	Stay with him, give aid, hide	Carry him with you, flee	Just leave	Leave him behind hidden, aided, and armed; go for help	Leave him behind hidden, aided, and unarmed; go for help

Is there an alternative which, if chosen, would enable Michael to defend his choice as morally right because it was not blamable under any of the appraisal standards? If there is, then Michael may say that he did his moral duty.

If Michael chose either of the "Leave him behind" options, he could defend himself by saying that he did all he was morally obligated to do for Kevin. The "Carry him" and "Stay with him" alternatives might require that Michael make a sacrifice of comparable worth (risking his own life), which is not an obligation under the moral appraisal standards applicable to his situation. These alternatives could be described as *supererogatory* . A **supererogatory** *act is one which goes beyond what a person is morally expected or required to perform.* The "Just leave" and "Kill Kevin" alternatives would require that Michael offer some excusing description. They could not be justified because the choice of either would violate one or more of appraisal standards. We could not know in advance what kind of reaction the community would make to either of these choices, without knowing what sort of an excuse Michael would offer with his description. Only after we hear his excusing description could we decide the degree of blame he deserves, or whether and how he should be praised.

Our account may have overlooked a special role obligation Michael had: the obligation of friendship with Kevin. Friendship imposes special role obligations and prohibitions upon us. There are moral expectations and concepts used in appraising our relationship with friends that do not come on the horizon in our ordinary interactions with others. As Kevin's friend, Michael might choose the "Carry him" or "Stay with him" alternative, instead of one of the "Leave him" options. The choice of one of these alternatives would be understandable as an obligation of a friend to another friend. In fact, if Michael were later praised for his conduct as though it was heroic, he might simply say, "I just did what a friend should do."

But could the "Kill Kevin and flee" alternative be justified by an appeal to friendship as a special role obligation? If Michael killed Kevin to end his suffering because he was his friend, and he later tried to justify this act, he would still have to recognize that at least one of the appraisal standards held by the general moral community would have been violated. We have already seen in an earlier discussion that the moral community prefers conduct according to general moral standards, rather than by special roles *whenever these are in conflict* . Accordingly, although Michael's blame might be diminished by an appeal to the friendship role as an excusing condition, he would still be offering an excuse, not a justification.

Suppose that Michael chooses an option that meets all of the moral standards applicable, but he is appraised with the responsibility description, "You should have done something else, it would have been better"? Then what can he say in reply?

For Discussion

1) Define the following terms:

Responsibility description	Ethical Relativism
Justification	Moral Absolutism
Excuse	Dilemma
Rationalization	Epistemology

2)   What implications does the description of affixing responsibility in moral appraisal have for the study of the theory of knowledge?

3)   Moral appraisals are often made under the description of a moral concept term.   What is the moral concept Susan recommends for appraising Russell in the following example? Would he be able to describe his conduct under a different concept?   Explain what considerations from this chapter you used in forming your position.

Susan and Christy share an apartment together near their work place. They are good friends and frequently double date, or have one or the other, or sometimes even both, of their boyfriends over to the apartment. From time to time, the boys stay overnight. Christy is getting serious about Russell. They are considering living together, and getting married. Susan does not approve of Russell, and thinks that he would make Christy perfectly miserable. She tells Christy that Russell is just after sex, and doesn't really care for her. In fact, she tells Christy that she can prove that Russell is lecherous (def.--"desirous of inordinate indulgence in sexual activity"). She proposes a test. She says she will "come on" to him, and that she's sure Russell will respond. Christy agrees to this test. So, one evening when Russell comes over to cook out and then watch a couple of movies, Christy finds an excuse to leave the apartment for a while, and Susan makes her move. Russell is appalled. He says, "I can't believe this. You call yourself Christy's friend." Just then,

Christy arrives home and hears the argument. She explains what
has happened to Russell.

4) Describe a case in which a person has a justification because his action
has been misdescribed. Assume that the first concept term below is the one offered
in appraisal, and that the second concept term is the redescription offered in
justification.

> The businesswoman offered a bribe/gratuity.
> Johnny is playing viciously/aggressively.
> What the girls did was vandalism/a prank.
> Suzy was cheating/her eyes wandered.
> Bill committed adultery/had a sexual indiscretion.

5) Design cases like those in #4 for attempts and omissions.

6) Design cases like those in #s 4 and 5, except show misdescription
because of the application of an inappropriate moral rule, not a moral concept.

7) Provide a realistically conceivable alternative which enables all the given
moral standards to be met in the following situations. If there is no such
alternative, tell why.

--Situation: Patient tells psychiatrist she intends to kill someone.

--Standards: "Psychiatrist should keep information obtained in a
                 therapeutic setting confidential (Special Role)."

                 "All persons should prevent unnecessary harm."

Alternative:_____

--Situation: A person faces draft into the military.

--Standards: "We should obey the law."

                 "We should not kill innocent persons."

Alternative:_____

--Situation: The accused is found guilty.

--Standards: "An eye for an eye, and a tooth for a tooth."

                 "We should rehabilitate criminals."

Alternative_____

--Situation: Radicals are elected to power in a country with which the U.S. wishes to have relations.

--Standards: "Countries should protect their national interests."

"It is morally right for all people to determine how they shall be governed."

Alternative:_____

--Situation: The poor are hungry and in need of shelter and health care.

--Standards: "Persons should have whatever they earn for themselves without force or crime."

"Persons should have sufficient primary social goods for survival."

Alternative_____

Chapter Six: Responsibility Descriptions: Excuses

Introduction

Persons whose untoward conduct is appraisable, and who do not have successful justifications for what they did, will find that their conduct will be described under some blaming description. What remains to be determined is the degree or extent of blame which will be assigned by the concepts and intensifiers employed in the description. Excuses are offered in an attempt to diminish blame, but they cannot remove it. In ordinary practice, only a justification could do that.

In this chapter, we want to describe some cases in which we actually do excuse a person's conduct, and see how the various excuses work.   In J. L. Austin's fascinating essay, "A Plea for Excuses,"[42] he clears a great deal of underbrush for us, and offers some intriguing methodological suggestions for how to look at this kind of practice. Among these suggestions, Austin says that a fairly comprehensive catalog of excuses would even require a survey of the dictionary for terms we employ to diminish blame. He also holds that if a word or expression has proved fit enough to survive in the history of language, then there is some meaningful use for it in practice. Austin also suggests that watching how excuses work will help us pick out the internal detail of the "machinery of conduct," which is considered morally significant. Specifically, he means that ordinary moral practice pays attention to the way excuses have to do with the **intentions, deliberations, and purposes** which characterize our conduct.

Austin points out that we very often confuse the discriminators "intentionally," "deliberately," and ""purposely," which turn up repeatedly in ordinary moral language.[43] However, actual practice shows that these discriminators are used in different ways to mark the aggravation of blame and the intensification of praise. In ordinary language, when we say that something was done *intentionally*, we want to mark that the person was "aware of what he was doing"; he "wanted to do it"; he "did it without coercion"; he "was in control of what he was doing." If the teacher asks,"Johnny, did you spill the ink intentionally?" she wants to know if he was aware of what he was doing, and if he was in control, and most of all if he wanted to do it. When we say that conduct was *deliberate* we want to stress that the person "knew what he was doing"; he "weighed out the alternatives and chose to do what he did." Should we read about a person setting himself on fire, we might say, "I can't believe someone would deliberately do that." Our point is that we cannot imagine someone weighing out various alternatives, and choosing such a painful end. When we say that something was done *on purpose or purposely* we want to communicate that the person "had a plan in mind," or that he did it "in order to bring about a certain outcome." The reason he did it was to make this other thing happen. If Bill knows that Mary's

---

[42]Austin, "A Plea for Excuses," pp. 175-205. There are other fine works on excusing descriptions. Louise Antony, "Why We Excuse," Tulane Studies in Philosophy 28 (1979); Michael Bayles, "A Utilitarian Theory of Excuses, Philosophical Review 78 (1969); Charles Blatz, "Mitigating and Meliorating Defenses," American Philosophical Quarterly Monograph Series 7 (1973); and Daniel Dennett, Elbow Room (Cambridge, MA: MIT Press, 1984).

[43]J. L. Austin, "Three Ways of Spilling Ink," in Philosophical Papers, p. 273.

boss is waiting to check her work, but he does not tell her, hoping that she will lose her job, then she may say, "Bill, you withheld that information on purpose."

Consider the following possible combinations of discriminations about actions, attempts, or omissions.

		Intentionally	Deliberately	Purposely
	Case One	Yes	Yes	Yes
	Case Two	Yes	Yes	No
	Case Three	Yes	No	Yes
Cases	Case Four	No	Yes	Yes
	Case Five	Yes	No	No
	Case Six	No	Yes	No
	Case Seven	No	No	Yes

Excuses diminish blame by discounting one or more of these features of conduct: either intention, deliberation, or purpose. Excuses are cases like #s 2-7, but not case #1. In case #1, the conduct was intentional, deliberate, and purposive. In this case the conduct may be praised intensely for being so, in which case the person needs no excuse. Or, it may be blamed intensely, in which case the person's conduct is inexcusable. In this chapter we are going to discuss several ways the discounting practice represented by cases 2-7 is done in ordinary moral language. For example, if we want to discount the intentional nature of an action, attempt, or omission, we may say it was an *accident or a mistake* . If we did something by accident or mistake, we may be blamable, but not as much so as if we did it intentionally. Or, we may try to diminish blame by saying that we thought about the alternatives and made the best choice we could given the circumstances. We did *the lesser of two evils*, we might say. If we are blameworthy under some appraisal standard, it may nevertheless be the case that our blame is diminished because the moral standard under which we are responsible is of lesser importance than others by which we abided. Or, we may say we thought about our decision and *made a reasonable effort* to conduct ourselves as the appraisal standards of the moral community require. Finally, we may try to show the undesirable outcomes were not the purpose for our conduct. We may say we were ignorant of the consequences, or that we knew blameworthy outcomes could occur, but we did not think them probable. Or, at the least, we may hold that the undesirable consequences were not our purpose; our conduct had some *double effect* .

If we cannot offer an excuse to discount one or more of these features of conduct, then blame will be intensified and this will be indicated in the description of a person's conduct. Consider the following example from an earlier chapter.

> *Larry is a lifeguard at the local beach swimming area. He has wanted this job for a long time, because he has always believed that girls are really attracted to lifeguards with nice tans and such. Well,*

> *one afternoon, while Larry is visiting with two great looking girls*
> *wearing bikinis, a surfer falls from his board and is hit in the head.*
> *The surfer is disoriented and bleeding. He begins to flail in the*
> *water and cry for help. Ordinarily, Larry would see the man and*
> *use his skill to save him. However, Larry is distracted, talking to*
> *the girls. He does not see the surfer, and the surfer drowns.*

Larry is appraisable for his omission to save the surfer under the special role standards applicable to lifeguards; or at least he is appraisable for omitting to make an attempt. If Larry offers an excuse to diminish his responsibility, what can he say? He can say that he was not aware of the surfer; he did not intend to let him drown. He may say that he was "distracted." Or, he can claim that his omission was not deliberate. Since he did not know that the surfer was drowning, then he surely did not decide to talk to the girls, instead of save the surfer. We may accept one or both of these excuses. But we will say that Larry was "negligent" or "careless." We will certainly blame him; perhaps even we will believe that he should be fired from his job. Or, maybe, we will allow him to continue, if he assures us that he will be more "conscientious" and "careful." But the use of the discriminators "negligent" or "careless," although blaming, are not as intense as some others. Larry could have omitted to save the drowning surfer in a more blamable way. If Larry had "refused" to save the surfer, certainly his blame would be more severe.

What is the difference between being "negligent" or "careless" and "refusing"? A very significant moral difference is marked by changing the discriminators. If Larry had seen the drowning surfer, thereby becoming aware that he was drowning, and if Larry had thought about whether he wanted to save him or not, and simply chose to stay in his chair talking to the girls, then he would have "refused" to help. Such a person should be fired from his job as a lifeguard, and he should be more blamed for having deliberately thought about helping and deciding not to than if he had been too "negligent" or "careless" to see the drowning surfer. The intensification of blame which would be placed on Larry under the "refusal" discriminator is a result of his being unable to offer a description of his conduct which can discount the intentional and deliberate nature of his conduct.

SOME EXCUSING DISCRIMINATORS

Intention

mistakenly	accidently	incidentally
didn't mean to	inadvertently	by mistake/accident
under the influence	under orders	under threat
under duress	couldn't help it	adventitiously
unaware	not paying attention	careless
lax	remiss	negligent
slack	inattentive	

Deliberation

whimsically	impulsively	impatiently
benignantly	off the handle	in a hurry
out of the blue	at the drop of a hat	the lesser of two evils
at random	under distraction	recklessly
rashly	heedlessly	thoughtlessly
after reasonable effort (to do otherwise)		

Purpose

didn't realize	with good graces	to no end
in good faith	for all I knew	it was risky
by chance	aimlessly	for no rhyme or reason

Excuses Having To Do With The Intentions Of The Agent

When we say that an action, attempt, or omission was *intentional,* we want to emphasize that the agent was "aware of what he did"; he "wanted to do it"; he "did it without coercion"; he "was in control of what he was doing." Excuses that discount this feature of conduct will diminish the blame which is due an agent for something morally untoward. We will consider two of the more common excuses having to do with the intentions of the agent and make some reference to other excusing discriminators which have to do with intentions.

1)   Accident

Let's reconsider our example of the baseball team batting practice discussed in an earlier chapter. You will recall that Jimmy, while taking batting practice, hit the ball foul. It carried over the fence and smashed the windshield on Big Robbie's car. Now, consider that we held Jimmy appraisable because of the accordion effect of his intentional action. He was willing to have it happen as a result of his intended act of hitting the ball that a windshield nearby would be struck. So, Jimmy must accept some responsibility for this action. However, what degree of blame attaches to Jimmy's action is yet to be determined. It is fixed by the responsibility description which is offered. Different descriptions may be provided depending on the situation.

Suppose Jimmy is standing at the plate, with the bat over his shoulder, not even facing the pitcher. If the ball is thrown, strikes his bat, and flies off, breaking the windshield, shall we hold Jimmy as responsible for harm as if he hit the ball intentionally? The answer is no. Under this description, the smashing of the windshield is an accident. An accident is not something we do intentionally. His excusing responsibility description will be simple. "It was an accident. I didn't intend to hit the ball; I was doing something else." The reason why this excuse works is because there is no originating intention to hit the ball. "Resting the bat on his shoulder" and "facing away from the pitcher" are actually acts which indicate that he does not intend to hit the ball.

We can now see something else. We might call the "breaking of the windshield" an accident even if Jimmy did hit the ball intentionally, provided that we do not stretch his intention so far down the accordion effect of his action. In order to consider this option, we will expect Jimmy to protest that he "did not intend" to break the windshield.

Persons routinely attempt to diminish blame by appealing to the excuse "It happened by accident" or "I did it accidently." However, our practice contains many examples of outright rejection of this excuse. Consider the following cases. It makes perfect sense for me to say, "I'm sorry, I stepped on your glasses accidently." But I could not excuse myself in this way, "I'm sorry, I stepped on the baby's head accidently." The reason why the latter excuse is rejected is that we expect persons to exercise care and attention around eyeglasses which might be breakable, but we expect them *always to get it right* when walking around babies lying on the floor.[44] Or, consider another illustration of the same point. It is one thing for me to drop my toothbrush into the tub while you are bathing, but quite another for me to drop my plugged-in hair dryer in the tub. This is the kind of accident that should never occur. If it were to occur, then I would be "negligent" or "careless." My blame could not be diminished by saying,"It was an accident" or that "I did it inadvertently."

2) Mistake

Ordinary moral practice makes a difference between an accident and a mistake. In an accident, conduct is not intentional. But in a mistake, one intends to do something but actually does something else. He "mis--takes" one conduct for another. Austin points out this difference clearly in a very famous example.

> *You have a donkey, so have I, and they graze in the same field. The day comes when I conceive a dislike for mine. I go to shoot it, draw a bead on it, fire: the brute falls in its tracks. I inspect the victim, and find to my horror that it is your donkey. I appear on your doorstep with the remains and say--what? "I say, old sport, I'm awfully sorry, etc., I've shot your donkey by accident?" Or "by mistake"? Then again, I go to shoot my donkey as before, draw a bead on it, fire--but as I do so, the beasts move, and to my horror yours falls. Again the scene on the doorstep--what do I say, "By mistake"? Or "by accident"?* [45]

Of course, what Austin must say to show that he properly understands the practice of excusing is "by mistake" in the first shooting and "by accident" in the second. In the first case, you intended to shoot the animal you drew a bead on, you just mistook it for your animal. But in the second case, you shot an animal which was other than the one you intended to shoot.

Here is a case in which it is conceivable that an agent's blame may be diminished by offering a mistake description.

---

[44]Ibid., p. 194.

[45]Ibid., p. 185.

*Suppose, for example, that I intend to take my umbrella from the
stand in our office. However, I take yours instead. Perhaps they
look alike, even virtually identical. Upon discovering your umbrella
missing, you could run after me crying, "Stop, thief, you have
stolen my umbrella!" Hearing your screams, I might stop and upon
examination of my action say, "I am sorry, I took your umbrella by
mistake."*

The question arises now, how would you know whether this was a true
description of what occurred? Well, the point of our discussion of the relationship
between justifying descriptions and epistemology applies here, as it does in every
other case of responsibility description as well. Since you have no direct access to
my mind, you cannot know "for certain" whether I intended to take your umbrella.
You will rely on various clues, such as the similarity in appearance of the
umbrellas, the frequency with which such things happen, and whether it is
conceivable that others could make such a mistake as well.

Still, even if you excuse me by accepting the description that I took the
umbrella by mistake, you might caution me to be more careful next time. And this
would be perfectly in order. You might take steps to show me something
distinctive about your umbrella, or else we might agree to keep our umbrellas in
separate places. It is noteworthy that mistakes, like accidents, could be described
as carelessness or negligence if the agent has overlooked matters he should have
noticed. In fact, these words are those we use in moral practice to describe failed
appeals to accident and mistake.

I once knew a young man who never brought a ball to the soccer game, but
who bragged that he would always come home from the field with a ball. He
would look around for some ball which had been kicked away from the others, spy
it, and slyly gather it up, half concealing it under his jersey. If any player called to
him, identifying the ball, he would reply ,"Oh, I took yours by mistake. It looks
like mine." Now, obviously this responsibility description will not do. The boy
brought no ball to the game, so the ball could not have been his. He could mis--
take the ball for his only if he had a ball. Practice shows, then, that there are
sometimes factual considerations which make it possible to determine whether an
event is appropriately described as a mistake or not.

If my umbrella is black, and yours red, it will not do for me to say, "I'm
sorry, I took yours by mistake." Unless I have some actual disability such as color
blindness, I should not make a mistake of this sort. In fact, excusing by appeal to
mistake would be entirely inappropriate. It is one thing to make a mistake about
similars, but it is no mistake to choose one rather than the other well-discriminated
thing. If I own a Volkswagen, and you a Mercedes, it will hardly do for me to
say, "I got in your car by mistake."

*Suppose that I intended to steal your umbrella but took mine by
mistake, would I be morally responsible in any way?*

The answer is yes. I am morally guilty of an intent to steal. Of course, a
legal system would not hold me guilty of anything. Law considers intention only
after a criminal act has been committed. But in this example, no crime has been
done. However, I do reveal something of my moral character by being the sort of

person who wants to steal your umbrella. This is something which you may wish to know when deciding whether to establish relationships with me or not. It may be important to you to know whether your possessions are safe in my presence.

Paying attention to someone's intentions is crucial in deciding blame relative to the mistake excuse.

> *What if Mr. Jones is awakened in the night by strange noises in the house, and thinking he is being robbed, runs downstairs with his pistol and shoots the "intruder," who is actually his visiting nephew coming home too late.*

We should use care in our responsibility description of this man's action. This killing is *not an accident.*. An accident would occur if while cleaning the gun, it discharged. *This is a mistake.* Mr. Jones intentionally shot his gun at the intruder, but he mistook his nephew for a robber.

3) Other ways of excusing by diminishing the role of intention

Cases could also be designed showing the use of the following intention excusing discriminators which vary the intensity of blame being assigned: incidentally, adventitiously, unaware, not paying attention, careless, lax, remiss, negligent, slack, inattentive, didn't mean to, inadvertently, under the influence, under orders, under threat, under duress, couldn't help it.

Can you think of others?

Excuses Having To Do With The Agent's Deliberations

When we say that an action, attempt, or omission was *deliberate,* we want to stress that the agent "realized what she was doing"; she "knew what she was doing"; she "weighed out the alternatives and chose to do what she did." Excuses which have to do with the deliberation given to our conduct may claim that the person *did the best she could have*; she did *the lesser of two evils,* because she weighed out the moral standards and the possible alternatives available, and she chose the alternative which preserved what mattered most morally. Or, another common excusing mechanism is that although a person did something which was blameworthy, she *made a reasonable and deliberate effort* to conduct herself in a praiseworthy manner, but a wrong still occurred. She did everything that could have been reasonably expected of her, everything a reasonable person would require. In the following we will explore these considerations further.

1. The Lesser of Evils

The making of a moral appraisal is a way human persons have of saying what matters to them. A person cannot be completely unconcerned about everything. Some things matter; they are important or significant in order to live a fulfilling and satisfactory life. However, not all things matter to this end equally. Some values, just as some kinds of conduct, are more important to encourage or blame than are others. In some respects, what matters to us as human persons is transmitted to us by the moral community through its moral concepts and standards. We actually find these values well-nested in the language and practice we learn.

But another very important way of recognizing what matters most is to observe the way we proceed in using the lesser of evils excuse. How we use this excuse communicates a great deal about our sense of values, and the way the moral community reacts to our use of this excuse tells us about how values are ranked within it.

The things which matter to persons sometime come into conflict. In moral practice, we recognize that some things are worse than others: murder is a graver offense than theft. Of course, both are evils. But it is more blameworthy to take a person's life, than to take his possessions, and this is well-established in ordinary moral practice. If we take his possessions, he may have an opportunity to regain them, or accumulate others. But if we take his life, his possessions do not matter. "To give aid" is better than "to refer one to where he might get aid." If we actually deliver the aid, we guarantee its occurrence; whereas if we only refer a person to a place from which he might get aid, we cannot be certain that he will receive it.

So, if we find ourselves in situations where we must make choices, and no matter what we choose, we will do something evil, then we are less blamed if we do the lesser of evils. This brings us back again to our discussion of moral dilemmas, first introduced in the chapter on justifications. Unless we are moral absolutists, we must recognize that there are **some** dilemmas: situations in which there is no alternative which will allow us to fulfill all of our moral standards, or keep all things that matter to persons in balance. When this conflict of standards and values occurs, what we find in moral practice is a keen appreciation for the prioritization of moral concerns expressed as an "I did the best thing that I could under the circumstances" or "I did the lesser of evils" excuse. But the implications of this are severe.

If indeed there are some situations in which there is no alternative which we can choose which meets all of our moral standards, then how are we to understand the theoretical concept of a "morally perfect" life? In order for a person to live a morally perfect life, he would have to meet several conditions. Of course, he would have to possess the will power always to choose an alternative which fulfilled all of his moral obligations and do so within his moral prohibitions. Such a person would also have to be able to control the basic ordinary exigencies and situational circumstances of life in such a way as never to find himself in a position of a genuine dilemma. And even if he could do all of this, the moral community might still appraise some of his conduct by saying, "You could have done better."

This means, of course, that moral practice shows us that not only is it important what values we have or obligations we recognize, but also that how we rank those values or obligations is itself appraisable. Not only are values expressed in the standards which guide conduct, but also we show what kind of person we are by the values and duties to which we give priority. If a person is confronted with the choice of whether to provide a robber with the combination to the bank vault or to allow him to kill his hostages, then the moral community will pay great attention to what he chooses to do, and others will base their decision about whether to have relationships with him and what kinds to have on the way he prioritizes his values in this situation. If he tells the robber the combination, thereby acting as an intervening agent by making the robbery possible, he may yet be excused because he has valued the life of the hostages more than the lost money. He has a good sense of what matters most in the moral community. The moral community wants persons with the "right" values, and it takes steps to teach and reinforce these. But it also wants persons who know how to rank values and differentiate between them in responsible ways.

Prioritization of moral concepts and rules is something we have already recognized to be present in the practice of moral appraisal. Earlier we noted that special role obligations are regarded as subordinate to the general concepts and rules for moral agents whenever they conflict. What we are doing now is extending our observations about this practice. We now find that persons not only prioritize among special roles and general appraisal standards, but also among general standards themselves. Philosophers who have observed this practice carefully have offered explanations for how it is done.[46] They have identified some of the things moral practice reveals about what a community considers when appraising our conduct of prioritization. In Moral Investigations: An Introduction to the Study of Current Moral Problems, Henry Ruf tries to explain how we rank moral standards by showing that some of them are *logically or rationally preferable* to others.[47] Consider the following arrangement of priority from the least important (A) to the most important (C).

(A) You should prevent suffering (harm).
(B) You should not cause suffering (harm).
(C) You should treat others as valuable in themselves and
       not as means to some other purpose.

Ruf holds our practice reveals that we consider it more blameworthy to *cause* suffering, than to *fail to prevent* it. If we fail to prevent harm to another person, some blame may attach to our omission, the degree depending on whether we have some excuse. But, at any rate, it is still possible that someone else may help, or that the need for help may end of itself. However, if we inflict suffering, then we guarantee that harm will occur because we become its cause. So, the logic of this analysis shows that it is more blameworthy to cause suffering than to omit preventing it. Accordingly, the rule prohibiting us to cause suffering would always take priority over our obligation to prevent suffering. "I may not have helped; but at least I did not harm," we might say to excuse our omission.

Let's expand this example a little further. It is even worse to destroy persons as persons, than it is to cause them pain, harm, or suffering. For example, imprisonment may cause individuals pain and suffering, but it is preferable to lobotomies which destroy the capacity to be a person. A surgeon inflicts pain and injury, but she may do so because it is necessary in order to fulfill her higher order obligation of trying to restore that patient to better health.

There is a rich grammar of moral prioritization found in our practice of appraisal which shows that appraisals of how one ranks his values and standards is

---

[46]Some interesting treatments of the prioritization of values may be found in the following: J. S. Mill, Utilitarianism, ed. by Oskar Piest (Indianapolis: Bobbs-Merrill, 1957), ch. II, pars. 6-8; David Ross, The Right and the Good (Oxford: The Clarendon Press, 1930), pp. 149-154; and Rawls, A Theory of Justice, pp. 40-46.

[47]Henry Ruf, Moral Investigations: An Introduction to the Study of Current Moral Problems (Lanham, MD: University Press of America, 1978), pp. 95ff.

also *a result of the history of appraisal in a given moral community.* Some communities exist in which death is preferable to disgrace or financial ruin. It is not clear why there would be a rational or logical reason for this preference. So, we have uncovered another way of prioritizing in addition to that identified by Ruf.

Such a realization poses some interesting difficulties. For example, what do we make of the fact that moral communities differ on their priorities in ways which do not seem to be resolvable on rational grounds? Does this mean that it makes no sense to speak of an all-embracing general moral community after all? Are we left only with specific historical and temporary moral communities which are merely representative of special roles or traditions? A description of moral practice itself cannot resolve this issue, because it is a theoretical one. One of the reasons this issue interests ethicists is that some of them hold that there are logical rules for how to prioritize all moral standards, and that these prescribe the way it *should* be done. Prioritizations of values or standards which are not rationally defensible should be appraised negatively.

However, even if descriptive ethics cannot resolve this theoretical issue, that does not mean that it has nothing to contribute to the conversation. For example, we may observe that there is nothing in everyday moral practice which would prevent a moral community from installing a hierarchy of standards and values which largely conforms to what we would find logically supportable as well. So, the conclusion that there is no logical or rational basis for our moral ordering is unjustified. But description alone cannot decide whether the differences in prioritizations always follow by some rule of logic.

Our moral practice of the ordering of values and standards uncovers another significant issue. Consider the problem occurring when a person is repeatedly forced to appeal to higher order values in a responsibility description. Let's take an extreme example.

> *If Hitler asks us, "Why shouldn't I torture my enemies?"*
> *We might say, "Because you should not force your will on others*
>   *and torturing is a way of forcing your will on others."*

> *If Hitler then asks, "But why shouldn't I force my will on others?"*
> *We might say, "Because you should not cause injury to others and*
>   *coercion is a type of injury."*

> *If Hitler asks us, "But why shouldn't I cause injury, if I want to?"*
> *We might say, "Because you should treat persons with respect as of*
>   *the highest value--and injuring them is an affront to this."*

> *If Hitler asks, "But why should I treat persons with respect?"*
> *What can we answer?*

What has happened in the course of this exchange is that we have reached an end to our standards. One way of expressing this is to say that we have come upon the final or fundamental building blocks of moral practice itself. That is, one could not practice morality, unless one utilized these concepts and rules. Another way of saying this is to observe that we have arrived at the highest values in the moral community.

Instead of using the analogy of a building introduced in the previous paragraph, another analogue might be more instructive. Imagine that this process can be compared to a tree. Let's say that we began far out on a high branch, with a prohibition against torturing one's enemies. Then, when questioned about why this should be valued, we appealed to a more basic concept, a rather large limb on the priority tree, the rule against coercion and injury. Further inquiry forced us from the limbs to the trunk of the tree, the moral standard that all persons should be treated with respect, as of highest value.

If we take this analogy, what happens when we are asked the next question? The final inquiry asks a different sort of question. It would be like asking, "Why this tree and not another?" When we reach this point we are being asked about the way we practice morality itself. Why do we have the moral concepts, rules, and values we do? Why do we not have some other morality? If this question is asking for more than a sociology of morals, it may not be answerable. If it is answerable, it will require a theoretical explanation, not a descriptive one, and thus it must be postponed until later in our study. What we will find is that some philosophers hold that the ultimate moorings of our moral practice can be rationally defended, whereas others think not. To show how important this issue is, consider the following points. We do not justify the belief that we still have two feet before we stand up. It would be silly to try to go around providing such an account. Analogously, asking for proof of one's moral foundations may be the same kind of thing.

Suppose one observed that holding up moral practice until one could justify all of its standards would be like holding up a geography lesson until one proved that the earth existed. Such a person might point out that there are all kinds of things one can ask about geography and geographical locations, but that one doubt or question which is not included in the practice of geography is the proving of the earth's existence. In fact, the person might go on to say that all of the other geographical questions were made possible only under the assumption that the earth exists. Would you think that this analogy could apply to moral practice as well? If so, then you might simply say that when Hitler asks his final question, he is really not asking a question at all, but only indicating that he does not know what this way of practicing morality is all about. **(Cf. Can Ultimate Moral Standards Be Justified Rationally? in Ch. 9)**

Let's redirect our description now by looking at an example of how **the lesser of evils** excuse actually works.

A woman learns that her son-in-law fathered an illegitimate child several years before he met her daughter. Suppose, though, that he has been married happily to her daughter for ten years. Let us say that the woman is sure her daughter is not aware of the child, and that she has reason to doubt that her daughter would ever find out on her own. Let's suppose the woman 's daughter does find out this information from another source. Then,when she sits down to talk to her mother about what to do, her mother tells her that she has known about the son-in-law's action for some time. The daughter becomes upset and says,"Why didn't you tell me the truth?"

In an attempt to diminish blame, the woman in our example may reply to her daughter, "I just didn't want to hurt you or your marriage; things were going so well." The woman has been confronted by her daughter with one obligation: "We should tell the truth", and her daughter is giving signals of blame. The woman has excused her action of not telling the truth by an appeal to "We should not cause harm or suffering," holding that acting according to this rule was of higher priority. That is, it was more important not to cause harm than it was to tell the truth. We cannot tell the daughter how much to blame her mother on the basis of this excuse, because we have no estimate of the probability that telling the truth would have actually caused suffering or harm. However, we can understand the woman's ranking of values.

The excuse that one was threatened or afraid is a common lesser of evils description. Consideration of threat as an excuse is as old as Aristotle (384-322 B. C.).[48] Threat and fear are excusing mechanisms that essentially say there was a greater evil which I was afraid would occur, or was threatened to occur, than the wrong which I did. Threats take many forms. A gunman may threaten to kill Betty, if she does not assist him in a robbery. Betty's excuse is that it was a lesser evil to assist in the robbery than for her to be killed.

Threats can vary in degree and this is certainly taken into consideration in the description of responsibility. Some threats are of no serious consequence at all. A child may threaten a parent, "If you don't buy me that toy, I'll jump up and down and cry." If the parent buys the toy he may offer the excuse that the child was going to throw a tantrum otherwise. The excuse essentially means, "It is a lesser evil for me to buy my child the toy, than to observe and maybe be embarrassed by the child's display." Of course, the parent might just say, "Go ahead, you'll only make a fool of yourself!" In which case, the child's threat is completely disarmed.

Logic suggests that threats of death should be regarded as the most serious, because what is lost is irreplaceable, and if it is the life of a person, it is of highest value. Threats of bodily harm and injury to persons should perhaps be the next most serious, then threats of loss of money, property or possessions. But there are also threats of exposure (blackmail), and loss of position, power, or prestige which are difficult to quantify, and are resolved case by case, according to what one may get the moral community to accept, and to which moral community one is offering the responsibility description. As we have seen, the actual practice of a moral community may not follow what one thinks should occur rationally or logically.

Try your hand at appraising this example.

> *Suppose the boss said to his married secretary, "Unless you have sex with me this weekend, I'll fire you." If the woman did have sex with him, and excused herself to her husband by saying "He threatened me," how would you evaluate her excuse?*

The issue is made somewhat more complicated by interjecting self-regarding values and obligations more fully. If a robber, holding hostages in a bank, threatens to kill Sam unless he opens the safe, then, of course, we will excuse Sam

---

[48]Aristotle, Nicomachean Ethics, Book III, Ch. 1, 1110.

for doing so. Money is replaceable; Sam is not. It is of lesser evil to lose the money, than to lose Sam. If the same robber says he will break Sam's arm if Sam does not push the bank guard out a fourth story window, that is a different matter. Sam should probably refuse to take the life of another person, even though by doing what he is asked he could avoid the infliction of pain on himself. Of course, different persons have different thresholds of pain. Some can withstand pain or torture for long periods of time. But for most persons the difficulty of doing what is morally right increases as the pain becomes more severe. We characteristically recognize in ordinary language that there is a threshold point, beyond which someone "just can't stand it." Still, the moral community seems to expect someone to stand it, if the alternative is killing another person. Of course, special moral communities exist in human culture which do not recognize pain or torture as an excuse at all. The military, for example, does not consider torture an excuse for divulging anything beyond one's name, rank, and serial number.[49]

Putting aside cases in which torture is involved, we can still appreciate other times when the cost of doing the right thing is so great, that the moral community recognizes that an agent's blame may be diminished. Some of these are examples of other-regarding value preferences. Consider the example below.

> *Captain Williams flies for U.S. Airlines on its transatlantic routes to southern Europe and Egypt. Shortly after taking off from Cairo, there is a disturbance on the plane. A disheveled man pushes past the flight attendant into the command center. He demands to be taken to Libya, and brandishes something that looks like a T.V. remote control. He claims that the control is a detonator for several sticks of dynamite in his luggage. "Take me to Libya, or else I will blow up the plane," he says.*

In this case, the terrorist's threat and the Captain's fear may be used as an excuse for changing the course of the plane and diverting to Libya. The threat is probably a sufficient reason for excusing Captain Williams from many other things as well: "reading propaganda statements over his radio," "denouncing his own government," "the disruption of personal lives and schedules caused by course correction," or "the expenses involved." These are less blameworthy than would normally be the case, because they are done to avoid the mass destruction which would result from an exploding jet liner. It is of lesser evil to do these things and have these outcomes occur than to suffer the death of all the passengers on the plane.

There is yet one more matter to be mentioned. Even if a threat is of the most serious kind, moral practice sometimes shows it to be irrelevant to what one should do morally. Being moral is sometimes costly, and there is a recognition of this fact in moral practice. There may be moral obligations and values worth dying for, or being tortured for, or losing one's job for, or paying a great deal of money for, or going to a lot of trouble for. Persons are appraised based on how they practice moral prioritization of this sort.

---

[49]Hospers, Human Conduct, p. 370.

2) After Reasonable Effort

Suppose Smith walks into a public telephone booth on a busy street to make a phone call. He finds several quarters on the tray. Perhaps he goes ahead and makes his call, and then imagine that he waits around for a few minutes to see if anyone returns to claim the quarters. While waiting, he sees another person whom he knows was at the phone booth earlier, and Smith asks if the quarters belong to her. Upon finding that they do not, Smith decides that he will go on his way, so he pockets the quarters and walks away, saying to himself, "I tried to return them, but I couldn't locate the owner."

There is more than one moral standard under which Smith's conduct can be described. By observing how he acts, we are provided clues that Smith wanted to describe his conduct under the moral standard, "We should return things which are lost to their rightful owners." Smith stays around a few minutes to see if the owner returns. He takes the additional step of inquiring of another person whether the coins belong to her. Such actions constitute an attempt to return things which are lost to their rightful owners, but do they constitute a "reasonable" effort to do so?

Think about how the description of what constitutes "reasonable" effort to return lost things alters in the examples below.

--Suppose, though, that instead of finding something like $.75 worth of quarters, he finds $75.00 in currency. Does this alter what constitutes a reasonable effort to return the money?

--Suppose that instead of finding only loose money, he finds a billfold or purse, with identification in it. How does this alter what counts as reasonable effort?

--Suppose that instead of finding money, he finds a lost child.

The excuse we employ says a great deal about the description of our conduct for which we are willing to accept responsibility. His taking the quarters with him introduces the possibility of a new moral standard under which his action may be describable. We may want to try a responsibility description of Smith's conduct under the rule: "We should not take things which do not belong to us." This is a broad rule. It captures situations like robbery, embezzlement, stealing, and even pocketing the extra change a supermarket cashier gives us by mistake.

When this standard is applied to Smith's action, several responses are open to him. He may provide a "That's not what I did" justification. He may hold that we have misdescribed his conduct. He may say he is only taking the quarters to hold them for the owner, to "protect" them or "hold them for safe keeping," and that we have not got it right to describe his action under this second rule. He may say that taking the quarters with him is only a continuation of his effort to return them. He does not intend to "take" them in the sense of "keeping" them. To determine the credibility of his justification, we may want to know whether he has plans to try to determine the unknown owner.

Suppose he claims that we have misdescribed his conduct because the quarters do not belong to anyone, they are public property, so taking them is a way of making them belong to someone, namely himself. How would you determine the credibility of such a justification as this?

If Smith's justification fails because it lacks the credibility which the moral community requires, then we may hold him responsible for "taking something which does not belong to him."   Smith certainly could have omitted taking the quarters. A reasonable effort not to take the coins is simply "not to take them," to leave them where he found them. If he objected to having his conduct described as "taking something which does not belong to him," then he should simply leave the quarters.   It would be no good for him to protest that someone else would just come along and take the coins, because, of course, it is no excuse for doing something wrong that someone else would also do it. We are concerned with Smith's conduct, not hypothetical persons who have not yet come into the appraisability picture. So, we might hold Smith blameworthy to some degree for taking the coins, even though the small amount of money involved and the circumstances suggest that the blame we would assign would be negligible.

Although the reasonable effort excuse is particularly well-suited to the ***attempts*** category of appraisable events, it is a transcategory excuse. Indeed, the "reasonable effort " consideration is often useful in determining whether mistake and accident excuses are acceptable and convincing. This is because of the relationship between making a reasonable effort and exercising due care and attention. "I'm sorry I stepped on the baby accidently" is a poor excuse against the charge of causing harm. It is not a good excuse because we expect that what counts as a reasonable effort to avoid stepping on the baby, is that we just never get it wrong! Anything short of that is not a reasonable effort.

3)   Other ways of excusing by diminishing the role of deliberation

There are many other ways of diminishing blame by choosing excusing discriminators relating to the role of deliberation. Unlike the "reasonable effort" excuse, which says that one did give careful thought and deliberation to one's conduct, and blame should be diminished *because* of this, there are other strategies to show that a person's conduct was *not deliberate, not thought out, or chosen after careful consideration* . Cases could also be designed showing the use of the following deliberation excusing discriminators: whimsically, impulsively, impatiently, benignantly, off the handle, in a hurry, out of the blue, at the drop of a hat, at random, under distraction, recklessly, rashly, heedlessly, thoughtlessly, and so forth. See if you can think of others. It may seem strange to think of appealing to the "thoughtlessness" of one's conduct as an excuse; but one must remember that we are describing the difference in intensity of blame between being "thoughtless" and doing an evil "deliberately." There is no question about whether blame is appropriate but only what degree of blame is to be assigned.

Excuses Having To Do With The Consequences Of The Event

When we say that an action, attempt, or omission was *on purpose* we want to communicate that the agent "chose with a plan in mind," or "in order to bring about a certain outcome." Or, that the reason for the conduct was "to make this other thing happen." The consequences or outcomes of conduct have been taken as serious moral considerations throughout history. In fact, some philosophers have built their entire ethical theories on the singular criterion, "Act so as to produce the greatest happiness for all affected." They have maintained that ultimately the only thing which matters is the consequence or outcome of our conduct. This is called a **utilitarian** theory, because it privileges the utility, usefulness, or effects of conduct as the supremely important moral consideration. Later in this work we shall describe utilitarianism more fully as a theoretical model which tries to understand the art of moral appraisal comprehensively. For now, however, let's consider only that consequences do play a role in the assignment of moral responsibility and illustrate how blame may sometimes be diminished by holding that untoward consequences were not within a person's purposes or desired objectives. (**Cf. Is Utility the Irreducible Basis for All Moral Appraisals? in Ch. 9**)

The following excuses exemplify two ways in which persons try to diminish blame by discounting the agent's knowledge about the possible consequences of his conduct. First, that the agent was ignorant about the possible untoward consequences. Second, by claiming that the agent's purpose for the event was different from that which is being regarded as blamable and untoward morally. The event had a double effect.

l) Ignorance of the Consequences

Paul was a doctor at a local hospital. One evening, while working in the emergency room , a young boy with a critical reaction to an insect bite was brought in. Paul knew of only one antidote for the reaction. But when he administered the drug, the boy had a reaction to the drug, went into shock and died. Paul excused himself by saying he did not know the boy would have a negative reaction to the drug.

Paul is describing his conduct under the *ignorance of the consequences* excuse. He says the boy's death happened because he "did not know" the boy would react as he did to the drug. The reason this excuse enjoys such wide usage in ordinary moral practice is that knowing just what the consequences of our conduct are is often not very easy to determine. Indeed, most of the decisions we make in life are such that we cannot know with certainty what the outcomes will be. Some of this uncertainty lies in our own limited knowledge, but there may also be some indeterminateness in the course of events themselves which creates the unpredictability of outcomes. When one considers both of these factors, then it seems clear that the conduct of human persons is often highly risky in the sense that the outcome of their actions, attempts, and omissions may not always be known.

We have discussed *ignorance of the consequences* considerations earlier in this work under the heading of *unavoidable ignorance*, and we have seen that such ignorance means that the person would not be appraisable at all. But now we should try to get somewhat clearer about how what Paul is claiming in his description differs from the unavoidable ignorance which makes an agent nonappraisable. If Paul is unavoidably ignorant, then he is not appraisable at all, and Paul would be suggesting that no one could have possibly known about the boy's reaction to the drug. However, Paul's claim does not seem to be of this sort. Paul's ignorance does not seem to be unavoidable.

Paul is a physician. In this role, he has a special obligation to know the possible side-effects of the drugs he uses. Moreover, he possesses special knowledge of the side-effects of drugs of this sort, knowledge gained through long years of study and practice. Accordingly, he has a much greater range of knowledge than someone not medically trained. If he knows that one side-effect of the drug itself is shock induced trauma and maybe death, regardless of the patient involved, then he should be especially careful in dispensing the drug to anyone. If the drug had never been used before, or there were no case history on its use, then he might be able to claim unavoidable ignorance. Otherwise, what he seems to be doing is claiming only that his ignorance of the consequences was such as to diminish his blame. Ordinary practice shows that the more serious the possible outcomes of our conduct, the more care we expect persons to exercise in choosing an alternative which minimizes the possibility of harm. Paul says he did not know one of the possible outcomes of his conduct would be the death of the patient.

Appropriate use of the "ignorance of the consequences" description requires that the range of the agent's ignorance be appropriate to what is expected in the situation, given the actors involved, and the objects employed. Another way of saying this is to say that we are required to make a reasonable effort to act within the limits of our knowledge. If we have done so, then we may successfully excuse ourselves as ignorant of the outcomes of our conduct should something happen which we did not anticipate.

If Paul had opportunity, we should expect him to have inquired of the patient, or of the patient's parents as to whether there was anything he needed to know before dispensing a powerful drug (e.g., whether the boy had any known drug allergy). We would want him to narrow his range of ignorance about this specific patient as much as possible. If he had no such opportunity, but he knew that one common side-effect of the proposed drug was death, then we would expect him to wait , if possible, until he could determine whether the boy was allergic or susceptible to a negative reaction.

What we expect from those using the ignorance of the consequences excuse varies depending on the nature of the decision situation. In practice, we distinguish between avoidable and forced decision situations. In an avoidable decision context, we have the latitude to delay or perhaps even omit deciding to choose. In a forced decision, we must make a choice; we cannot omit or delay. In our example, Paul is in a **forced** situation. What makes it a forced situation is the certainty of an undesirable outcome if Paul omits to act. As described, he must decide to administer the drug or else the boy will certainly die. In such a case, we tend to be more tolerant of any omission to narrow his range of ignorance on Paul's part. The certainty of an undesirable outcome if one does nothing changes the relative responsibility of the agent involved to narrow his ignorance of the probable outcomes.

CERTAINTY OF NEGATIVE OUTCOME, IF DRUG IS OMITTED

Administer the drug	Death, from injury	Cure	Severe sickness, but not death	Death from drug

CONDUCT

Omit the drug	Death, from injury			

There is a way in which knowing an outcome with certainty may make a situation an avoidable decision situation. If Paul can avoid giving the drug, and the shock and trauma will subside in due time, and this is known with certainty, then we should certainly expect that he will omit to give the drug. We will blame him more intensely if he takes risks by giving the drug, especially without narrowing his range of ignorance about the patient's likelihood to react negatively to the drug.

If Paul can delay giving the drug, we will expect that he will omit the drug

CERTAINTY OF POSITIVE OUTCOME, IF DRUG IS OMITTED

Administer the drug	Death, from injury	Cure without suffering		Death from drug

CONDUCT

Omit the drug	Shock subsides recovery comes naturally			

until he can gain further knowledge which will narrow his range of ignorance about the patient. Perhaps administering the drug would bring a "cure without suffering". But there may be some risk in administering the drug to try to bring about such a cure. In the case of the example described immediately above, the physician acts more responsibly if he follows the adage, do nothing which might make the patient worse.

A third type of *ignorance of the consequences* case is the one in which the outcomes of both omitting the drug and administering it are uncertain. It is just these sorts of situations in which the *ignorance of the consequences* excuse is most frequently used, and it is used to excuse undesirable outcomes resulting from proceeding with conduct which was risky.

This complicated decision context is one in which there is a risk that the boy may die, even if he is given the drug, or perhaps because he is given the drug. Paul may not know with certainty that the boy will die if the drug is omitted, or be cured if the drug is administered. Paul must make his **decision at risk and under uncertainty**. He must assess the probabilities of recovery without receiving the drug, over against the possibilities of cure resulting from the drug. Against these, he must also consider the relative probabilities of the other possible outcomes.

Performing this assessment has been given a technical name by ethicists. It is called a **utilitarian calculus**. A **utilitarian calculus** *is an estimate of the possible consequences of our alternatives, predicting which of these consequences* *is most probable, and choosing from the ones that are most probable, those which also are most desirable for the greatest number of persons.* As you can appreciate, the use of such a utilitarian calculus is not an exact science, but it is still well founded in our ordinary practice of morality. We expect persons making an appeal to the *ignorance of the consequences excuse* to be able to give an account of

UNCERTAINTY OF OUTCOME
DECISON AT-RISK

Administer the drug	Death, from injury	Cure	Death from drug

CONDUCT

Omit the drug	Death, from injury	Shock subsides recovery comes naturally

this process, explaining how they have considered such weightings in the decision. Some ethicists believe that there are decision rules which should guide us in these matters, and that persons who conduct themselves by these rules will be less blameworthy. We are reserving discussion of these until a later time because there are some theoretical issues involved in taking such a position. (**Cf. Are There Decision Rules for Situations of Limited Knowledge? in Ch 9**)

2)   Double effect

Mary has been kidnapped. For three days she has been held captive in a shack in the wilderness. Even though her family has agreed to the ransom demands, her captor is planning to kill her. "I just can't take the chance that you will identify me," he says. As he is pushing her out of the cabin, he turns to pick up a gun which is in a nearby chair. Mary notices a knife on the counter, grabs it, and stabs him in the back so that she can flee. The captor dies. Was her action morally excusable?

In our example, we are told something about Mary's purpose in the stabbing of her captor. She stabs him "so that she can flee." What this means, then, is that her purpose is not to cause his death. She wishes to flee in order to protect her own life. That is her goal. As this goal is being accomplished, however, an unexpected event occurs. The captor dies. Mary's appeal to the moral community represents that his death was not desired as a goal in itself. The end toward which she is directed is escape as self-protection; the additional outcome of achieving this end is the captor's death.

Under all normal conditions let us stipulate that we recognize the moral duty not to kill other persons, even though we probably should form a moral rule about killing that already contains qualifications, since in ordinary practice some excuses have been so readily made that they should be included in the general rule (e.g., "Do not kill persons, unless in self-defense"). Self-defense is a well recognized way of diminishing blame for a very grave moral offence. The double effect excuse is one way of explaining why the moral community recognizes this as a legitimate appeal.   The **double effect** could be expressed in this manner *conduct which produces a harmful effect is excused, if the harmful effect is not desired for itself, but is inseparable from some good effect that is sought.*

This description fits well with self-defense scenarios. Typically, in discussions about self-defense situations, our moral practice prioritizes conduct as follows, from the highest priority (#1) to the last excusable resort (#3).

1) Our highest moral priority is to avoid a situation which would endanger our lives. We should retreat, escape, take precautions, and so forth.

2) If we are in a situation in which we cannot get away or retreat, we are expected to end the confrontation in such a way as to diminish our blame as much as possible. So, we use only the amount of force needed: subdue without the use of a weapon; if a weapon must be used because of relative equality of strength, it should be used as a threat first, then only to incapacitate.

3) If the confrontation has escalated so that one is in immediate peril of one's life, with no evident incapacitating alternative and with the only force which will diminish this peril being deadly force, then such conduct may be excused as self-defense. In self-defense, the death of another person is not desired in itself, but is the result of the desire to protect oneself. The death of the other person is a double effect.

The double effect excuse has enjoyed rather widespread use in ordinary moral practice whenever considering the morality of self-defense. Of late, this excuse has also been employed as a strategy for diminishing blame in certain cases of abortion, particularly within the Roman Catholic moral community. In order to illustrate the application of this excusing condition, consider that abortions may sometimes be regarded as self-defense under the double effect rule. The good outcome, which is desired for itself, is the life of the mother. The undesired outcome, which is, however, inseparable from preserving the life of the mother, is the abortion of the fetus.

3)   Other ways of excusing by diminishing the role of outcomes and consequences

There are many other ways of diminishing blame by choosing excusing discriminators relating to the role of the purposes or outcomes one is directed toward. For example, "in good faith," "aimlessly," and "for no particular purpose." See if you can design some cases which employ such discriminators.

For Discussion

1) Distinguish between Accident and Mistake as moral excuses.

2) Design a case in which a person's action, attempt, or omission is morally blameworthy, but whose blame is diminished because the event may be described under one of the excuses given in this chapter. Try to develop an example for each excuse covered.

3) If the moral standard below is one of finality, write (F) in the blank. If it is derivative, write a (D) in the blank, and then write at least one higher order standard from which it is derived in the space between the items.

_____a.   "Prejudice is wrong."

_____b.   "The least severe punishment which accomplishes the desired end is the morally right one."

_____c.   "We should not pollute the environment."

_____d.   "Persons should be free to make their own decisions regarding their bodies."

_____e.   "It is wrong to have more than one sexual partner at a time."

4) The examples below make an appeal to an excusing condition to diminish the agent's moral responsibility. Tell which excuse you think is being used.

1)   A: "I cannot believe that you did such a horrible thing as to amputate Joe's leg."

      B. "I deeply regret thus crippling him, but it was the only way to save his life."

2)   A: "You killed him, there's nothing more to be said. Killing is as wrong as it can be."

      B: "But I didn't mean to. I checked and there was no ammunition clip in the rifle."

3)   A. "Mary, you should have prevented that assailant from robbing that woman on the parking lot."

      B: "I did my best. I honked my horn and screamed. I even threw rocks at him. But I wasn't going to come into hand-to-hand combat with a man twice my size."

Chapter Seven: Responsibility Descriptions --
Rationalizations

Introduction

Justifications and excuses seldom function in isolation from one another as the previous chapters may lead one to think. Multiple excuses are often provided for an action, attempt, or omission. Sometimes if an offered justification or excuse is rejected, a person may alter his strategy and provide some other description intended to defend his conduct or diminish his blame. If one cannot be justified, perhaps one can offer an excuse and diminish his blame. Our strategy is to defend our moral character and conduct to the fullest extent possible.

In ordinary practice, an excuse is acceptable if it is believable as "something that could have happened to anyone" or "something any other person in your position would do."[50] However, just understanding this is not sufficient to appreciate why some excuses are rejected, let alone why various attempts at justification are rebuffed. We say that someone is just **rationalizing** his conduct if he has offered a justification or an excuse, but we have not found his description convincing.

Why Relativism Fails As A Justification Strategy

All ethics are relative; there aren't any standards binding on everyone. What's right is what I believe is right, and wrong is what I believe is wrong. You have no right to impose your moral beliefs on me, and I can't impose mine on you. So, don't judge me.

An appeal to moral relativity such as that made above may be used as an attempted justification strategy just because it holds that there are not generalizable standards to which persons agree, and by which a person's conduct may be appraised. If there are no generalizable moral standards, and one's moral norms are derived strictly on an individual basis, then one need not justify himself to anyone else.

Moral Relativism *is a theoretical model of philosophy which denies that there are moral standards which are binding on all persons.* The appeal of moral relativism lies in its interpretation of the moral disagreement which occurs in ordinary practice. It takes this disagreement as evidence that there must be no universal standards within the moral community. The relativist argument is something like this: if Rob and Susan disagree about what is morally praiseworthy or blameworthy, then there must not be any universal standards.

---

[50]C. R. Snyder, Raymond L. Higgins, and Rita J. Stucky, <u>Excuses: Masquerades in Search of Grace</u> (New York: John Wiley & Sons, 1983), p. 43. This work discusses how excuses sometimes function and fail. For some work on how justifications function and sometimes fail, particularly moral relativism, see <u>Ethical Relativism</u>, edited by John Ladd (Belmont, CA: Wadsworth, 1973); and Gilbert Harman, "Moral Relativism Defended," <u>Philosophical Review</u> 84 (1975).

Relativism is significant because it undercuts all moral appraisal, and denies that there is anything like a moral community, because it ultimately reduces all moral appraisals to matters of personal taste and individual preference. A community requires some webbing of values and standards which hold it together. However, it is precisely this webbing that relativism is calling into question. In the final analysis, according to relativist theory, there are only individual moral appraisals. Moral relativism rejects both the right of others to make moral judgments of our conduct or character, and our right to make such appraisals of their conduct, because it denies that there are any generalizable standards to use in the making of such evaluations. Since it is this mutual interchange of appraisal which defines the moral community, the relativist position is a radical deconstruction of the practice of morality as a fundamental component in the fabric which knits a community together and gives it its identity.

We could have a clearer understanding of moral relativism by showing what it is **not**. It is not the recognition that persons differ about the appropriate description of their conduct in moral language. One need not be a moral relativist to recognize that one person may describe his action as borrowing, while another says it was stealing. This is not moral relativism. "Borrowing" and "stealing" are moral concepts in this difference of description. No one is doubting the blameworthiness of "stealing" or the harmlessness of "borrowing." So, there is actually agreement on the concepts. The difference is over what description is to be accepted. However, moral relativism is a much more radical idea. It says there is no agreement about moral concepts either. In effect, a moral relativist is saying that persons can use the concept of "stealing" and mean to do something other than blame with it. Such a view, should it be tolerated in the moral community would undermine the process of moral appraisal and threaten the webbing which knits the community together. For this reason, it is the case that to call someone a "relativist" seems almost to have become a way of blaming someone.

The reason why we have grouped moral relativism under our discussion of rationalizations should now be fairly clear. If we have been right in our procedure for studying moral appraisal by describing what we actually do in ordinary practice, then there seems to be no way to derive relativism from our experience, unless it is treated as an aberration. Our description of persons talking about human conduct reveals that they do make value assessments of themselves and of others. Furthermore, persons characteristically recognize the legitimacy of others by requiring them to justify or excuse certain conduct, or even for being the type of persons they are. These descriptions and evaluations utilize both well-defined and hardened moral concepts like "murder" and "stealing" and those which are more in flux.

We have also noted that those who are not a part of this process are either regarded as nonappraisable entities because of considerations discussed earlier, or else they are ostracized as morally bankrupt because they **refuse** to recognize the moral community's appraisal power over them, and to participate themselves in this process. Description alone cannot tell us whether relativism is a third category, or whether it is simply a signal of refusing to recognize one's place in the moral community.

What we have seen from our description of moral practice is that persons find it necessary, as well as desirable and significant, to make moral appraisals. These appraisals form the main body of considerations required for establishing any sort of relationships of importance with other persons. So, far from establishing the relativist position, our actual practice does just the opposite. It actually implies that no community can exist without some coherent set of moral appraisal standards; and that the very existence of a community is partially defined thereby. And from the standpoint of descriptive ethics, this is the strongest possible reason for regarding moral relativism as a rationalization, not a justification. The clearest explanation for why a relativist strategy fails as a justification of one's conduct, then, is that human persons are simply unwilling to give up the benefits derived from moral practice; and they would have to do this if relativism were legitimized.

Why Some Excusing Descriptions Fail

In ordinary moral practice, excuses are often intertwined with each other. They form a complex nest of interlocking descriptions. I may say, "I'm sorry, I dropped the plugged-in hair dryer into her bath accidently." (accident) I may follow with, "I did not know that it might electrocute a person." (ignorance of the consequences) "I tried to catch it before it fell into the water." (reasonable effort) One way of explaining why we do this is to say simply that "that's the way it happened." Another explanation is that we are interested in diminishing our blame, and we pile up excuses in case one of these descriptions fails, perhaps another will succeed.

But our present task is to see whether a description of moral practice can tell us anything about the basis on which we decide when an excuse fails. Is any of the above excuses very strong? Might we not say that my action was careless, or that it would have been much more reasonable to have made an effort to stay far away from the bathtub with my hair dryer than to try to keep it from falling into the water to which I stood too close?

A common strategy found in moral practice for rejecting excuses is to use one kind of excusing consideration to criticize another. Recall the incident of Jones mistaking his visiting nephew for an intruder in his home, and firing the gun to shoot him. We may say, "it was *careless* of Jones to shoot his nephew," and we would be right. It was a mistake, but it was an avoidable one. The gravity of the consequences of this action was so great, that we would expect him to exercise more care to be sure he got it right. We may say to Jones, "Had you made a *reasonable effort* to identify the 'intruder' the whole ugly and tragic incident might have been avoided." There are several other ways in which an excuse is tested in ordinary moral practice.

1) The excuse is inappropriate to the gravity of the event.

As we noted in our discussion of the *accident* excuse, there are times when an event is so serious that we are just expected always to get it right. It may be an excuse to say, "I stepped on the eyeglasses by accident" but it is no excuse to say, "I stepped on the baby's head by accident." The difference is that one of these actions is much more serious than the other. The degree of carefulness we are expected to exercise when walking around babies is different than that which we are expected to employ even when walking where eyeglasses may fall. This also holds true for *mistakes*. John can make a mistake about which umbrella was taken out of the stand, especially if his looks like another. But he had better not make a mistake about whom he goes to bed with. Going to bed with a woman other than his wife is not something that he can excuse by saying, "Oh, it was a mistake; I thought she was you."

At the very root of the ordinary practice of excusing is the idea that some things are more blameworthy than others. The *Lesser of Two Evils* is an excusing strategy which lessens responsibility precisely because it makes explicit appeal to the fact that the agent has taken into account the gravity of his conduct, and conducted himself in such a way as to minimize evil. We noticed also how what constitutes a *reasonable effort* excuse varies dramatically depending on the gravity of the conduct involved. Conduct excused as "reasonable effort to return $.75" was not the same as what was excused as "reasonable effort to return $75.00" or "reasonable effort to return a lost child." Likewise, being excused on the basis of a *threat* depended on the gravity of the threat. All things being equal, "losing a job" is less serious than "permitting an airplane full of passengers to be blown up." So, doing something blameworthy out of fear that one would lose his job may be excusable, but perhaps not as readily as someone's doing a wrong out of fear that an airplane full of passengers would be blown up otherwise. And in the case of the *ignorance of the consequences* excuse, we found that persons generally are excused for taking less risk than when they do not show an appreciation for the gravity of the possible consequences.

2) The excuse is not accompanied by regret and responsive adjustment.

In practice, when making an excuse, one usually introduces the description in one of the following ways: "I am sorry"; "I can't believe I did that"; "I am so upset that these consequences occurred." It is a fairly obvious observation, yet still an important one, to note that in order for an excuse to diminish blame we almost always expect that the person offering the excuse will express regret about his conduct or its outcome. Expressions of remorse are expected, not just as a courtesy or an etiquette of wrongdoing. They are essential to the preservation of character descriptions and the acceptance of the excuse.

Of course, merely expressing regret is not enough. We are not inclined to excuse a person's wrongdoing over and over again merely because he says, "I'm sorry." We have additional expectations too. One of these additional expectations is discussed by Peter French. He labels this expression **The Principle of Responsive Adjustment (PRA).** While we may not wish to take the theoretical move of calling this practice a "principle," French's observations still help us understand what we do in moral practice. The principle may be paraphrased as : "I will not do it again, and I have taken steps to insure that it does not reoccur." [51]

Consider that we might excuse someone who said, "Oh, I'm sorry! I took your umbrella by mistake" the first time it happens. But then, again, we expect that next time he will be more careful. We anticipate that he will take some steps to be sure he gets the correct umbrella in the future. If he takes our umbrella again, we will be less likely to excuse him.

---

[51]French, <u>Collective and Corporate Responsibility</u>, pp. 155ff. Another view is Irving Thalberg, "Remorse," <u>Mind</u> 72 (1963).

Let's consider a more grandiose example, one discussed in detail by French.[52]

On the morning of November 28, 1979, flight TE-901, a DC-10 operated by Air New Zealand Limited, took off from Auckland on a sightseeing passenger flight over a portion of Antarctica. Sometime just after 12:45 p.m. the plane crashed into Mount Erebus. The mountain is 12,000 feet tall. The plane was at 2,000 feet. Passengers were taking photos, there was perfectly visibility for 23 miles. There were no survivors.

The Royal Commission appointed by the Governor-General of New Zealand found several causes for the crash. Among these the most important two were the following.

1) Captain Collins, the pilot, had plotted his flight plan the night before the flight, but the direction of the last leg of the flight fed into the computer navigational system was changed six hours before takeoff, and no one informed the Captain.

2) The nature of the cloud base in the area and the unrelieved whiteness of the snow-covered terrain produced the "whiteout" visual illusion which flattens the terrain. The flight crew never saw a mountain, even though they flew right into it on a day when the visibility was perfect.

Air New Zealand Limited offered several excuses directed specifically at these two causes. Those involved with changing the flight plan said they made the *mistake* of thinking someone else would inform the Captain of the changes. There were no required forms to be filled out about such changes, or written policies about whose responsibility it was to notify the crew, so each thought someone else would notify them. The flight crew was excused from responsibility because they *did not know* there was a mountain in front of them, and their visual checks would not have confirmed otherwise.

Keeping in mind the consideration of responsive adjustment would mean that although we might diminish our blame of New Zealand Limited in this case, they would not be excused in the future for repeating the same mistakes, or allowing a pilot to get himself into a position where his ignorance of the terrain would cause the same risks to be taken. We would expect the airline to adjust its policies to insure that such disasters did not occur again. We might expect that it would implement policies about who is to be informed and by whom, whenever flight plans are changed. We might expect a discontinuance of low level sightseeing flights because of the risk of the whiteout effect. If Air New Zealand did not take such steps, or ones very similar to them, we would hold it to blame for a repeated incident, and fail to accept the same kinds of excuses which we had accepted before. For our purposes it is important to note that responsive adjustments are applied, not just to airlines, or corporations, but to individuals as well, whenever we have previously accepted excuses they have offered.

---

[52]Ibid., pp. 145-164.

3)   The excuse is contrary to fact.

Examples when an excuse is contrary to the facts are sometimes difficult to provide. We have already seen that "deciding what the facts are" is often a matter of determining "what one will accept responsibility for." If someone says, "I didn't mean to; it was an accident," or "I didn't intend to," or "I didn't know this would happen," often we do not know whether to accept the excuse or not. Knowing what an agent's intentions are, and how far down the accordion effect of his conduct we should stretch the intentional nature of his conduct is hard to know. Likewise, it is difficult to determine what an agent had knowledge of, or should have had knowledge of. Our tendency in such cases is to appraise a person in light of past conduct and established character descriptions and to consider matters such as remorse and evidence of responsive adjustment as evidence that blame should be diminished.

However, if someone says, "I didn't promise to meet you," when there is a witness to the promise, then this claim is just contrary to fact. If Michael the soldier says he had no other choice but to kill Kevin, when Kevin was injured on the battlefield, that is just contrary to fact. He did have other choices. If our young soccer player who likes to take balls which do not belong to him says, "I'm sorry, it looks like my ball" that is contrary to fact, because he has no ball with him for this one to look like. These are some of the procedures we use to determine "what were the facts" and whether the excuse offered is compatible with them.

4)   The excuse is available to everyone, anytime

Appeals like "Everybody has to live his own life, and I have to live mine" or "After all, I'm only human" are not generally regarded as excuses appropriate to diminish blame. The main reason why they are not appropriate is that they are too general. They apply to anyone in any circumstances. Literally anyone could use such excuses for anything. Whereas, in ordinary practice, the point of excuses is differentiating by nature. They are based on an appeal which says, "I did it, but there were extenuating circumstances that made this case unlike the normal ones we blame." Or, "I did it, but I am not as blameworthy as would usually be the case in such wrongs, because my case is exceptional in this way...." We expect persons who offer excuses to be able to tell how their situation was unique, different, extenuating, or extraordinary, and therefore worthy of reappraisal.

We must now make some very controversial remarks. Specifically, I want to address the use of what is called the **weakness of the will** excuse.[53] The philosophical term used for "weakness of the will" is *incontinence*, meaning a lack of self-control. If a person knows some conduct to be the morally appropriate one, everything considered, if it is the thing he morally ought to do, and yet he does

---

[53]There is some very fine work on this subject. Donald Davidson, "How Is Weakness of the Will Possible?" in Moral Concepts, edited by Joel Feinberg (New York: Oxford University Press, 1970), pp. 93-113. Robert, Audi, "Weakness of Will and Practical Judgment," Nous 13 (1979). Alfred Mele, Irrationality: An Essay on Akrasia, Self-Deception, and Self-Control. (New York: Oxford University Press, 1988). Weakness of Will, edited by G.W. Mortimer (New York: St. Martin's Press, 1971). Gary Watson, "Skepticism about Weakness of Will," Philosophical Review 86 (1977).

something else, then he may say, *"My will is weak."* "I knew it was wrong, but I just couldn't help myself," he may say. Plato (427?-347? B. C.) told a story about a man named Leontius which may clarify what is meant by weakness of the will. While on a walk, Leontius noticed something.

> He noticed the bodies of some criminals lying on the ground, with the executioner standing by them. He wanted to go and look at them, but at the same time he was disgusted and tried to turn away. He struggled for some time and covered his eyes, but at last the desire was too much for him. Opening his eyes wide, he ran up to the bodies and cried, "There you are, curse you; feast yourselves on this lovely sight."[54]

Leontius did something he wanted to avoid. He was incontinent. He did not have the will power to control his eyes or his desire to go and look at the horrible sight. Perhaps many of us can relate to such feelings. We know we should make an attempt, or do an action, or omit in a morally right way, but we simply do not. Our wills are weak. We do not do what we know we should. We do what we know we should omit. Aristotle spoke of the incontinent as "abandoning his choice," or "abandoning the conclusion he has reached" to "do the thing he knows to be evil," or as one who "...is convinced that he ought to do one thing and nevertheless does another thing."[55]

What is intriguing about this excuse is that we sometimes say of a person "He is weak-willed," and in doing so we mean to offer a vice description. We mean he has a character flaw. He does not do what he knows he should. This, by itself, would be a good reason for being very cautious about the kinds of relationships we have with him.

Some philosophers have offered theories about the weakness of the will in an attempt to explain what it really is. R.M. Hare thinks the explanation for weakness of the will is that it is making a decision on emotion: allowing our passions to outrun or overpower our reason.[56] Donald Davidson does not believe that there is an explanation for why we sometimes choose in this manner.[57] He considers weakness of the will to be a mystery. But these are theoretical interpretations of weakness of the will. If we confine our observations to descriptions of ordinary practice, we find that an appeal to weakness of will is an excuse which is available to anyone, anytime, for any blameworthy event. Accordingly, it is a perfect example of a kind of excuse which usually fails to diminish blame.

---

[54]The Republic, translated by F. M. Cornford (New York: Oxford University Press, 1945), p. 137.

[55]Nicomachean Ethics, Book VII, Ch. 9, 1151a; Book VII, Ch. 1, 1145b; and Book VII, Ch. 1, 1146b, respectfully, in McKeon.

[56]R. M. Hare, Freedom and Reason (New York: Oxford University Press, 1970), p. 77.

[57]Davidson, "How Is Weakness of the Will Possible?" p. 113.

J.L. Austin believed that the use of the weakness of the will appeal in ordinary language is as a euphemism for moral weakness, and that this is best shown by the fact that we tend not to accept this as an excuse. He wrote

> Plato, I suppose, and after him Aristotle, fastened this confusion upon us, as bad in its day and way as the later, grotesque, confusion of moral weakness with weakness of will. I am very partial to ice cream, and a bombe is served divided into segments corresponding one to one with persons at High Table: I am tempted to help myself to two segments and do, thus succumbing to temptation and even conceivably (but why necessarily?) going against my principles. But do I lose control of myself [become incontinent]? ... Not a bit of it. We often succumb to temptation with calm and even with finesse.[58]

For Discussion

1) Do you think there are certain actions, attempts, or omissions which would be morally blamed in every society? Morally praised?

2) If you answered #1 in the affirmative, how would some of the moral concepts or rules about such conduct be expressed?

3) Are the excuses below rationalizations? If so, why? If not, why not?

    a) "Well, nobody is perfect."
    b) "It's my life, and I have to live it."
    c) "I'm only human."
    d) "I'm just under so much stress."
    e) "It's a free country."
    f) The policeman said he killed the burglar because the burglar shot at him first, although witnesses say the burglar fired no shots.
    g) Mildred, your friend from another college is visiting for the weekend. Mildred is a smoker. One evening when you leave the apartment to go to a party, Mildred leaves a burning cigarette on the chair. When you arrive home the apartment is a sooty wet mess from the fire started by Mildred's cigarette. Mildred says, "I'm sorry, I forgot it."
    h) Chrissy is dating Kevin. One night they go out with some of Kevin's friends, and Chrissy noticeably flirts with Sam. Kevin confronts her with this after they are alone. Chrissy cries and says "I'm sorry, it won't happen again." Later that month, Kevin and Chrissy go to the college to visit and Sam is there. Chrissy repeats her behavior. When Kevin pulls her aside she says, "I'm sorry, it won't happen again."
    i) William killed sixteen unarmed women and children in a village during the military assault. He stood them all up in front of the grave he had made them dig and then shot them. When confronted with his action he said, "I was only following orders."

---

[58]Austin, "Plea for Excuses," p. 146 (my brackets).

j) Mary offers to pay Kim Lo $1,000 from her commission if Kim will help her get the contract to do the U.S. publicity for his car manufacturing firm. Kim Lo agrees, and Mary's P.R. agency gets the job. When confrontedwith her action, Mary says, "It's just good business; everybody does it nowadays."

4) Make up your own examples of failed excuses, one for each of the categories discussed in this chapter.

5) When an excuse discriminator like "accident" or "mistake" is unacceptable, we often redescribe the person's conduct by saying it was "careless," "reckless," or "negligent". Make a list of "failed excuse discriminators" for other excuse strategies.

Chapter Eight: Responsibility Descriptions Using Virtue and Vice Concepts

Introduction

Sometimes we use virtue and vice concepts when we make moral appraisals. For example, we may say "Sherry, that was an *honest* thing to do." or "Mike, that was *cruel* ." On the other hand, we sometimes predicate or attribute virtues and vices to persons. That is, we sometimes "characterize" them--appraise their characters. "Margaret is the most *opinionated* person I have ever met." "Sarah is *sensitive* and *tender-hearted*." We might hope that language would show that some virtue or vice concepts may be used only of events, and others only of persons. However, the matter is not as simple as that. Some concepts are used of both events and persons. For example, we may as readily say, "Mike, that was a *cruel* thing to do." as "Mike is *cruel*."

It is possible then for these moral concepts to do duty that intensity discriminators cannot do. We do not say, "Tim is accident," although certainly we say "Tim did that accidently." Of course, we could say, "Tim is an accident waiting to happen," but this seems to be a metaphorical use of "accident" in a way that saying "Mike is cruel" is not. We could conclude, then, that virtue and vice concepts, although they are capable of being used as conduct discriminators, may also function as attributing a moral appraisal to a person.

Of course, we have already introduced some moral concepts which also make conduct discrimination, especially those whose main task is to refer to conduct. Take, for example, that we may say, "Manson, you *murdered* those people," discriminating this conduct from others. But we may also say, "Manson is a *murderer*." In doing so, we discriminate this person from other persons. Such uses also hold for concepts such as lie/liar, theft/thief, adultery/adulterer, and so forth. Of course, in ordinary practice there is some connection between employing virtue and vice concepts of conduct and the attribution of these concepts to describe persons, but it is not clear on the basis of description alone how this is done. The question of how this connection is made is a theoretical one. (Cf. **Is There a Theoretical Explanation for the Move from Conduct Description to Character Ascription?** in Ch 9)

From Conduct Description to Character Ascription

Consider the following two examples as ways of introducing how moral language functions when this connection is made.

Let's suppose that Mary and Helen are shopping. While looking through the various sweaters that are on sale, Mary spies Tricia, whom she dislikes intensely . Mary notices that Tricia has just come out of the dressing room with a sweater in her hand. Tricia says to a friend with whom she is shopping, "I really want this sweater, it's the only one of its kind on sale, and my boyfriend will love it." Just then, her friend motions for Tricia to come over to where she is. Tricia lays down the sweater momentarily, intending to come back and buy it. Seeing the sweater there, Mary goes over, picks it up, and buys it, without looking at the price, style, or even the size. Tricia returns to get the sweater and is alarmed and disappointed to find it gone. As Mary and Helen walk by, Mary holds up the sweater and says to Tricia, "Looking for this Trish?" and laughs. As they leave the store, Helen asks Mary, "Do you like that sweater?" "My gosh, no!" Mary replies. "I just didn't want Trish to get it, since she liked it. Did you see how mad it made her?"

If we know all of these girls, and we overhear Mary and Helen talk as they leave the store, we may well be morally outraged. "Do you mean that you bought that sweater intentionally?" we may ask. Now, of course, we know that there is a straightforward sense in which Mary bought the sweater intentionally. "Purchasing" of the sort Mary did must be done intentionally.[59] So, why would we use the word *intentionally?* Do we use it with its usual meaning? Well, yes, if we recognize that *one* of its ordinary usages is to determine intensification in appraisal of conduct. It seems to be playing this role as an aggravation word in a responsibility description. But we may inquire of Mary further, "You *deliberately* bought the sweater because you knew Trish wanted it, right?" We want to know if Mary weighed out buying the sweater, or if she did it on an impulse. We know that she knew Trish wanted it, and we want to know whether Trish's wanting the sweater carried determinative weight in Mary's choice. "You bought that sweater *purposely,* just to hurt Trish, didn't you?" we may ask.

We want to know whether the purchase of this sweater had anything whatever to do with keeping warm in the winter, or matching a new skirt, or such. Mary's comments to Helen as they left the store suggest that the purpose in buying the sweater was to annoy and irritate Trish. We may offer the description that Mary has done a **spiteful** thing, but we may also say, "Mary, you're a **spiteful** person."

Look at a second example.

Jack and Estel work for a large manufacturing firm. Homer is the plant manager, and he is planning to promote Estel to Director of Transportation and Shipping, a powerful position with a very high salary. When Homer asks Jack for a recommendation of Estel, Jack, who does not like Estel, implies that Estel would not be the best man for the job. Based on Jack's biased recommendation, which Homer does not know is personally motivated, Estel is passed over for the promotion. When Estel asks why he did not get the job, Homer tells him directly that Jack gave him a poor recommendation. A year later the man who did get the job leaves the company, and Estel this time is promoted. A few months later, the plant is forced to lay off two hundred workers. Jack is among those in Estel's section who may be laid off. As Estel and Homer consider whom to discharge, Homer says, "This is a good time for you to get rid of Jack." "What do you mean?" Estel asks. "Well, I

---

[59]Of course, you could purchase something by mistake. If you were at an auction and did not know the rules of auctions, you might scratch your nose, and find that you had bought a painting.

just thought after what he did to you last year, knocking you out of the promotion the first time it came open, that you'd just as soon be rid of him."   Estel replies,"It's true that we seem to have a personality conflict. But did you know that Jack has six kids, one of whom is in college? He's actually not a bad worker either; there are some better, but he's a good worker. No, Homer, I could never lay him off just because he doesn't like me, or tried to hurt me."

Estel was intentionally wronged by Jack. But instead of revenge, we may say that Estel acted **magnanimously** in his treatment of Jack. We may also say, "Estel, you're a **magnanimous** person."   After all, Estel *intentionally* does not discharge Jack. He is fully aware of what he is doing, keeping a man who does not like him.   Furthermore, there is no indication that Estel is motivated by trying to change Jack's opinion of him, or to make Jack into a friend. He is showing a loftiness of spirit, and a generous disdain for meanness or retaliation. The decision to retain Jack is *deliberate*. Estel has other options. He is weighing them out. He counts in his deliberation all that he knows about Jack. Jack is a mediocre to good worker, has a large family with many expenses, and is the person who, except for fate, would have kept Estel from his promotion. But Estel chooses to retain him. What is interesting about his *purpose* is that he seems to be acting with a view toward what is best for all concerned. He is balancing the interests of the company with Jack's interests, and he is keeping rein on any ill feeling he has toward Jack.

What happens now if we do some reflection on how language is operating in these appraisals? First, we would notice that it is not absolutely "provable" that Mary's act was *spiteful*, or that Estel's omission to discharge Jack was *magnanimous*. Neither could we "know for certain" that Mary was spiteful or Estel magnanimous. Consider, for example, that someone like Jack, upon hearing that he was retained, and cynical in his dislike for Estel, might say, "Well, I knew he wouldn't have the nerve to get rid of me; I'd sue the company." Or, he might say, ""Well, he wanted to keep me on to badger and harass me; it's his way of getting even with me." Jack might have some difficulty accepting the description of Estel's omission as magnanimous. This kind of give-and-take occurs in ordinary moral practice. If we ask, was Estel's act *really* magnanimous? the answer would require our knowing which description prevails.

Using Character Traits to Guide Conduct

We often overlook the fact that virtue and vice concepts as character descriptions may be used to direct conduct just as surely as moral rules do. We may say, "You should not be *dishonest* " or "You don't want to be *dishonest,* do you?" as well as "Do not do X because it's *dishonest* ," or "Persons should avoid *dishonest* conduct."   Moral practice certainly takes into account conduct guiding concepts and moral rules.   But it also shows that the type of person one is, or wants to be, or should want to be may be every bit as important a reason for making the moral choices one does, or for living as one does. Moral communities encourage persons to consider the type of character they have, or want to have, as sufficient reason for acting, attempting, or omitting in certain ways. Aside from what duties or obligations a person has, the agent may want to consider what he is making of his life--what narrative others tell about him, or the story that he can tell about himself using virtue and vice concepts. Accordingly, what is permissible for persons in general someone may certainly judge not right for himself. He may do so by reference to his own virtue ideals.   In discussing this function of ordinary moral practice, Edmund Pincoffs writes that an

> ...agent may care if what he is doing is just, if it is loyal, if it is cowardly, and, merely sentimental, or decent. He may worry that in acting or approving as he proposes, he would be negligent, vindictive, or intolerant. He may be asking, that is, not what anyone should do, but what, given the circumstances, he should do-- whether the proposed action or practice would be worthy of him, would be consistent with his standards and ideals. What is incumbent on anyone is incumbent on him. But to confine his deliberation to duty, prior agreements, or possible consequences for the general happiness would be to leave out much of what concerns his status as a person who has standards and ideals that he does not necessarily prescribe for everyone.[60]

Virtue and Vice Traits as Reasons for Preferring or Avoiding Persons

Virtue and vice descriptions in ordinary moral practice are used as reasons for preferring or avoiding persons. Predicating virtues and vices of persons is an indispensable use of language when performing the necessary task of distinguishing between persons within the moral community. If we find out that Jim Bob may be described as 6'4" and weighing 265, that he wears cowboy boots and dips Skoal, then we know something about him which will help us decide whether we want to have relationships with him and what sort we want. But there is much that is wanting in this description. *We do not really know what kind of person Jim Bob is* . The way we have of communicating such important information includes the use of virtue and vice language.

If we find out that Jim Bob is *honest, loyal, decent, amiable, and sensitive,* then we know some of the really important things about him. And the other previously stated facts of his description may seem less decisive. At the very least, they are viewed in a new light. Likewise, if we are told that he is *cruel, dictatorial, patronizing, vindictive, and belligerent* he would probably be much less preferable; just as a person, let's say. So, utilizing a virtue concept (*honest, loyal, decent,* etc.) of a person is the equivalent to providing a reason for preferring that person--considered morally. Whereas, using a vice concept is the sufficient grounds for avoiding a person--considered morally.[61] If someone asks, "Why don't you like Jim Bob?" We may reply, "Because he is cruel and vindictive." If we do make such an answer, then others will understand perfectly why we do not like or prefer him. We need not make any other explanation beyond offering our appraisal description. Of course, someone may differ with our description of Jim Bob. He may say that we have misdescribed Jim Bob. But he will not disagree

---

[60]Pincoffs, Quandaries and Virtues, p. 44.

[61]Ibid., p. 83.

that *cruel* and *vindictive* people are undesirable just as persons; he will be disputing whether "Jim Bob" is cruel and vindictive and this is a very important difference about what is being disputed.

We have been discussing Jim Bob's preferability. But "preferable" has many uses. If you were going to war or to a gang fight, then the Jim Bob who was cruel and belligerent might be preferred as the fellow you would want on your side. In such a situation, you might rightly say that the amiable, sensitive, and decent Jim Bob would not be nearly as desirable.

Untangling the relationship of preference to virtue and vice usage is an important task for ethics. For example, what should we make of an appraisal like this: "Fagin is a courageous thief"? This seems like an odd use of language. Is it possible to praise Fagin with a virtue concept like *courageous* while at the same time saying he is a thief? After all, saying that someone is a thief is a way of blaming him, and warning others about him. Or, consider this. Could a person who unjustly obtains resources, say someone like Robin Hood, use these resources charitably? Can an unjust man act charitably? Would we say this unjust man is benevolent or charitable? Or, would we refuse to use the concept "unjust" of a man who does charitable things with his ill-gotten gain?

There is a sense in which all of these puzzles are generated by our failure to appreciate how moral language is functioning in actual practice. The reason we might think that we prefer someone for having what in other contexts would certainly be a vice, and the fact that we might think we are praising someone for doing something that is wrong, and that we might even find a use for descriptions which seem to say that an immoral person does things which are praiseworthy, is that we are thinking of virtues and vices as all of the same type, when this is not so. There are different types of virtues and vices which reflect the various ways in which someone can be preferable.

Pincoffs has made a careful effort to categorize virtues, thus showing an appreciation for the different types of preferability which occur in ordinary practice. Pincoffs believes that our use of virtue concepts falls two main categories. **Instrumental Virtues** are those which enable people to pursue their goals effectively or to perform tasks well, whether as individuals (agents) or as a part of a group. The instrumental virtues may be reasons to prefer someone irrespective of moral considerations. Certain characteristics may even help someone achieve an end that is not considered morally proper by the community. So, it is perfectly possible to have a "courageous thief." What we are praising is the thief's manner of performing his task, not the stealing itself. We may say that someone is "efficient." This is an instrumental virtue. Whenever we need to perform a task, we prefer efficient persons to those who are inefficient. But the Nazis were "efficient killers." Strangely enough, one can "admire" or "praise" the performance of a task without condoning or praising the conduct itself. Simply because something is "efficient" does not mean that it is the morally praiseworthy thing to do. Likewise, if someone is a "competent" plumber, I will certainly prefer that he fix my pipes, rather than an "incompetent" plumber. Although the "competent" plumber may be an "adulterer" or "cruel" person under a moral description, if I want him to fix my pipes his being an adulterer may not be relevant to my preference. For plumbing, he is preferable. But when it comes to relationships, however, I may wish to avoid him.

Noninstrumental Virtues, according to Pincoffs, are those traits desirable for their own sake, and not because they are related to the performance of a task. Pincoffs divides these virtues into several categories. The *aesthetic* noninstrumental virtues make persons attractive, either because the person has character traits which are admirable in human persons as noble, or because the person has traits that add beauty to life by being charming. The *meliorating* noninstrumental virtues make our common life as human persons more tolerable. Persons may possess traits that help mediate in times of disputes, quarrels, and conflicts in common life. They are the peacemakers or negotiators who make common life more tolerable because they help us get along. Or, they may have such an even temperament that living with them is just easier than living with others. And, of course, there are social settings in common life in which we prefer persons who possess *formal* virtues. *Moral* noninstrumental virtues are of both the mandatory and nonmandatory types.[62]

While Pincoffs description is helpful, it is not without its shortcomings. Consider the virtue chart exhibited on the following page. We should recognize that there are certain theoretical implications of this chart which may not completely reflect ordinary moral practice, thereby leaving some aspects of moral appraisal uncaptured. We should not treat the chart as absolute, and we should recognize its deficiencies as a descriptive mechanism. We cannot make a concept fit in one and only one category whenever it is used in such a way as to fit in many categories. Neither should we ignore uses which transcend the table entirely.

A descriptive account of moral practice will leave us with several observations on Pincoffs' work. 1) Some virtue/vice concepts have more than one use, thus having to be placed in more than one place on Pincoffs' chart. Consider that being *conscienceless* could be classified as nonmeditating, as well as immoral. *Kindly* may be a noble aesthetic description, a temperamental melioration trait, and a mandatory moral distinction. In order to get a feel for how difficult it is to know how to categorize a virtue on Pincoffs' chart, try to take the table of uncategorized personality traits and place its virtues onto Pincoffs chart. 2) Some moral concepts may mark virtues under some descriptions and vices under others. For example, *imperturbable* or *impulsive.* To be impulsive may be an agent instrumental vice, yet under some descriptions it may be used to mark a certain charm and excitement which a person brings to life. Other examples of concepts which are sometimes used as virtues, and sometimes as vices, are *meek, zealous, simple,* and *ambitious.* Of course, we must be wary not to think that it is always the case that every virtue may also have a vice usage. "Being opinionated" is the vice of "having convictions," let us say. We do not find a virtue use of *opinionated* in ordinary practice. 3) Use of virtue and vice concepts in moral practice exposes some difficulties with the most fundamental characterization of the table: its division into instrumental and noninstrumental. "Being moral," for example, may be both a moral virtue (which is called noninstrumental by Pincoffs) and yet also an instrumental virtue. It could be instrumental because "being moral" makes it more likely that we will achieve a desired goal, if the goal is establishing community between persons. Under this description, "being moral" is not valued "just for itself," which is Pincoff's definition of a noninstrumental virtue, but it is valued because it helps one achieve a desired end. 4) Some of the names for the table categories Pincoffs gives are themselves virtues or vices (e.g., *noble, charming* and

---

[62]Ibid., pp. 84-86.

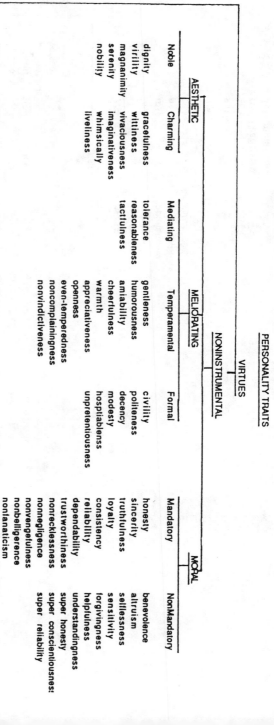

Taken from Edmund Pincoffs, Quandaries and Virtues

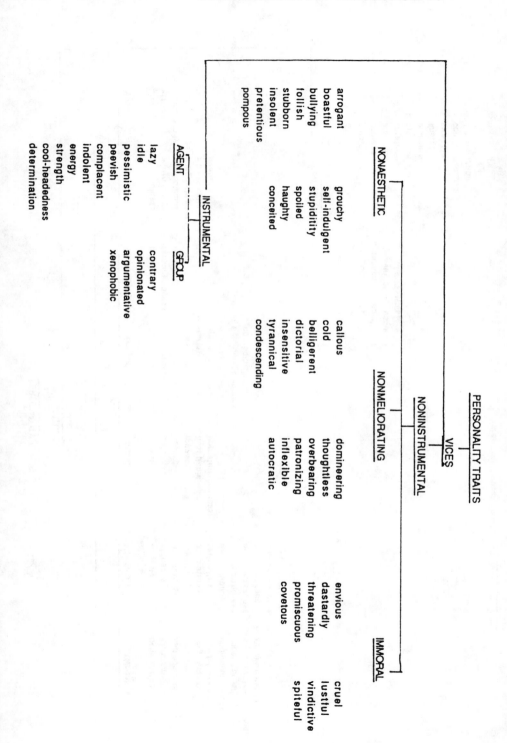

UNCATEGORIZED PERSONALITY TRITS

Taken from Edmund Pincoffs, <u>Quandries and Virtues</u>

able	curious	idle	prescient	sympathetic
affable	dastardly	imperturbable	presumptuous	tactful
affected	decent	impulsive	pretentious	tender
affectionate	dedicated	independent	proud	tender-minded
agreeable	dependable	inflexible	prudent	tense
alacritous	devout	ingenious	quarrelsome	thoughtful
ambitious	dictorial	ingenuous	queer	thoughtless
amiable	dignified	inscrutible	querulous	threatening
argumentative	disciplined	intelligent	quick-witted	thrifty
arrogant	disgraceful	interesting	quizzical	timid
avaricious	distant	irritable	reasonable	tolerant
belligerent	distinguished	jingoistic	refined	torpid
benevolent	dominating	jocular	reliable	truthful
bilious	domineering	just	religious	uncomplaining
boastful	ebullient	kindly	repressed	undemonstrative
brainy	energetic	knightly	reserved	understanding
brave	enigmatic	lazy	repectable	uxorious
brooding	enterprising	learned	respectful	vigorous
bullying	envious	light-hearted	revengeful	vindictive
calculating	equable	lively	secretive	virile
callous	euphemistic	lustful	self-confident	vivacious
cantankerous	excitable	magnanimous	self-contained	waspish
careful	exhibitionistic	manly	self-controlled	watchful
cautious	fair-minded	mannerly	self-disciplined	weak
changeable	fearful	meek	self-indulgent	weak-minded
charitable	flattering	mercenary	selfish	well-intentioned
cheerful	foolish	mercurial	self-pitying	whimsical
civil	foresighted	methodical	self-reliant	wise
claustrophobic	forgiving	moderate	self-respecting	withdrawn
clever	frank	modest	self-satisfied	witty
cold	friendly	morbid	sensitive	worrying
complacent	frugal	nefarious	serious	xenophobic
complaisant	gallant	neurotic	shy	yielding
conceited	gay	odd	silly	youthful
condescending	generous	open-minded	simple	zany
conscienceless	gentle	opinionated	simple-minded	zealous
conscientious	good-living	orderly	sensible	
contrary	good-natured	patronizing	sinful	
cooperative	good-tempered	peevish	slavish	
cosmopolitan	grouchy	persistent	sober	
courageous	hasty	pessimistic	spoiled	
courteous	helpful	petulant	stimulating	
courtly	honest	phlegmatic	stubborn	
covetous	hospitable	picayune	stupid	
credulous	humble	polite	submissive	
cruel	humorous	pompous	suggestible	

moral). This raises a problem, because they could be shown as instances on the table, not as categories which set up the table. The easiest way to see this is to try to construct a vice chart of your own using the table of uncategorized personality traits and your dictionary. One is faced almost immediately with the difficulty of establishing sub-categories which are not also themselves specific vices.

In spite of these concerns, Pincoffs' chart is helpful in some significant ways. It helps us see that while some virtues are primarily directed toward others, there are self-directed virtues as well. This is Pincoffs' way of showing us that our use of moral virtues in ordinary practice includes self-appraising and self-referential appraisals, and not just those which are directed toward how we relate to others. So not all moral virtues or appraisals of moral character have to do with others. Not all moral practice is other-centered. To hold any such theoretical view is, therefore, to run directly counter to actual moral practice. There is also a moral language which indicates the practice of self-appraisal (e.g., *vain; self-controlled*) and takes note of the fact that our own self-reflection about the type of person we are, or are becoming, is made possible because there is a language available for this function. As we have already seen, such self-referential descriptions may influence our conduct toward others. If we want to be more self-controlled, it is likely that our conduct toward others will be altered by this desire.

Another way in which Pincoffs' work helps us understand moral appraisal is by uncovering our practice of preferring or avoiding persons for qualities that we do not praise or blame them for having. Again, this seems to discount certain theories of ethics which hold that all moral description is based on what a person has **willed** to do, attempt, omit, or be. Pincoffs helps us understand that moral concepts are used not only of those traits and dispositions which become a part of one's character as a result of his decisions and exercise of will. Sometimes we prefer persons who have traits which did not come by reason of choice or will power, but by their temperament. Since language seems to suggest that this is true, then we may conclude that some theoretical questions historically regarded as quite significant, really do not need to be answered at all. For example, consider a classic question like, "Who is *really* honest, the man who is tempted to steal but does not succumb, or the man for whom stealing is no temptation?" If we accept that there are preferences which are well-founded in moral practice independent of the question of will, this question may not be as relevant as at first it seems. That someone is honest is what is important; how he came to be so may be significant only to those interested in moral education. Still, however, one of the distinguishing marks of moral virtues and vices seems to be that they do have something to do with conduct under the control of persons; the will is relevant. Otherwise, why would we consider persons who have no control or who are unable to conduct themselves morally as nonappraisable? So, we find both an emphasis on simply being honest, whether temptation is overcome or not, and on striving to overcome temptation and be honest.

Some virtues seem necessary for all persons in the moral community, and some vices seem to be universally abhorred. As Pincoffs says, we do not imagine that there will be any common life of persons in which justice, persistence, courage, and honesty will not be virtues. This is true, at least, given the fact that the conduct marked by these concepts exemplifies traits which human persons find necessary for well-being and flourishing in community. Of course, if either persons or their environment changed radically, then some virtues might become obsolete, and they might even perish from language, or, if retained, they might come to be regarded as simply arbitrary. As Pincoffs observes, if we lived in a world in which our every desire were fulfilled immediately, then there would be no place for *perseverance* or *fortitude* as virtues. These concepts would become anachronisms. We would not know what to do with them. There would be no use for them. In time, they would either be given new meanings, or else they would fall into disuse and eventually die. Conversely, if we were immune to pain, psychological as well as physical, then *cruelty* would be not vice; it would not exist. We would not speak of persons having this trait because there would be no conduct to exhibit it. *Benevolence, sympathy, justice,* and *kindness* are virtues given only certain facts about our common life. This is also true about moral concepts such as *stealing, lying,* and such.[63]

There are also virtues and vices which are concerned not only with particular abilities or traits, but also with the practices we exercise within the community of human persons as well. Whether we are *fair* or *just* depends in part on how we appraise or judge others. So, not only do we form character descriptions of others in making moral appraisals; but we also provide the conduct which enables character descriptions to be made of ourselves, as others observe us making moral appraisals. Someone can be *judgmental* or *censorious* rather than fair or just. Such language in the moral community seems to show that persons feel the need to safeguard the process of moral evaluation and protect persons from abuses of the practice. The practice of moral evaluation is related to the edification of both the community and its individuals, and the way this practice is done is itself appraisable.

Consider an appraisal which is applied to the individual himself. Being *conscienceless* is a vice which does not mark any specific moral deficiency, but the fact that a person is morally depraved. Such a person does not function appropriately in the moral community, not primarily because he has no values himself, but because the normal mechanisms available to the moral community for the control of conduct and presentation of appropriate aspirations for human persons do not work on this person. A conscienceless person is impervious to blame, excommunication, or shame of any sort. Of course, the use of such a concept is rare and imprecise, at least to the extent that it is difficult to conceive of any person who is totally immune to the workings of the moral community. Still, however, the concept is used; and when used it marks a character vice of a certain sort: specifically, the fact that the person does not even admit that vice descriptions may be applied to him. This vice is the way the community has of blaming someone for not recognizing its moral power over him. It distinguishes such a person from those who are "morally innocent" or "mentally deficient" and *unable* to appreciate the power and significance of moral appraisal and therefore are not appraisable at all.

Character Description and Self-Deception

Sometimes another person sees our action as virtuous, but we do not see it so. Estel, for example, might say that he was only doing his duty. He might be embarrassed if Homer praised him. Perhaps Estel knows something about his

---

[63]Ibid., pp. 7ff.

intentions, deliberations, or purposes that Homer does not. But moral practice discloses that the opposite danger is probably more to be avoided. Persons want to be praised and recognized, even if they are undeserving. An overabundance of humility does not seem to be a problem.

However, a person who refuses to reflect on his intentions, or rationalizes his conduct, or denies his purposes may become *self-deceived*. **Self-deception** *is the intentional evasion of acknowledging a truth about oneself.* The self-deceived are persons who think they deserve to be praised when they do not, perhaps because they are denying their true and less than honorable intentions or purposes. Such people can be dangerous to the moral community.[64]

Mike Martin has made a study of self-deceiving patterns as they occur in the practice of morality. These patterns include the following: willful ignorance (intentionally and deliberately omitting to inform oneself); systematic ignoring (repeatedly disregarding moral liabilities and conduct); emotional detachment (blocking, hardening and freezing emotions one would have if he admitted his true character and conduct); self-pretense (pretending to oneself that one's conduct and character are not *seriously* amiss morally and letting on to others that one is morally responsible and respectable); rationalization (convincing oneself that one's conduct is morally excusable, without regard for the witness of the moral community to the contrary).[65]

Self-deception often leads to *hypocrisy*. **Hypocrisy** *is assuming a false appearance of virtue, pretending to have moral beliefs and character higher than is actually true.* Hypocrisy is a blaming concept in moral language because those who are hypocritical, or who practice hypocrisy, deceive others and violate relationships built upon an understanding of moral commitment which is not present. Of course, not all of the self-deceived are hypocrites. One may be intentionally hypocritical without being self-deceived at all.[66]

Authenticity is a virtue in so far as the avoidance of self-deception is virtuous. **Authenticity** *is both the capacity to accept one's character and the willingness to acknowledge to oneself one's values and how these values are exercised through conduct.* However, a person may be authentic and immoral. A person could be honestly immoral.

One may feel guilty because of his self-deception when he discovers it. But guilt and blameworthiness are distinct. Some self-deception has nothing to do with moral blameworthiness. Considerations which turn up in moral language when determining whether self-deception is blameworthy, and to what degree it is, are as follows. 1) The gravity of the moral concepts and rules which are threatened by self-deceiving conduct. 2) The actual degree of harm or injury done to others, and to oneself. Actually some self-deception may be morally permissible, even

---

[64]There are some exceptional discussions of self-deception. See Martin, Everyday Morality, pp. 93ff. and Herbert Fingarette, Self-Deception (Atlantic Highlands, NJ: Humanities Press, 1969).

[65] Mike Martin, Self Deception and Morality (Lawrence, Kansas: The University of Kansas Press, 1986), pp. 7-9.

[66]See Eva Feder Kittay, "On Hypocrisy," Metaphilosophy 13 (1982): 283.

admirable. Occasionally persons who deceive themselves into thinking that they are conducting themselves with altruistic intentions may still do much good. 3) The extent to which it is reasonable to expect that one should have known himself more thoroughly. Sometimes evidence which might influence one's belief about one's conduct or character is incomplete or unavailable, even to the agent. Self-deception may be inevitable, or at least inescapable. 4) The degree of control one has over his self-deception. 5) Whether one uses self-deception in hypocritical ways.

If we take note of the persons whom we describe as self-deceived, we will find that they are not all of the same type. Some persons are self-deceived because they genuinely are not in touch with their moral life and conduct. They honestly believe themselves to be a different sort of person than the one they present to the moral community. So as a deceiver the person is guilty; whereas as genuinely deceived, he is also an innocent victim. [67] Others know exactly the kinds of persons they are. Indeed, they must know this in order to conceal it from others and from themselves.[68]

For Discussion

1) Following the pattern set up by Edmund Pincoffs, make your own virtue and vice charts. You may find the table on uncategorized personality traits helpful.

2) Construct cases patterned after those of Spiteful Mary and Magnanimous Estel which demonstrate how character traits may be expressed in conduct.

3) Construct a case in which an agent is displaying self-deceiving conduct, relying on one or more of the patterns noted by Mike Martin.

---

[67]Herbert Fingarette, Self Deception (Atlantic Highlands, N.J.: Humanities Press, 1969), p. 1.

[68]This is a point made by Jean Paul Sartre in Being and Nothingness, trans. by Hazel E. Barnes (New York: Washington Square Press, 1966), p. 89.

Chapter Nine: Theoretical Questions About
the Practice of Moral Appraisal

Introduction

It is fair now to comment more thoroughly on how the descriptions we have been making of moral practice raise important theoretical issues. Up to now we have tried to avoid any extended discussion of these philosophical concerns. But now it seems necessary and desirable to introduce theoretical reflection for the following reasons.

First, a basic introduction to ethics should serve the general function of providing a student with an appreciation of the classical philosophical positions taken on key moral issues and of providing an acquaintance with the noteworthy philosophers who represent these views. Such learning increases cultural awareness and instills respect for some of the moral questions which Western Civilization counted as significant.

Second, it is possible that ordinary moral practice supports one of the classical theoretical explanations as more plausible than the others. If it is found that some philosopher's views are a more accurate depiction of how we actually proceed than are those of someone else, then we should read the one rather than the other.

Third, our ordinary way of proceeding in moral appraisal may not be the **best** way to proceed, or the way we **should** proceed. Perhaps some theoretical analysis might provide a corrective to our common moral practice. Maybe employing this analysis would lead us to the conclusion: "Well, we say this, but we *should* say something else." Some ways in which this might occur are as follows. It is possible that ordinary moral practice tolerates or permits certain conduct which we can show by theoretical means to be morally reprehensible. Or perhaps our moral considerations and distinctions may be so sloppy, irrational, or so biased as to render them in some way deleterious to the fulfillment and well-being of human persons. If any of these matters could be shown true based on theoretical analysis, then we should alter our way of proceeding in ordinary moral life.

Fourth, a description of how we proceed in moral appraisal leaves unanswered some questions which it may be quite important to have answered. For example, whether one's moral standards are simply arbitrary or whether they may be defended rationally, or whether they can be known by direct experience because they refer to objectively real properties of events. Or, whether there are identifiable considerations which make an entity worthy of moral consideration, such that all persons should recognize these. Or, whether there are decision rules for situations of limited knowledge which can be defended rationally. Or, whether there is a theoretical explanation for the move from conduct descriptions to character ascriptions. Or, whether it is possible to construct a single comprehensive moral theory which can justify appraisal standards and provide a complete application apparatus .

We have made note throughout the text of several of these key theoretical issues and how they are raised in ordinary moral practice itself. The questions which we have identified are discussed below. Of course, these are be no means the only ones which could be addressed. But perhaps studying these issues will stimulate us to ask other questions about moral practice, and our search for the answers to these will itself make us more responsible moral agents.

Are Moral Appraisal Standards Objective or Subjective?

It is clear from our analysis of moral practice that we use moral concepts in making appraisals. But to what, if anything, do these concepts refer? How did they originate? Did humans invent them or did they discover properties which events and persons possess and create language to name these? Does a moral appraisal depend on my feeling or belief, or is there something more objective involved? Is "seeing" cruelty in a person's conduct somehow analogous to "seeing" a tree outside my window? Is the source of moral language objective and independent of the user, or is it his subjective interpretation of what he observes? What is at stake here may be expressed in terms of the theoretical debate between moral objectivism and subjectivism. In what follows we will mention two objectivist theories, and describe one prevailing way of approaching this issue from a subjectivist view.

Moral Realism is one of the most fundamental and historically significant objectivist theories. A very fine contemporary exposition of moral realism has recently been offered by David McNaughton in his work, Moral Vision. He holds that moral concepts and rules refer to actual facts about the conduct and character of persons.[69] These moral facts belong to the furniture of the world, just as do empirical facts about trees or buildings. For example, "Trees have limbs," "Buildings are made of brick," and "Setting the cat on fire is cruel" are statements of the same category. They are all factual descriptions.

McNaughton believes moral facts are directly-perceivable; that is, they are not our subjective interpretations of what has taken place, neither are they simply how we read a person's character. We do not first see other observable facts and then make an individual moral judgment about these facts based on our feelings or opinions. Rather, the process of description is something like this. When we describe an act as a murder, McNaughton believes we mean that **murder** is as much a part of the factual description of the event as *where* the event took place (the kitchen), *who* was killed (Mrs. Smith), and *how* the killing was done (with the butcher knife). The killing's being a murder is as directly-perceivable a fact as is the kitchen, Mrs. Smith, and the butcher knife.

At the same time, McNaughton thinks that moral concepts (facts) are unanalyzable. We cannot give a complete definition of a moral concept. Of course, there may be insurmountable obstacles in giving a complete definition of the kitchen, Mrs. Smith, and the butcher knife too. But what McNaughton means when he calls moral concepts unanalyzable is that describing a killing as a **murder** is to say something *more* and *other* than to describe the performance of the killing. Let me try to clarify this claim by comparing moral facts to color facts. When we say "The coat is green" or "The dress is pink" we are using unanalyzable color concepts. *Green* and *pink* cannot be defined, except by pointing to examples of these colors. Of course, we may go to the dictionary and get some definition like "Pink is any group of colors bluish red to red in hue, of medium to high lightness,

[69]David McNaughton, Moral Vision: An Introduction to Ethics. Oxford: Basil Blackwell, 1988). There are other works concerned with moral realism as well. Two are David Brink, Moral Realism and the Foundation of Ethics (Cambridge: Cambridge University Press, 1989) and J. McDowell, "Aesthetic Value, Objectivity, and the Fabric of the World," in Pleasure, Preference and Value, edited by E. Schaper (Cambridge: Cambridge University Press, 1976).

and of low to moderate saturation." But does that tell you what pink is? Probably not. Since the definition relies on other color concepts, it may only serve to confuse you, whereas, pointing to an example of something pink will define it for you. You will be able to identify pink objects the next time you are asked to do so. If you want to buy a pink shirt or dress you will be able to do so.

Now McNaughton believes moral concepts are analogous to color concepts in this way.[70] Someone may ask, "Where is the *murder* that you say you perceive?" But this is like asking for the definition of a color concept. How do I know that I understand what a murder is? Well, roughly speaking, I know this in the same way that I know what pink is. I can identify it when I need to do so.

It may seem like an easy objection to moral realism may surface at this point. One could argue that if the realist position is the correct theoretical explanation of the origin of moral concept terms, if "murder" is a property which makes up the world like people, and animals, and things do, or at least like things such as colors do, then it seems that we would not disagree about when to apply a moral concept.[71] Persons do not disagree, at least not often or seriously about whether a shirt is pink. So, we ought not to disagree about moral appraisals either. We should not disagree over whether someone is being cruel, or spiteful, or kind. However, moral realists have considered this problem, and they hold that cases of disagreement over the uses of moral concepts and the discriminatory judgments we make using them (e.g., "Murder is wrong"), arise for one or more of the following reasons.

1) The person is teasing us or deceiving us, as for example, when a child answers a question about the color of the sky by saying; "Uh....it's orange!!" The child actually knows what concept to use; but he is deceiving us about his knowledge, saying something other than what he knows is true, either to joke, or to be deceptive, or to be obstinate. Moral realists simply believe that some moral disagreements have the same point of origin. Persons are trying to be obstinate or else they do not want to admit what they know to be the case. Persons really know what moral concept to employ, but because they wish to be deceptive or avoid blame, they will not use the appropriate moral description of conduct, whether their own or someone else's.

2) The person has made a mistake because of poor moral education or training. Realists develop the analogy between color concepts and moral concepts more fully in order to make their point. If we consider that some persons have a highly developed color sense and vocabulary because they have had extensive education or training, we may be able to see how this illuminates moral differences too. For example, if I am considering painting the scenery outside my cabin in Wyoming, someone may inquire what color the sky is. Blue I answer. But such a reply might really frustrate a trained artist. "What shade of blue?" the artist may inquire. The artist may appreciate the differences in sky hues, and be able to identify them much more accurately than I can.

---

[70]Ibid., pp. 91ff.

[71]J.L. Mackie offers some very strong criticisms of what he calls the property theory of objectivism, which would apply well against the moral realist position in Inventing, pp. 20-46.

Likewise, because of poor moral training, a person may simply not be able to use moral vocabulary correctly. For moral realists, persons are not sensitive to the moral facts about events and persons in the same way, or to the same degree. So, a person whose moral sensibilities are not well-trained may make a mistake, or may not know whether or not a moral concept is applicable, and this leads to moral disagreement. Yet, the moral fact captured by a moral concept may be present, even if such a person does not perceive it.[72]

A realist could expand this description even further. He might say that training can radically change one's perceptions and experiences. If we can increase our ability to use a rich and diverse color vocabulary, then we certainly may perceive things differently than before. The same also holds true for expanding our moral vocabulary. Consider the following analogies.

I may attend a symphony and appreciate the music. But to be sure, the conductor is in some sense hearing a "different symphony" than I am. He perceives the trumpet entry, noting whether it is too soft (or loud),or flat (or sharp), whereas I may miss the whole thing. He "hears" tones which I do not--at least he is aware of them. The musicians are, after all, playing the same score for him as for me. Literally, they play the same notes for him as for me. But the conductor is trained to hear what I do not.

Likewise, a gourmet surely tastes different seasonings in the food than I do, and he does so because of his training. My auto mechanic hears noises in my engine which I do not. I may look at an X-Ray for hours, without seeing what the physician sees; *yet it is there nonetheless*. The notes, or seasonings, or noises in my engine, or hair-line fractures on the X-Ray are all there whether I perceive them or not. The problem is not with reality, but with me. The explanation for such differences in perception is that I am not sufficiently or properly skilled. I do not have the right training.[73] Accordingly, a moral realist would assert that if we want to minimize the frequency and intensity of moral disagreement, then we should be about the business of training persons to perceive moral facts more clearly.

Sometimes moral disagreements arise not because a person is *insufficiently* trained morally, but because he has received *improper instruction* in moral appraisal--those who have taught him how to practice morality have done so inadequately. For instance, he may have had poor moral examples, thereby contributing to a truncated, erroneous, or underdeveloped ability to make moral appraisals. He misses what he should "see" because he has been warped.

Another objectivist approach to the origin of moral concepts is called the **Divine Command Theory**. Some philosophers believe that moral realism is a faulty theoretical system because the analogies upon which it is based are reducible to subjectivist descriptions. What they mean is that so-called "color facts" are subjective. There is no pink or green in an actual object itself. These colors are

---

[72]McNaughton makes some other strong arguments against relativism in morality based on the fact of cultural diversity, in Moral Vision, pp. 150ff.

[73]McNaughton uses some of these arguments, in Ibid., pp. 58ff.

manufactured perceptions based on light quanta filtered through our optic mechanisms. So, neither are there "murder facts" or "cruelty facts." Since these philosophers do not accept Realism as a theoretical explanation, and since they see Subjectivism as a dangerous basis for moral concepts because it reduces them down to personal interpretation and opinion, they turn to some other external explanation for the origin of moral concepts. The objective source they find is God.

Moral concepts are embodied in the divine commands of God, such as the Ten Commandments and other moral rules. Divine Command Theorists do not say that we have the moral concepts and rules which we do because these concepts are moral facts which are a part of the real world. Neither do they believe that the justification for a moral concept is that it promotes the general good, or even our own good. Perhaps a moral concept does, in fact, contribute to these ends. But this is not their justification. Divine Command Theorists hold that moral concepts and rules are established by God, and that is sufficient reason for us to believe in them and to order human communities by them. They are eternally true, regardless of what any human thinks about them. Some important advocates of the Divine Command Theory include Robert Adams and Philip Quinn.[74]

A common objection to Divine Command Theory is that sometimes religious texts report that God commanded a person to do something that appears to be immoral. In our earlier discussion of special role obligations and prohibitions we observed that there are times when such role standards conflict with our general moral standards. This is true of all special roles, not just those standards one holds because of one's religious tradition. But it is true of the religious role. One way a Divine Command Theorist can respond to
this criticism of his theory's consistency is to make an appeal to what is called *the teleological suspension of the ethical*. This expression, coined by Soren Kierkegaard,[75] states that obedience to divine command takes precedence over allegiance to all other norms and authorities. The case from which Kierkegaard derives this criterion is Abraham's near-sacrifice of Isaac reported in Genesis 22:1-14. According to the narrative, Abraham was directed by God to sacrifice his son, Isaac. Clearly, then, Abraham was commanded by God to perform an action which under general moral standards would be prohibited ("Do not murder" or "Do not kill innocent persons"). Indeed, Kierkegaard's case rests precisely on noting that the action is contradictory to general moral duties and prohibitions. Kierkegaard calls Abraham the "knight of faith" because he acted from religious devotion and not from a morality established by humans.

However, while a claim such as this may have some theological merits, ordinary moral practice shows that the dangers for harm and injury are very great

---

[74]Robert Adams, "A Modified Divine Comand Theory of Ethical Wrongness," in Religion and Morality: A Collection of Essays, edited by Gene Outka and J.P. Reeder (New York: Anchor Books, 1973); Philip Quinn, Divine Commands and Moral Requirements (Oxford: Clarendon Press, 1978); and The Divine Command Theory of Ethics, edited by Paul Helm (London: Oxford University Press, 1979).

[75]Soren Kierkegaard, In Fear and Trembling, in A Kierkegaard Anthology, edited by Robert Bretall (Princeton, NJ: Princeton University Press, 1946).

whenever general moral standards are disregarded. Historically, whenever morality has been subordinated to religious intuition, serious repercussions usually follow. In the recent past, the cases of the Ayatollah Khomeni, Jim Jones and Charles Manson illustrate what we mean.

There are some other difficulties with Divine Command Theories which deserve note. One problem is that it is unclear how we are to know what it is that God has commanded. Although it seems obvious to their adherents that the Judeo-Christian texts and traditions are the appropriate source for God's command, such a view ignores the rich pluralism of religions across the world. There are Hindu and Buddhist texts, New Guinea shamans, Zen masters, the Qur'an, and many others which may have much to contribute to moral practice. An adherent to the Divine Command Theory would need to develop some compelling argument for which religion provides us knowledge of God's commands. At the very least, if a supporter of the Divine Command Theory could identify a common terrain of "divine commands" in all religious traditions (some of them are not theistic, of course), then he would still have to provide an account for the differences, if he ever privileged one religion's teachings over another.

But there is more to it than this. Even if one accepted the belief that God's commands came only through the Judeo-Christian texts, it is still difficult to form a comprehensive and noncontradictory set of commands from the Bible. Consider that the Bible commands us "Do not kill." But it also teaches, "Do not allow a witch to live" and "Whomever shall have sex with a beast shall be executed." Of course, we could find ways to make all this consistent. We could say that the commandment "Do not kill" really means "Do not murder." But if it does, then why did not God say that? And if it does, then how do we distinguish "murder" from "execution" and "euthanasia" and "suicide"? These are matters which seem to be left to human interpretation, but they are just the sorts of things that we need to be able to do in order to be able to practice morality. The distinctions are not provided in the Bible. Furthermore, there seem to be some very significant moral situations left uncovered by the Bible. For example, what is the moral status of pornography, or should one pay taxes, when part of the funds are used to support war-making? On the very fine-grained distinctions we have noticed in our description of moral practice the Bible is almost totally silent. But should not God provide some instruction for these matters too? Even if God gave us our moral standards, these are only a small part of what it means to practice morality.

Of course, what many philosophers consider the most difficult obstacle for the Divine Command Theory has not even been mentioned. In his dialogue Euthyphro, Plato (427-347 B.C.) called attention to the fact that a Divine Command Theory does not satisfactorily explain *why* God commands something. The classic dilemma of all Divine Command Theories, according to the Euthyphro, may be expressed thusly: Is something morally right because God commands it, or does God command it because it is morally right? Critics of Divine Command Theories have shown how this dilemma is very important. If we say that something is praiseworthy because God commands it, then God has no more reason to approve benevolence than to disapprove of it, and praise and blame become wholly arbitrary functions of God's discretion. If God's will were that benevolence be blameworthy, then it would be. So, the argument goes that it would be a dangerous theoretical foundation for moral standards to rest them on the capricious will of any being, even God. Critics believe the dilemma cuts the other way too. If God commands something because it is morally praiseworthy, then the conduct's being praiseworthy is independent of God's command, and it must lie somewhere else. What is morally praiseworthy is as open to discovery by us as by God. So, God's command would be superfluous, and we should look for the more fundamental reason that something is praiseworthy or blameworthy.

Divine Command Theorists have felt it crucial to develop a response to only one horn of the Euthyphro dilemma. They wish to respond to the objection that saying something is praiseworthy because God commands it means that God has no more reason to approve benevolence than to disapprove of it, and praise and blame become wholly arbitrary functions of God's discretion. What they want to hold is that one must consider God's nature or character more carefully than do the critics. Their point is that since it is God's nature to be good, pure and perfect, then God would not command such a thing as benevolence to be blameworthy or evil.

The **Moral Subjectivists** agree with the Divine Command Theorists that Realism is flawed. However, they also believe that the Divine Command Theory cannot overcome the problems mentioned above, even though they do not hold that the moral teachings of religions are necessarily incorrect or worthless. They simply argue that moral standards derive from another source--from human persons themselves.

According to the Subjectivists, moral standards are primarily understood as those moral concepts which have come to be a part of our language simply because the community of human persons has agreed that some actions, attempts, and omissions are to be encouraged as desirable for the overall project of making it more likely that persons can realize a full and rewarding life; and that some conduct is to be discouraged because it undermines this goal. The origin of all moral standards is just this simple.

Subjectivists hold that moral concepts are born in experience itself. They ask us to imagine that at one time in the history of human development, there were only individual persons making isolated moral appraisals of specific conduct. For example, at one time there were only individual appraisal judgments for the sorts of ways human persons could relate to each other sexually. Here and there one person, and then another, made some moral appraisal of some sexual conduct. Eventually, for the distinguishing of these ways of relating, and for highlighting the relative seriousness and nature of the various activities for the overall project of making it more likely that persons could realize a full and rewarding life, a vocabulary arose. Concepts like *adultery, masturbation, fidelity, homosexuality, beastiality,* and *prostitution* came into being. These concepts carried the blame or approval of the community with their use, and they also informed persons about the particular type of conduct being described.

Imagine the period in which a moral concept such as *adultery* was in its emergent stage. Before there was the concept *adultery* there were certainly acts of voluntary sexual intercourse between a married person and someone other than his spouse. Some people disapproved of these acts, and others maybe did not. But following some indefinite period, this kind of sexual activity was over and over again judged to be undesirable for the project of making life more livable and enriching for human persons. Persons came to believe that this kind of sexual relating was such as should be prohibited, in order to make it more likely that persons could realize a full and rewarding life. To mark this specific type of blamable sexual relating, moral agents began to use the concept name **adultery**. As a result, whenever we use the concept of adultery as we do now, it describes not only a particular type of act, but also it expresses moral disapproval and blameworthiness.

According to Subjectivists, what happened in the history of the moral community is that persons *hardened their individual judgments into a moral concept.*[76] Such hardening of individual appraisals **IS** the justification of moral standards for subjectivists. There is no justification other than this. Humans decided that conduct marked by some concepts would be discouraged and blamed, and conduct marked by others would be encouraged, admired, and praised; and no further justification is needed nor possible, according to Subjectivists. Subjectivists hold that a moral concept does not make conduct objectionable or praiseworthy. The conduct already is objectionable or praiseworthy; the concept is just our way of marking this. Being objectionable or praiseworthy is *why* we use the moral concept.[77]

Subjectivists have tried to show how their position differs from Moral Realism. According to subjectivists, moral concepts such as murder are not facts to be found in the world of things. Murder belongs to a different logical category from facts. Murder is not a thing. It is not a property of a thing. It is not a fact. It is a concept. What this means is that moral language is about a world which human persons invented. They invented this world because "given a generally held belief that we must maintain a certain environment, the absence of which makes human life not worth living, we need to identify specific kinds of acts and other events for the purposes of blaming, praising, encouraging, discouraging, promoting, preventing, guiding."[78]

In criticism of the realist analogy of moral concepts and color concepts, Julius Kovesi says, "There is no 'gap' between something being yellow and the judgment 'this is yellow'."[79] However, in the case of material objects there is a gap between the thing itself and the concept used of it. For example, there arecertain facts or properties which a car possesses. It is fairly rectangular, it is made of steel, and it has weight. However, a car does not, in addition to having these properties, also have the property of *carness* by virtue of which it is a car. It is a car because it has a certain set of properties. Kovesi thinks that moral concepts are more like our language about material objects than about color concepts. Killing Mrs. Smith in a certain manner is a murder, but murder is not some additional property of fact alongside of the butcher knife, the kitchen, and Mrs. Smith.

Peter French illustrates the Kovesi position by describing what Adam might do.

[Adam} learns that Cain has killed Abel by, let us stipulate hitting him over the head with a heavy rock. He realizes that such actions would if generally practiced destroy the hope of most people to realize a full and rewarding life....He wants to admonish Seth and

---

[76]Ludwig Wittgenstein, On Certainty, quoted in Peter A. French, The Scope of Morality (Minneapolis: The University of Minnesota Press, 1979), p. 102.

[77]G.J. Warnock, The Object of Morality (London: Methuen & Co., Ltd., 1971), p. 55.

[78]Ibid., p. 48.

[79]Julius Kovesi, Moral Notions (London, Routledge and Kegan Paul,1967), p. 10

his other children not to do as Cain did, but he realizes almost immediately that there is a major difference between this injunction and telling his wife and children not to eat of the fruit of a particular tree, when all he has to do is point to the special tree and say, "Don't eat of this fruit." In this case he clearly does not mean to convey or not only to convey that he does not want them to hit each other over the head with large rocks. What he intends is to identify any acts that have certain features that are exemplified in Cain's act,...He forms the concept of murder by associating the ideas,...of an act being (1) an intentional killing of any human being (2) who is innocent and not an immediate threat to the life of the agent, (3) in part, at least, because of the agent's expectation of personal satisfaction or aggrandizement as a direct outcome of his act.[80]

Murder is not just the "hitting on the head," or the "shooting," or the "poisoning," or the "stabbing." Murder is the conceptual description which *captures* all theseparticular ways to kill. It is the concept for which Adam is searching.[81]

Kovesi holds that once we understand a moral concept such as *adultery* or *murder,* or *lie,* the addition of *right* or *wrong* is unneeded. The latter discriminators do not add new information. So, moral rules that contain moral concepts are really unnecessary. Understanding the concept *murder* is to know that it is conduct to be avoided. "Murder is wrong" is simply redundant. *Wrong* might be a sort of reminder word, but we could as well get along by saying things like "He murdered" or "It was a murder." Once we understand the meaning of the concept of murder, we know it is wrong-that the community will blame such conduct.[82]

Up to now, we have seen how Subjectivists account for the justification of moral concepts as moral standards. But critics of Subjectivism ask , "What if there is no moral concept functioning as a standard in some area of activity?" Subjectivists reply that one thing which may be happening is that we are not sure under what concept to describe an action, attempt, or omission, so it may look as though no concept is functioning. For example, suppose that we want to know whether assisting someone in ending his life is *murder*. Now we are not arguing about whether *murder* is wrong or not. We know that. However, we do not know whether our conduct fits under *murder* .

Another explanation offered by Subjectivists for the absence of a hardened concept is that morality is fluid. Subjectivists hold that moral language is alive. Human persons are engaged in the process of creating and recreating moral concepts, as well as applying them. So, the absence of a moral concept may simply indicate that the moral community is in the process of making up its mind about the

---

[80]French, The Scope of Morality, p. 85.

[81]For a technical but informative discussion of supervenient properties of actions and persons see Jaegwon Kim, "Supervenience and Nomological Incommensurables," American Philosophical Quarterly 15 (April 1978): 149-156.

[82]Kovesi, pp. 26-27; 103-109.

moral status of the conduct. Subjectivists believe that new moral concepts are being invented as we learn more about the conditions necessary for worthwhile life, and as the conditions of existence in our complex world offer new opportunities and challenges to that end. This process goes on in the day-to-day conduct of moral appraisal which culminates in the assignment of some degree of praise or blame.

Subjectivists hold that in those areas where we lack moral concepts, the moral agent is directed largely by special roles: institutional and relational obligations.[83] So, what obligations or prohibitions we have outside of those to be described under general moral concepts are tied to our special roles, contracts, agreements, and relationships.[84] Everything else is open to what Peter French calls, "the constantly repeated attempt to achieve the best judgment on the full merits of each individual case."[85]

As we conclude this treatment of the question of whether moral standards are objective or subjective, some final observations are in order. 1) If we focus on moral language, as the Subjectivists do, it may serve as an objective source for our interpretations in a manner that will satisfy at least some of the things Objectivists are trying to preserve. The concepts, rules, and procedures we find in moral language are, after all, not of our own making, although we certainly ratify them, reshape them, and participate in creating new ones. However, we never do this alone. No one can simply will to create a new moral concept or procedure. Its presentation must stand the scrutiny of the entire community, perhaps for generations to come. Likewise, we are not free to offer whatever justifications or excuses we want. There are well-recognized patterns in language, and the single most important factor which insures conformity to these is not an appeal to Moral Realism or Divine Command, but the pressure and presence of the moral community itself. 2) One wonders what the ultimate point of the Objectivist/Subjectivist debate is. If there is a substantial common terrain of moral standards, whether one is an Objectivist or a Subjectivist may not matter a great deal. The standards will be similar and usable in ordinary practice. Perhaps this is what matters in the final analysis.

Are There Theoretical Criteria for Determining Which Entities are Worthy of Moral Consideration?

We have discovered that moral language is used to make appraisals of the conduct and character of some entities, but not of others. However, we have also noticed that concerning those entities about which we do not make moral appraisals, we do provide moral consideration for some, but not for others. Why do we have a language of moral consideration for some entities, but not for others? Is there something about the entity itself? If so, what is it?

---

[83]C. H. Whiteley, "On Duties," in Moral Concepts, edited by Joel Feinberg (Oxford: Oxford University Press), p. 54.

[84]French, The Scope of Morality, p. 94.

[85]Ibid., p. 67.

It is a theoretical question to ask **why** we should use moral language about our treatment of certain entities. While we can make descriptive observations about which entities are accorded such consideration, this does not seem to be enough. Consider that one might argue that there were times and societies in which black persons, or Jewish persons, or women were disenfranchised from the protection and benefits of moral consideration. Accordingly, a set of theoretical criteria for inclusion in moral consideration might prevent undesirable exclusions in the future, or at the very least, it would provide a ground from which appraisals of such omissions might be made.

The various approaches to answering this question have been vigorously debated. Probably the most widely criticized theoretical view of which entities are to be accorded moral consideration is known as anthropocentrism. **Anthropocentrism** *is the view that human persons are to be valued more highly than all other things in nature, and that natural entities receive whatever consideration given to them from humans only because it is in the interest of humans to accord it.* This view is thoroughly described, although certainly not advocated, by Lynn White.[86] In anthropocentrism, the natural environment is accorded moral protection. Trees, water, animal species, and natural resources are considered, insofar as doing so benefits humankind. If the natural environment is to be preserved, it is only because it is in the interest of humans to do so. If it is determined to be in the greater interest of humans to snuff out a species in order to build new cities or mine new resources, then, according to those holding an anthropocentric view, there is no moral reason to refrain from doing so.

Peter Singer is very critical of anthropocentrism. He believes animals are deserving of moral consideration, regardless of whether this investment of value also happens to benefit human beings. According to Singer, animals are worthy of moral consideration because they have the capacity to suffer--to know when they are having pleasure or pain.[87] Animals are conscious and capable of feeling pain or pleasure, they have preferences and interests just like humans do. To ignore this fact is to be guilty of what Singer calls speciesism. Anthropocentrism is the classic example of speciesism. **Speciesism** *is a prejudice or attitude of bias toward the interests of members of one's own species and against those of other species.*

Another critic of anthropocentrism, Tom Regan, expands Singer's view. He holds that mammals, at least, deserve moral consideration not only because they are capable of pain and pleasure, but also because they have beliefs, desires, memories, preferences, and a welfare which is different from their potential use for or by humans.[88] Regan says that this means that animals have an inherent value. He also holds that because of their inability to speak for their moral consideration,

---

[86]Lynn White, "The Historical Roots of Our Ecological Crisis," Science 155 (1967).

[87]Peter Singer, Animal Liberation (New York: Random House, 1975), Chapter One. Joel Feinberg holds a similar view in "The Rights of Animals and Unborn Generations," in Rights, Justice and the Bounds of Liberty (Princeton, N.J.: Princeton University Press, 1980), p. 168.

[88]Tom Regan, The Case for Animal Rights (Berkeley: University of California Press, 1983).

they are dependent upon surrogate agents to do so, but in this respect they are no different than human babies and severely mentally handicapped persons.

Paul Taylor has advocated a more radical position. According to Taylor, just being a thing "with a good of its own" which can be furthered or damaged by other agents qualifies an entity for moral consideration. Taylor's criterion casts a much wider net of moral consideration. It includes both animals and plants, but not inanimate things.[89]   Something can have "a good of its own" without being sentient, but not without being animate. Trees and flowers are included in the class of things accorded moral consideration; rocks and water are not.

These theoretical models and their criteria for what entities to include in moral consideration do not in themselves offer a solution to the serious possibilities, indeed probabilities, that the moral good of such entities will sometimes conflict with that of human persons. Shall we save the spotted owl, or harvest the timber? Shall we preserve wilderness, or drill for oil? Must we fall back on anthropocentric resolutions to these difficult decisions? The moral community now seems to be working out its patterns for such issues.

Can Ultimate Moral Standards be Justified Rationally?

We have described the practice of how a person might justify a moral appraisal by appealing to some concepts or rules which are of a higher order, from which the lower order standards of appraisal are derived. But what happens when one asks about the ultimate justification of these final standards?   It is clear that we use rules and concepts such as "We should treat all persons with respect," but what if someone questioned the legitimacy of this standard? Is there a philosophical basis for the norm, or is it simply a product of the moral community in which one is a member?   Is there a rational way to defend one moral standard as preferable to other possible candidate standards about the same conduct?

Although ordinary language warrants the use of moral standards, it does not provide an uncontroversial set of such standards. [Accordingly, persons are sometimes called upon to justify a moral concept, rule, or special role obligation which they use in appraisal. There are many important philosophical accounts about how this may be done. There is even an account which says the question about the ultimate justification of moral standards cannot be answered. This account says that when we ask "What justifies the rule, 'You should treat all persons with respect'?" the spade turns and we can go no further. According to this view, there is a point at which the justifying of standards comes to an end. For the fundamental bedrock of the form of our moral life no rational justification is possible. We must say simply that "This is the way we do morality."

In the following paragraphs, however, we will turn our attention to those philosophers who have attempted to show that the fundamental standards of morality are rationally defensible and explicable.

In the late eighteenth century, Immanuel Kant (1724-1804) placed almost exclusive emphasis on moral rules as appraisal standards when he argued that the standards used in moral appraisal should be imperatives (commands) which state what we must do, what we have a duty to do. Those philosophers who have

---

[89]Paul Taylor, "The Ethics of Respect for Nature," Environmental Ethics 3 (Fall 1981): 197-218.

agreed with Kant that moral appraisal standards are statements of our duties are called deontologists. The word "deontology" has a Greek origin: *deon* -meaning "duty" and *logos* -meaning "knowledge of" or "science of." So, **deontologists** *hold that ethics is the science of our moral duties. Knowing what is moral is a matter of knowing what is our duty.* Being moral, for Kant, consisted in persons doing their duty.

Kant believed that there were many moral duties: to be honest, to keep promises, to be fair, to help others, to show gratitude, to develop our talents, not to hurt others, not to lie, etc. He believed that we could demonstrate what our moral duties are by subjecting all possible candidate duties to a rational test. So, the justification for moral standards depends on their satisfying this test. Some commentators on Kant's moral works believe there is only one version of the test by which all candidate duties can be justified. Others believe there are three different tests. And still others think that there is actually only one test, but the test is expressed in three different ways. Kant himself is the source of this confusion. He says that in order for a conduct guide to be a moral duty, and to function as a standard in moral appraisal, it must be derivable from, or rationally consistent with, **the Categorical Imperative**. However, he then gives three formulations of the Categorical Imperative in his work, Foundations of the Metaphysics of Morals. To add to this obscurity, he then proceeds to talk about every specific moral standard (duty) as **a** categorical imperative.

The formulations of the Categorical Imperative given in Foundations of the Metaphysics of Morals are the following:

1. "Act so that you treat humanity, whether in your own person or in that of another, always as an end and never as a means only."

2. "Act only according to that maxim by which you can at the same time will that it should become a universal law."

3. "Act only so that the will through its maxims could regard itself at the same time as universally lawgiving."[90]

The idea seems to be that if one wanted to know whether there is a moral duty to "be honest," then he should inquire whether this imperative "always treats humanity as an end and never as a means," or whether he could will that this command "should become a universal law." Still another way of expressing what is going on whenever the categorical imperative test is used is to ask yourself the following question about any specific choice you are about to make. "What if everyone did that?" If you could will the universalization of the conduct, then it is a moral duty.

Some philosophers claim that each of these formulations would yield the same catalog of duties, thereby freeing us of the interpretive decision about which of them Kant meant to be his test for moral standards. It seems clear that the first formulation (#1) would be compatible with the second (#2) and third (#3), and since the second (#2) and the third (#3) seem symmetrical, so we probably do no

---

[90]Immanuel Kant, Foundations of the Metaphysic of Morals, translated by Lewis White Beck (New York: Liberal Arts Press, 1959).

violence to Kant's intention to read him in such a way that duties should be determined by using all of these tests. When we do so, we can see that the catalog of moral duties usable as standards for making moral appraisals would be quite large.

One significant contribution of Kant's categorical imperative is that it can rule out some candidate moral rules as unacceptable. Consider that "Lie when it suits your own purposes" could never be a moral standard because it could never pass these tests. We could not imagine everyone acting by this rule. If this imperative were universalized, communication would break down. Persons would no longer be able to take each other's statements seriously, so both sincere and deceitful statements would lose their meaning. Promising would become empty. Trust of others would be so critically undermined that virtually all relationships would be radically altered or completely severed.

Another one of Kant's most important contributions is the distinction he draws between **categorical** and **hypothetical** imperatives (duties). When Kant speaks of **a** (not the) categorical imperative, he means a duty which has no personal names or situational exceptions in it. It is a categorical duty because it is supposed to direct everyone in the moral community, without regard for self-interests or distinctive contextual extenuation. It is a duty which every rational person *must* act on. On the other hand, a hypothetical imperative is a duty only if one is directed toward the purpose it addresses. *"If you want to be successful in this company, then you ought to be prompt."* If you do not want to be successful in this company, then you are not obligated to be prompt. In the case of a hypothetical duty, one may reject the "if" clause (the antecedent). If one does, then the duty expressed in the "then" clause (the consequent) does not hold. Hypothetical imperatives, in Kant's sense, resemble what we have called special role obligations or prohibitions, but they should not be confined too narrowly. Philippa Foot, for example, holds that moral imperatives are all hypothetical in her essay, "Morality as a System of Hypothetical Imperatives." She argues that the antecedent to all moral imperatives is something like this "If you care about the things we do, then....." or "If you want to contribute to human well-being and flourishing, then...."[91]

What we have called moral concepts, Kant would simply place in rule form, in much the same way as we saw with the Realists. However, Kant would do so for entirely different reasons. Both Kant and the Moral Realists would agree that "Murder is wrong" may function as a moral rule for appraisal of the conduct of persons. But the Realists would say that rules describe the facts that moral concepts name; whereas Kant would say that rules do not name facts, but they represent universalizable categorical duties to which it is rational for persons to agree.

A more modern version of regarding moral standards as duties is in the philosophy of David Ross (1877-1971) in his work entitled The Right and the Good. Ross did not really try to provide a theoretical method for determining what was a duty, as Kant had done. He began instead with moral practice, and uncovered the duties he found present in our language of assessment. He called these **prima facie** duties. He organized prima facie duties into the following categories.

---

[91]Philippa Foot, "Morality as a System of Hypothetical Imperatives," Philosophical Review 81 (1972): 305-316.

1. Duties deriving from my previous actions.
   a. Duties of fidelity: those arising from my promises and commitments.
   b. Duties of reparation: those arising from any harm I have caused to others.

2. Duties of gratitude: those arising from favors and unearned services and benefits which others provide for me.

3. Duties of justice: those supporting fair distribution and opposing unfair distribution of the benefits and goods of society in accord with merit.

4. Duties of beneficence: those relating to providing help to others.

5. Duties of self-improvement: those relating to improving our own virtue, intelligence, and talents.

6. Duties of non-maleficence: those requiring that we not injure others.[92]

Ross' view has the virtue of categorizing the duties which are found in ordinary moral practice. However, he offers no theoretical justification for why there are these duties and not others.

The work of philosophers like Kant and Ross has been inverted somewhat by **Rights Ethicists**. In general, deontologists believe that every moral duty generates a correlated right. *If I have a **duty** not to injure you, then you have a **right** not to be harmed.* But some philosophers believe that this process is reversed. Rights Ethicists hold that persons have *inherent or inalienable* rights, and that moral duties arise because of these rights, not vice versa. One of the most helpful works representing this approach to the justification of fundamental moral standards is <u>Philosophical Issues in Human Rights: Theories and Applications</u>, edited by Patricia H. Werhane, A.R. Gini, and David Ozar.[93]

---

[92]David Ross, <u>The Right and the Good</u> (Oxford: Clarendon Press, 1930), pp. 21-22. Some other versions of deontological theory are C.D. Broad, "Obligations, Ultimate and Derived," in <u>Broad's Critical Essays in Moral Philosophy</u>, edited by David R. Cheney (London: George Allen and Unwin, 1971). Bernard Gert, <u>The Moral Rules</u> (New York: Harper and Row, 1970) and Alan Gewirth, <u>Reason and Morality</u> (Chicago: University of Chicago Press, 1978). Divine Command Theory is a special version of deontology: Robert Adams, "A Modified Divine Command Theory of Ethical Wrongness," in <u>Religion and Morality: A Collection of Essays</u>, edited by Gene Outka and J. P. Reeder (New York: Anchor Books, 1973); Philip Quinn, <u>Divine Commands and Moral Requirements</u> (Oxford: Clarendon Press, 1978; and <u>The Divine Command Theory of Ethics</u>, edited by Paul Helm (London: Oxford University Press, 1979.

[93]<u>Philosophical Issues in Human Rights: Theories and Apllications</u>, edited by Patricia H. Werhane, A.R. Gini, and David Ozar (New York: Random House, 1986). Other recent works illustrative of this approach, but with different emphases, include Ronald Dworkin, <u>Taking Rights Seriously</u> (Cambridge: Harvard University Press, 1978) and Max L. Stackhouse, <u>Creeds, Society, and Human Rights: A Study in Three Cultures</u> (Grand Rapids: William B. Eerdmans, 1984).

Philosophers in this tradition consider the most basic rights to be human rights. These are simply rights that one has by virtue of being human. We are most familiar with this belief because it is expressed in the American *Declaration of Independence* : "We hold these truths to be self-evident; that all men are created equal; that they are endowed by their creator with inherent and inalienable rights; that among these are life, liberty, and the pursuit of happiness." Different rights ethicists provide lists of rights which add to those given in the "Declaration of Independence." There is even a United Nations statement of "Universal Human Rights." Rights ethicists hold that since rights are inalienable, they cannot be taken away from us.

Arguably the most significant work in deontological theory in recent years was published in 1971 by John Rawls, a professor of Philosophy at Harvard. The work is entitled A Theory of Justice. Rawls' main concern in this book was with the appraisal standards used for determining what constitutes social justice. However, much that he did has been adapted to show how moral standards can be justified also. Although Rawls may be called a deontologist, and is sometimes associated with the label of Neo-Kantian Morality, his approach is also firmly rooted in what has come to be called the **Social Contract** tradition. His method for justifying moral standards is based on setting up conditions under which it would be theoretically possible to achieve a contract or agreement from all persons as to the standards which constitute the fundamental bedrock of morality.

Rawls holds that all persons freed from their biases, and operating rationally, would choose the same fundamental principles. In order to portray the conditions under which this agreement can be achieved, Rawls challenges us to assume what he calls **"the original position"**.[94] The original position is simply an imaginary state in which one regards himself as free from any moral system whatever. It is conceiving of one's moral belief system as a blank slate.

Once a person's belief in his inherited and accepted moral standards is suspended in this fashion, then the rational process of justifying moral standards may begin. The most important condition under which this process is conducted is what Rawls calls the **Veil of Ignorance**. In order to explain Rawls' position on the necessity of the veil of ignorance, imagine the problems faced by the parties who are trying to reach universal rational agreement on moral standards in the following situation. If we were transported to a place where there was no moral system, but we still had complete knowledge of such traits as our social class, sex, nationality, and race--much as we do now--then we would probably agree only to those standards which seemed to be to our advantage. In fact, Rawls holds that it would be rational to do this. Knowing our race and sex, for example, it would be rational for us to choose from a set of options on moral standards those which put us in an advantageous position. But the problem with such a procedure is obvious. Since other persons would know the same things about themselves, then what would happen is that others would not agree to the biased principles which we

---

[94]John Rawls, A Theory of Justice (Cambridge: Harvard University Press, 1971). Rawls is within what is called the social contract tradition. Since the time of Thomas Hobbes, Jean Jacques Rousseau and John Locke, some philosophers have held that the basic rules and laws guiding society originate from the needs, and in Locke's case, the natural laws, found in the state of nature before any laws were made. Rawls' original position is comparable to the social contractualists' state of nature.

supported, and we would not agree to theirs--or at the very least, this process would be greatly complicated. [95]

So, Rawls recognizes that another move is required in order to arrive at moral standards to which all rational persons may agree. We must have a mechanism by which we can eliminate the arbitrariness and bias of our "situation in life" and insure that our moral standards are justified by the one thing all persons share in common: reason. It is the function of the veil of ignorance to remove such bias.

Let us imagine that we are under a veil of ignorance. What would this entail? We would be behind a veil of ignorance if we did not know our place in society, our sex, degree of education, race, natural assets, abilities, talents, intelligence, or health. If we did not know our age, religious creed, national origin or citizenship, occupation, or even whether we have a family or how many persons are in it, then we would be behind the veil.

Since we can not rely on the knowledge of these matters to make a decision about what moral standards we choose, then we will have to rely upon reason . All other people, who are also under this veil of ignorance, will have to do the same thing. It will be rational for all persons to agree only to those limits on their behavior or to accept only those duties which all others will accept too. Then, once the agreed upon standards of morality are in place, and agreed to by all, we can imagine that the veil of ignorance is removed. At this point, we enter society, becoming aware of our lot, but armed with the moral standards to which we mutually agreed while behind the veil of ignorance. These standards will be the best possible moral guidelines we could possibly have because they will be both rationally justified and impartial.

As an illustration, we may consider this example. One principle which it would be rational to advocate behind the veil of ignorance is, "No person should suffer job discrimination on the basis of race or sex." Of course, we can certainly imagine other principle options for guiding action relative to getting a job. For example, "Those who are white males should be given priority in employment and advance." Or, "It is right to treat all females as inferiors in business." Why would it be rational to choose the principle "No person should suffer job discrimination on the basis of race or sex" instead of one of the other candidates? Well, think about it in this way. Since we do not know what our race or sex will be whenever we emerge from behind the veil of ignorance, then it would be reasonable for us to insure that whatever race or sex we will find ourselves to be, that such considerations could not be used as a ground to discriminate against us in the matter of securing a job without moral censure and blame. We would want a moral standard to protect us, which disapproves of human conduct which was discriminatory on such arbitrary criteria. Likewise, every other person behind the veil of ignorance would want the same thing, because it is rational to want it, under the limiting conditions of the veil of ignorance.

There is another way of thinking about how Rawls' method works. Imagining that we are behind the veil of ignorance, it would be rational in order to

---

[95]Ibid., pp. 142ff. See Rawls' discussion of the rationality of the parties in the original position. Another version of doing morality by agreed norms is David Gauthier, Morality by Agreement (Oxford: Clarendon Press, 1986).

maximize one's self-interests, with the least amount of risk, to assume that one would emerge into society in the least advantaged situation. So, the best way to protect oneself from the conduct of others, and at the same time to insure one's greatest advantage, would be to assume that one was in the most vulnerable position imaginable and consent to moral standards which would protect and defend the most vulnerable.

Rawls' method has several similarities to that employed by Immanuel Kant. One of the most important of these is that Rawls holds that moral appraisal standards must be justified apart from any specific experiential situation. He believes that a truly universalizable standard which is impartial cannot be derived from any actual set of circumstances without altering our present way of thinking and believing morally.

Richard Brandt is a contemporary **utilitarian** philosopher whose views in his work A Theory of the Good and the Right are sometimes compared to those of Rawls.[96] Brandt, like Rawls, recognizes that individual bias may influence our choice about moral standards. The basic difference in approach is that while Rawls wants to generate agreement to moral standards in the original position, and behind a veil of ignorance, Brandt holds that rules are derived from our assessment of which actual outcomes of concrete situations are the best for all concerned. Brandt's way of controlling bias is somewhat different than that of Rawls. Instead of a veil of ignorance, Brandt says that only *fully rational persons* can establish moral rules which are impartial enough to receive universal consent. Fully rational persons are persons who have undergone *"cognitive psychotherapy"*.[97] This means that such persons have done the following types of things.

1) They have identified and controlled their irrational desires or aversions, and have chosen their moral standards only after doing so.

2) They have selected moral standards on the basis of an ideally vivid representation of all relevant available information. They have not overlooked morally significant facts.

3) They have not overlooked outcomes or wrongly estimated the probability of outcomes for the actions, attempts, or omissions about which they are forming moral standards.

4) They have weighed outcomes of action in an undistorted holistic way; considering the interests of all persons effected, they have developed standards respecting those interests.[98]

---

[96]Richard B. Brandt, A Theory of the Good and the Right (Oxford: Clarendon Press, 1979), p. 295. Michael Bayles, Contemporary Utilitarianism (New York: Anchor Doubleday, 1968) is a helpful survey of utilitarian theory. David Lyons, Forms and Limits of Utilitarianism (London: Oxford University Press, 1965) has an analysis of the theory. A somewhat different approach than Brandt's is followed by Anthony Quinton, Utilitarian Ethics (New York: Macmillan, 1973).

[97]Ibid., pp. 115-126; 152-162; 208-212.

[98]Ibid., p. 202

As we conclude our discussion of this theoretical issue, we should note that there are philosophers who do not consider any of these models satisfactory. What bothers these thinkers is that each of these approaches is attempting to explain the justification of fundamental moral standards for what we have called the general moral community of all human persons. However, someone such as Alasdair MacIntyre holds there is no general moral community of human persons. In his book, Whose Justice? Whose Rationality? MacIntyre argues a position that would belie the entire search for universalizable moral standards. According to this view, there is no general moral community--only specific moral communities of persons. There are specific traditions of morality, each with its own fundamental core standards, but there is no coherent set of moral standards. These communities may certainly overlap, as well as differ. But what is not the case is that there is an overarching general moral community, the fundamental standards of which take precedence over the communities plural.[99] Fundamentally, according to MacIntyre, there is no such thing as impartiality. Persons always stand within a specific moral community, or more accurately, within several communities at the same time. Moral standards survive in language provided that persons within the community find them appropriate and useful to human flourishing and well-being.

Is Utility the Irreducible Basis for All Moral Appraisals?

We have recognized that moral practice takes into consideration the consequences or outcomes of conduct when establishing the degree of an agent's responsibility. Is it possible that all moral appraisals are ultimately reducible to a matter of the utility or outcome of our conduct?

Utilitarianism is the name for the view that there is a single criterion for deciding what it means to be morally praiseworthy or blameworthy: *"Act in such a way as to produce the most happiness for all concerned."* "Happiness" in this definition does not mean merely physical pleasure. Nor should it be understood as meaning only short-term happiness. Another way of expressing utilitarianism is *"Act in such a way as to produce the greatest well-being, over the long term, for the greatest number of persons involved."*

Some utilitarians believe that this criterion is itself the one and only standard to be used in moral practice. The kind of calculus it requires, which measures the amount of happiness or well-being to be gained for those involved, is to be made in each and every situation, without regard for other concepts or rules. These thinkers are called **Act-utilitarians** (popularly known as "situation ethicists"). According to act-utilitarianism, something like a "promise" should be kept only because of the desirable outcomes of keeping the promise in a specific case. If, in any situation, keeping the promise would cause more ill effects than breaking it, then the promise should be broken. There is no absolute duty to keep a promise. Likewise, it might be situationally permitted, on the same grounds, to lie, steal, commit adultery, and so forth.

Other utilitarians, who think that calculating the consequences of each act individually interjects bias and arbitrariness into the appraisal process, hold that

---

[99] Alasdair MacIntyre, Whose Justice? Whose Rationality? (Notre Dame: University of Notre Dame Press, 1988).

moral rules as standards are necessary for appraisal. These thinkers are called **Rule-utilitarians.** They hold that a moral rule is justified if it "Obligates conduct which generally produces the greatest happiness for the greatest number of people effected." Or, if it "Prohibits conduct which generally produces more harm and unhappiness for the greatest number of people effected." Rule-utilitarians include what we have called moral concepts in their rule formulas (e.g., "Persons should not murder"). Likewise, they recognize the use of special role obligations as moral standards in much the same way, and on basically the same grounds, as the Realists and Deontologists.

While there is some dispute about this categorization, I regard John Stuart Mill (1806-1873), the famous British utilitarian, as holding the rule-utilitarian view.[100] Mill was aware of the ordinary functioning of moral rules in appraisals. He considered them to be generalizations: rules of thumb about what generally tends to produce good or bad effects. He did not disregard them, except in those cases in which the rules conflicted. In such situations, Mill advocated an act-utilitarian resolution to the conflict, but even then, one of the rules was vindicated as of higher priority.

Richard Brandt is a contemporary rule-utilitarian. We have already seen how important Brandt believes it is to have impartiality in rule formation. We have seen also that he believes that moral rules should be established by fully rational persons. We can now observe that he holds that the rules to which fully rational persons will agree will also maximize the best outcomes for the greatest number of persons.

Brandt believes that rule utilitarianism has definite advantages over act-utilitarianism. Some of these are as follows. 1) Persons will be able to plan on specific behaviors by others because they know the rules for action, attempt, and omission, and expect that others know these as well, and will follow them. 2) Persons need not worry about the outcomes of others' moral deliberations. They will feel personally secure, because they will not have to wonder what another agent is thinking in a particular situation. The assumed mode of action, attempt, or omission will be according to the moral rule. 3) The agent benefits from his ability to know at any time whether he is under a duty and what that duty requires of him. 4) The agent knows that if his duties are discharged he is free to do as he pleases, so there is a zone of permission.[101]

But let's return to the claim that the irreducible basis for determining a person's moral responsibility is the outcome of his conduct. What should concern us theoretically about this claim is that a description of ordinary moral practice makes it clear that we do take into account more than the outcomes of conduct. For example, recall the story of Jean Paul, Bridgette, and Alf climbing the mountain. If Jean Paul cuts the safety rope, thereby sending Alf to his doom for the purpose of saving the others in the party, then he may have done what was best for the greatest number of persons involved in that situation. But we did notice that if Jean Paul is thinking "There, now, I am rid of him. I can have Bridgette," then he will be

---

[100]John Stuart Mill, Utilitarianism, edited by Oskar Piest (Indianapolis: Bobbs-Merrill, Co., 1957).

[101]Brandt, A Theory of the Good and the Right, p. 295.

appraised as morally blameworthy for his conduct. This seems to imply that intention and not just the outcome of the conduct is a matter to be considered when making a moral appraisal.

Are There Decision Rules for Situations of Limited Knowledge?

In moral practice we observed that moral blame or praise may be lessened or intensified according to the community's description of whether a person conducted himself within the limits of his knowledge of the consequences of his conduct. This much we know by description. But are there any theoretical or logical decision rules which can guide an agent in choosing conduct alternatives which are more likely to show him to be a responsible agent ?

The most complex decisions are those made while one is at risk, under uncertainty about the outcomes of one's conduct. In situations of risk, ordinary moral practice shows that we tend to blame agents less if they have not run too far ahead of their knowledge. We privilege the choice which leads to the least harmful outcomes. If an agent has tried to stay within the limits of his knowledge, but still an untoward outcome results, then we are prone to diminish his blame to some degree.

Some philosophers have studied these most complex types of decisions thoroughly and have developed theoretical rules for making the "best" decision. Michael Resnik's work, Choices: An Introduction to Decision Theory, is an excellent summary of some of these rules. To illustrate some of the reasoning used by Resnik, and other decision theorists, let us recall our earlier description of the case involving the emergency room physician. One decision rule which Paul could employ to increase the probability that he was conducting himself within the limits of his knowledge is this: *"Choose the action the worst consequences of which are at least as good, or even better than any other action alternative."* [102] Decision theorists call this the **maximin decision rule.**

Suppose that in Paul's decision context the worst outcome of "Administer the drug" was "death," but the worst outcome of "Omit the drug" was also "death." Could the maximin rule have helped Paul know what to do? The worst outcomes are the same, but in "giving the drug" there is a possibility that the boy would improve. Yet, in "omitting the drug" there is a possibility that the danger will subside naturally. We cannot know the relative probability of the outcome of the patient's improving, over against the danger subsiding naturally, unless we know more about the drug and the patient. The problem with applying the maximin rule to this case is that the worst outcomes are the same.

But suppose the worst outcomes were different. If the worst outcome of "administering the drug" was "death" and the worst outcome of "omitting the drug" was "suffering short of death," then the maximin rule would tell Paul that the more proper moral course would be "omitting the drug." Paul would be blamed for taking a greater risk to gain an immediate cure by administering the drug, given his

---

[102]Michael D. Resnik, Choices: An Introduction to Decision Theory, (Minneapolis: University of Minnesota Press, 1987), pp. 26-33. See also, Nicholas Rescher, Risk (Lanham, MD: University Press of America, 1983) and Holly Smith, "Culpable Ignorance," Philosophical Review 92 (1983).

ignorance about the possible reactions the patient might have to it, even if he did so to minimize short term suffering. The reason he would be more blameworthy is that the worst outcome of administering the drug was death.

Resnik also discusses **the expected value decision rule**. It says, *choose the conduct which will yield both the most desired outcome and also has the greatest possibility of success*.103 To illustrate this procedure, consider a nonmoral example for a moment. A baseball manager makes a poor choice if he sends a .050 hitter to the plate in a crucial situation, rather than a .500 hitter. What he wants to do is choose the action which yields the most desired outcome (a hit), and also has the highest probability of achieving that outcome (sending a .500 hitter to the plate).

In Paul's emergency room case, the most desired outcome of "giving the drug" is "cure." What is the possibility of this being the successful result of giving the drug? We do not know exactly. However, since Paul is knowledgeable about drugs and their side-effects, he probably has some statistical knowledge about what percentage of the population might manifest allergic reactions to this drug. If the percentage is high, then he is at greater risk, and more blamable if he gives the drug and it fails. However, if the percentage is low, it may be rational to "act according to the percentages" and risk "giving the drug." If he succeeds, we may still say truly, "You took a risk." If he fails, we may say, "You took a risk, but we can understand why; the percentages were in your favor, so your blame is diminished." Of course, taking risks with human life is very different than taking risks with baseball.

A further study of decision theory is in order, but it is doubtful that these "rules" actually function in such a way as to provide a sure-fire method for insuring that persons choose within the limits of their knowledge. We probably cannot rely on them totally for assessing the degree of blame or praise to be given to a person under the ignorance of the consequences excusing strategy, but they may still be helpful.

Is there a Theoretical Explanation for the Move from Conduct Descriptions to Character Ascriptions?

There is ample descriptive evidence of a connection between one's conduct and the virtues and vices ascribed to one's character. However, ordinary moral practice does not provide us with a complete understanding about how this connection is made, much less with how it *should* be made. What enables us to move from a description of a person's conduct to the characterization of person under a virtue or vice trait?

One theory for how the move from conduct description to character ascription is justified may be called the **numerical connection theory**. This theory says that character ascription under the same concept used for conduct description is justified on the basis of the number of times the conduct is repeated. "This is not the first spiteful act Mary has done," we might say. The assumption of the numerical connection theory is that when Mary has done "enough" spiteful things, we are justified in saying "Mary is a spiteful person."

103Resnik., pp. 45ff.

There are real problems with this point of view. In the first place, the claim that the move to use a virtue or vice concept in character description is justified by calculating the number of acts, attempts, or omissions which are to be taken under that same description does not tell us how many "spiteful" things must Mary do or attempt to do in order for us to say, "Mary is spiteful." Just how many times must one do spiteful things in order to be spiteful? Sometimes we describe a person as "spiteful" after observing them do only one "spiteful" thing. How could the numerical connection theory account for this? In fact, it seems that the connection between conduct and character is based more firmly on the gravity or severity of the conduct than upon the number of times it is done. The usual answer to these objections offered by one who holds the numerical connection theory is that if a person repeatedly or habitually does something, then we are justified in making a character ascription. But this probably is not a satisfactory answer. What, after all, is the meaning of "habitual"?

There are other ways of explaining how the connection between conduct and character is drawn. For example, consider the views of Aristotle. Aristotle is the most noted virtue theorist in the history of philosophy. He developed an intricate and intriguing theory for explaining how the move from conduct description to character ascription is made. For Aristotle, morally virtuous conduct was found in the **Golden Mean** between two kinds of vice: *Excess* and *Deficiency*. At one extreme in the range of conduct is excess (too much), while at the other extreme is deficiency (too little). Both excess and deficiency are vices. So every virtue is the middle way between vices. So, we can make a character ascription when a person conducts himself to excess, to defect, or in moderation. The excess and defect descriptions will be in vice concepts; the moderate one in a virtue concept. Speaking of virtues, Aristotle wrote

> It is a difficult business to be good; because in any given case it is difficult to find the midpoint--for instance, not everyone can find the center of a circle; only the man who knows how. So too it is easy to get angry--anyone can do that--or to give and spend money; but to feel or act towards the right person to the right extent at the right time for the right reason in the right way--that is not easy, and it is not everyone that can do it. Hence to do these things well is a rare, laudable and fine achievement.[104]

---

[104] Aristotle, Nicomachean Ethics, Book II, Ch. 8, 1109, in McKeon. Although Aristotle is the most prominent virtue theorist, many other recent works have described virtue language and its place in moral appraisal. A good place to begin is with Gregory Pence, "Recent Work on Virtues," American Philosophical Quarterly 24 (1984) or with Pincoffs', Quandaries and Virtues. A few of the other notable works are Philippa Foot, Virtues and Vices (Cambridge, MA: Basil Blackwell, 1978); Peter Geach, The Virtues (Cambridge: Cambridge University Press, 1977); The Virtues, edited by Robert Kruschwitz and Robert Roberts (Belmont, CA: Wadsworth, 1987); Gregory Trianosky, "Virtue, Action and the Good Life: A Theory of the Virtues," Pacific Journal of Philosophy (1988); Vice and Virtue in Everyday Life, edited by Christina Hoff Sommers (San Diego: Harcourt, Brace, Jovanovich, 1985); and James Wallace, Virtues and Vice (Ithaca: Cornell University Press, 1978).

Aristotle believed that learning to be virtuous requires practice. By confronting moral situations in life, by expressing discipline and self-control, we can become virtuous. Commenting on Aristotle's theory of establishing virtues, John Finnis says it involves

being able to bring one's own intelligence to bear effectively on the problems of choosing one's actions and life style and shaping one's own character; positively, it involves that one seeks to bring an intelligent and reasonable order into one's own actions and habits and practical attitudes.[105]

Aristotle's work <u>Nicomachean Ethics</u> is filled out with discussions of the excesses and defects of conduct and character. The following table shows the virtues as discussed by Aristotle.[106] Although Aristotle says virtue is feeling and acting towards the right person, to the right extent, at the right time, for the right reason, in the right way, J. L. Mackie once observed that these criteria are too circular to be of much help.[107] Not only are the criteria circular but even though Aristotle held that virtues, as well as vices, were acquired by practice and habit, this theory does not account for those cases in which we make character ascriptions based on one observation. Are we to conclude that these are always unfair or erroneous?

A Subjectivist account for the move from conduct description to character ascription holds that the move is basically like any other responsibility description found in ordinary practice. It is not provable that "Mary is spiteful" because she did this act, or even a thousand others. "Mary is spiteful" whenever that description begins to stick, whenever she uses it of herself or others begin to use it of her. It may perhaps be tried on her many times before it sticks, but when it does hold, then "Mary is spiteful." With this observation, of course, we can again appreciate something of the power of the moral community--as well as of our own self-appraisals. Typically, when applied to persons, virtue and vice language is used to describe the habits and dispositions we see a person exemplify in one's conduct, but this is not always the rule. Yet according to Subjectivists, there is no rule about how many times Stacy must have been observed engaged in "cruel" conduct in order to be called "a cruel person." This description is simply put forward for each relevant member of the moral community to consider.

---

[105]John Finnis, <u>Natural Law and Natural Rights</u> (New York: Oxford University Press, 1980), p. 88.

[106]Mike W. Martin, <u>Everyday Morality: An Introduction to Applied Ethics</u> (Belmont, CA: Wadsworth Publishing, 1989), p. 42.

[107]Mackie, <u>Inventing</u>, p. 186.

Summary of the Virtues As Discussed by Aristotle

Sphere of Action; Kind of Situation	Type of Emotion, Desire, Attitude	Vice of Too Much (Excess)	Virtue (Mean)	Vice of Too Little (Deficiency or Defect)
Responses to danger	Fear, confidence	Foolhardiness	Courage	Cowardice
Satisfying appetites	Physical pleasure	Overindulgence	Temperance	Inhibition
Giving gifts	Desire to help	Extravagance	Generosity	Miserliness
Pursuing accomplishments	Desire to succeed	Vaulting ambition	Proper ambition	Unambitiousness
Appraising oneself	Self-affirmation	Vanity	Proper pride	Sense of inferiority
Self-expression	Desire to be recognized	Boastfulness	Truthfulness	False modesty
Responding to insults	Anger	Irascibility	Patience	Apathy
Social conduct	Attitudes to others	Obsequiousness	Friendliness	Rudeness
Indignation at others' undeserved good fortune*	Distress	Envy	Righteous indignation	Malicious enjoyment
Awareness of one's flaws	Shame	Shyness	Modesty	Shamelessness
Conversation, humor	Amusement	Buffoonery	Wittiness	Boorishness

*This entry may seem puzzling. Aristotle writes: "Righteous Indignation is a mean between Envy and Spite [or malicious enjoyment], and they are all concerned with feelings of pain or pleasure at the experiences of our neighbors. The man who feels righteous indignation is distressed at instances of undeserved good fortune, but the envious man goes further and is distressed at *any* good fortune, while the spiteful man is so far from feeling distress that he actually rejoices [at others' misfortune]."*

Taken from Mike Martin, Everyday Morality

Do We Need a Single Comprehensive Moral Theory?

A person may undoubtedly practice moral appraisal well without being able to provide a theoretical explanation for why he does what he does, and certainly without having made a conscious or rational decision to be a Deontologist, Realist, Subjectivist, Utilitarian, or Divine Command Theorist. Likewise, the justification of moral standards is a profoundly interesting issue; we can usually practice moral appraisal without deciding on some type of justification theory for our basic moral standards. Within our moral communities we often do not have to defend these standards. This would be like having to satisfy ourselves that we still have two feet whenever we wish to stand up, or proving that the earth existed in order to make statements about geography. We simply do not go through any process to establish such a thing.

Of course, we may surely say that some move or expression in ordinary moral practice is like what a great philosopher in the history of ethics said. The realists, deontologists, utilitarians, and subjectivists may all derive some support for their theories from actual moral appraisals. We may say things like: "Well, this is like what Kant says" or "This reminds us of a point made by Aristotle, Mill, Ross, Rawls, or MacIntyre." But such remarks are a far cry from saying that moral practice can be theoretically systematized into any single theory.

I believe that it is impossible to construct a comprehensive theory about the practice of morality. Ordinary practice is just too messy and fluid to yield any theory which captures everything which needs to be done in moral appraisal. Actual moral practice should be conceived as analogous to these sorts of things:

b) A doctor diagnosing a patient's illness
c) Learning to speak a foreign language
d) Being a wine taster
e) Throwing and working clay on a potter's wheel
f) Driving a stick shift car

Now, for these things one could develop rule books, offer instructions and observations, but always there would be something missing. Moral practice is an **art form**. Furthermore, it is an art form which is alive and in process, constantly changing. To offer a theory of what it is would require killing it. In fact, I suggest that this is exactly what happens in the formulation of a moral theory about what we do in moral practice. All moral theories are readings or interpretations of the actual practice of moral appraisal. They are inaccurate to the extent that they ignore or depreciate concepts and moves made in ordinary practice in order to retain the coherence of the theory.

It is, of course, a different matter to consider whether one needs a comprehensive theory about how morality **should** be practiced. I also have some reservations about whether this is possible. My principal reservation about a philosopher's being able to develop a theory about how we should do moral practice is that no theoretician may ever be merely a spectator. There are no completely objective standpoints. Even though Rawls and Brandt try to point to some way in which we can imagine what it would be like to be totally impartial or to be a fully rational person, I doubt that this is really possible. The reason for this is that philosophers are members of a moral community--indeed of several communities--and they cannot disengage from this membership. The danger inherent in this fact for all who would develop comprehensive theories is that they might allow their own experience to overshadow or condition what they believe to be rational, or excusable, or justifiable. But even if such a standpoint could be achieved, perhaps it **should** not be sought. The benefit of being a member of a moral community, while at the same time describing moral practice, is that one feels the nuances present there. A full appreciation for these nuances might be lost in the so-called objectivity of the veil of ignorance or cognitive psychotherapy. It may be that it is how actual practice handles these nuances which it is most important to learn about morality.

For Discussion

1) How do you think the following practices could be compared to the nature of moral appraisal as discussed in this text? First, try to think of as many similarities as you can, and then note dissimilarities. Offer an analogy to moral practice of your own:

   a) Doing the work of a brick mason
   b) A doctor diagnosing a patient's illness
   c) Learning to speak a foreign language
   d) Being a wine taster
   e) Throwing and working clay on a potter's wheel
   f) Driving a stick shift car

2. Do you think it is necessary to prefer one theory of the justification for ultimate moral standards over the others? If so, which one would you defend? If not, why not?

3. Consider the following candidates for moral standards. Explain how they might be justified by one of the methods discussed in this chapter.

   a) Respect others.
   b) Persons should admit their errors.
   c) Don't waste food.
   d) Treat others as you want to be treated.
   e) Do not take things which do not belong to you.
   f) Help those in need, whenever it does not require the sacrifice of
        something of equal worth on your part.
   g) Do not coerce others.
   h) Don't date another person's (girlfriend, boyfriend)
   i) Tell a lie, if your reputation is at stake.
   j) Be kind, if you get credit for it.
   k) Children should be seen, not heard.
   l) Persons should have those primary social goods (food,
        shelter, health care) which they need to survive

4. Choose one of the theoretical models and do a free write explaining how you would teach it to the young (i.e., a moral pedagogy or moral education theory).

5. Make a list of five moral rules or concepts suitable as appraisal standards which could be justified by one of the following:

    a) Appeal to the categorical imperative
    b) Rational selection behind the veil of ignorance
    c) Utilitarian choice after cognitive psychotherapy

6. How is the position of the moral realist different from that of the subjectivist?

7. Offer a justifiable set of at least three moral standards (concepts, rules, and/or special role obligations) which are relevant for appraisal in one or more of the following categories:

    a) Sexual activity
    b) Distribution of Primary Social Goods (e.g., food, shelter, health care)
    c) Medical care and dying
    d) Business ethics
    e) Parenting activity
    f) Persons Related to the Environment
    g) Persons and Animals

CONCLUSION: MORAL APPRAISABILITY AS A BENEFIT OF PERSONS

Being a member of the general moral community brings certain benefits our way. The most important of these is the willingness of others to form relationships with us. These relationships are not only necessary for our survival, but also for our opportunity to be happy, to have a sense of fulfilled purposes and achieved goals, and to flourish during our lifetime. This willingness of others to form such relationships depends greatly on the perception they have of the kind of person we are.

If they observe our practice of morality, and our acknowledgement of others' moral appraisals, then we will be received into the relationships we need and want. At some point, every human who is not mentally deficient in some irreducible way crosses this threshold. Doing so is like opening up a charge account. It is as though we have been extended moral credit because we have shown in our language and conduct that we have the capacity for moral appreciation and appraisal. It is very important to maintain this kind of credit, for the reason that its loss would mean the disintegration of confidence in us as someone worthy of just those kinds of relationships which we need and want.[108]

Once we possess moral credit, then our conduct may either contribute to or deflate its value. If we act, or appear to act, in such a way that our conduct could be described as a breach of moral expectations, we will be made accountable. In these circumstances, other persons deserve an explanation, or an apology, or some redress for this breach. They deserve this because they have chosen to risk relationships with us in various ways, or because they have come to do so through the course of life's events. At the same time, since our moral credit has been called into question, we are entitled to offer a justification for our action, or an excuse, or to ask for forgiveness and to give assurances of better conduct in the future.[109] If we hurt someone and that person tells us to go away, if he says he does not wish to hear our explanations or descriptions, then he is denying us something very basic in moral practice. He is not giving us what in legal language might be termed, "our day in court" or "right to be heard." If there is no remedy to this state of affairs, we will soon turn indignant over the way we are being treated in the moral community. The reason we react so strongly to such situations is that descriptions of our moral reputation and responsibility are immensely significant to us. We know what is at stake if our credit is ruined.

On the other hand, if we are unwilling in times of accountability to reveal our thinking, intentions, justifications, and excuses to others who are entitled to know because we have wronged them; or if our description falls short of being one which is acceptable by others, then our moral credit will be damaged. Often, a serious aspersion will be cast on our character. We may find difficulty in winning the confidence and trust of others, which means we will be denied the relationships we need and want in order to flourish. Or, at the very least, these relationships may be severely limited or altered from their previous form.

---

[108]Pahel, "The Public Process of Moral Adjudication," p. 191.

[109]Ibid.

> *Imagine Scott harms Trish, and Nicole sees what happens. It is*
> *possible that Scott may offer Trish an excuse for his action, and*
> *even be forgiven by her. However, Nicole may think that Trish*
> *was too easy on Scott--that she excused him and/or forgave him*
> *when she should not have. So, Nicole may choose to disassociate*
> *with Scott, or continue to blame him morally.*

If Scott wants and/or needs a relationship with Nicole, then he will have to find some way of restoring his moral credit with her. Nicole may place more strict expectations on Scott than did Trish, requiring some different kind of excuse, or she may demand that Scott demonstrate some sort of responsive adjustment in order to get back into her good graces. However, if she refuses to discuss the situation, then she is denying Scott something very important. The moral issue may actually shift. The real issue now becomes Nicole's refusal to allow Scott an opportunity to restore his moral credit. What Scott did to Trish may become of secondary importance now; and Nicole may be rightly required to justify or excuse her refusal to regard Scott's right to be heard. Nicole may be acting unreasonably or irrationally. She may not fully appreciate the role of extenuating circumstances, and/or strategies of justification, and/or the role of responsive adjustment.

Since we are members of more than one moral community, some of them may be more demanding than others. Not all moral communities, and certainly not all individuals within them, function rationally. Scott may feel that being a member of the general moral community of human persons is of no benefit. But the problem here is not membership in the community; it is the approach taken by one individual within that community.

Likewise, being a member of a moral community which functions unhealthily may be detrimental to the self-esteem of the individuals within it. When this occurs, members of a moral community sometimes use a grammar of appraisal directed toward the community in general. Persons may say, "We're going to hell in a hand basket;" "What on earth has gotten into people?" "What's the matter with people today?" "It's just not the same community it was years ago."

However, what we cannot lose sight of here is that when we find ourselves in such positions, we try to restore an appropriately functioning moral community. We want to recreate the crucial function of moral practice. We do not discard the need for moral communities. We could not do so, even if we tried.

There are times when we are not **primarily** required to provide an account of our actions to just anyone who wants it. "I don't have to justify my actions to you," we might say.

As Kenneth Pahel says,

> Many of the occasions for appropriate moral accounting are a
> function of the special roles we play and the agreements we have
> made with others. Thus we may feel the pinch of our moral
> accountability particularly as a parent, an employee, a promisor, a
> customer, or simply as a speaker in an act of communication. [110]

---

[110]Ibid., p. 197. Whether this "pinch" of moral accountability will eventuate in guilt or shame, and how these function within the moral community is itself a fascinating area of study. See Guilt and Shame, edited by Herbert Morris (Belmont, CA: Wadsworth, 1971).

If my younger son accuses me of showing favoritism to my older son, then it is to the younger that I am primarily accountable, and I must provide him with an acceptable description of my action, or lose some moral credit. This sometimes settles it. So, moral appraisal is sometimes brought to an end. Of course, my son may want to review his decision, and even reverse it, if my subsequent actions belie the accepted defense or excuse I offered. Yet, even though I am primarily obligated to offer a response to my son, I may also be expected to provide a justification or an excuse to other persons as well.

Suppose someone said to me, "You are treating your youngest son immorally, favoring your older one." A person may make such an appraisal, even though he is not the son being harmed. This person may be appraising me simply because my action is a morally blameworthy way of treating **any** person whatever, not just my son. In this case, I must provide a justification or excuse for my conduct.

I am accountable for moral wrongs I do to members of the general moral community, and not just for wrongs I do to those with whom I have some specific role accountability. There are certain actions and dispositions for which everyone wants me to feel accountable. I need not have a relationship to a drowning child to be appraisable for my conduct if I walk by, seeing the child going down for the third time, having it in my control to save him, and I just say, "the heck with it," and walk on by. I will be appraisable, and I stand to lose considerable moral credit.

In the moral community, there is no one person who sits in the role of judge. Instead, that authority seems to be shared by each member of the moral community, and it may be pressed by different persons to varying degrees. Sometimes the role of whom one is accountable to depends on who has been wronged, or whether the wrong was based upon a role or relationship one had, or whether the wrong is an affront to the moral community of persons at large. So, moral appraisal is a constant process. One way of interpreting this is that there is a continuous relativism and breakdown of descriptions of responsibility because everyone participates in the appraisal process of every other moral agent. Or, one may focus on unhealthy moral communities which are judgmental and demeaning.

However, moral practice seems to point in another direction. As we have seen, there are recognized and recurring patterns, expressions, and procedures for weaving the descriptions of our moral responsibility. These are embodied in some relatively stable forms of language having to do with moral concepts, rules, justifications, and excuses. The appropriate use of these forms and strategies increases the probability that we will have access into the kinds of relationships which we desire and need. But what we must never miss is that moral judgment is a product of an actual public dialogue about what descriptions to use of the conduct and character of particular persons. You and I are a part of this process. We are not passive automatons who have received a well-crusted-over morality. We are, or at least we can be, active participants in the forging of the shared morality so needed for personal well-being and satisfaction within the moral community.

Glossary

Absolutism. The responsibility description which holds that it is always possible for a person to choose at least one alternative which is consistent with all the moral standards whch apply to any specific case, and that anything short of this is blameworthy.

Accordion Effect of Actions. Those consequences of conduct for which a person may be held appraisable even though not consciously intended.

Agent. The entity to which conduct is traceable as its cause.

Anthropocentrism. From the perspective of moral philosophy this is the view that human persons are to be valued more highly than all other things in nature.

Appraisability. Whenever a member of the moral community has his conduct evaluatively described by means of a moral concept, rule, or some special role standard.

Appraisal. To evaluate the worth or significance of an entity's conduct, or character.

Attempt. Exercises of effort to cause an event, but which fail to achieve their ends.

Authenticity. Both the capacity to accept one's character and the willingness to acknowledge to oneself one's values and how these are exercised through conduct.

Categorical Imperative (The). The supreme and absolute moral law by which all rational beings may know their moral duties.

Categorical Imperatives. Moral rules which are meant to apply to all human persons.

Conduct Discriminator Words. General value concepts which name forms of conduct and carry blame or praise along with the name (e.g., murder, spite, kindness, elegance, nobility).

Deontology. Any ethical theory according to which doing what is praiseworthy is doing one's duty, where moral standards are reducible to statements of duty, without regard for intention or consequence.

Dilemma. A'situation in which one is aware of two or more conflicting moral requirements, expectations, or values, and yet is unable to satisfy all of these.

Divine Command Theory. The theory which holds that the only true and correct moral standards are derived from God by means of religious texts, traditions, and spokesmen.

Ethics. The philosophical discipline which makes a systematic effort to understand the practice of moral appraisal.

Excuse. A responsibility description which does not deny moral wrongdoing, but cites extenuating considerations in an attempt to diminish blame.

Expected Value Decision Rule. "Choose the conduct which will yield both the most desired outcome for the greatest number, and which also has the greatest possibility of success."

General Moral Community. That community constituted by the moral language of concepts and rules which seem to be common to all persons as persons.

Golden Mean. Aristotle's theory that virtue lies in the middle ground or mean between excess and defect for each individual in a specific situation.

Hypocrisy. Assuming a false appearance of virtue, pretending to have moral beliefs and character higher than is actually true.

Hypothetical Imperatives. Moral rules which apply only to those who accept the conditions expressed in the imperative (e.g., If you want to_____, then you ought to_____).

Instrumental Virtues. Those virtues which enable persons to pursue and fulfill their goals effectively, or to perform tasks well.

Internal Decision Procedures. Deliberative and self-conscious processes by which a group may be held accountable as a whole in distinction from random collections of persons in which only individuals are accountable.

Intensity Discriminator Terms. Words used to take note of the manner in which some conduct was undertaken in order to regulate the degree of responsibility assigned in the appraisal (e.g., negligently, recklessly, carelessly, inadvertently).

Intervening Agent. One who makes it possible for an event to occur, or attempts to do so, when otherwise the event would not occur.

Justifications. Descriptions of conduct according to which a person defends himself or his conduct as not morally blameworthy.

Maximin Decision Rule. "Choose the conduct the worst consequences of which are at least as good, or even better than any other alternative."

Moral Community. Any group of persons who share a common moral language and traditional practice.

Moral Concept Words. Conduct discriminators which represent hardened forms of moral appraisals, carrying blame or praise along with their names (e.g., adultery, stealing, lying, vindictiveness).

Moral Consideration. The assignment of worth to any person or entity which occurs whenever moral language is used to appraise the conduct of members of the moral community toward the person or entity.

Moral Innocence. The state in which a person is not yet able to understand the effects of his conduct, or appreciate the gravity thereof.

Moral Objectivism. The theory that moral standards and values are logically independent of human activities of preferring, recommending, and condemning.

Moral Persons. Those entities which possess the abilities to form intentions, to make decisions based on deliberative reasoning, to communicate a capacity to appreciate how their conduct affects others, to reflect self-consciously and form a resolve to change or alter their conduct and/or create one sort of character rather than another.

Moral Prioritization. The practice of ranking values and standards.

Moral Realism. The theory which holds that there is a moral reality which is independent of our appraisals and beliefs, and this reality determines whether or not those beliefs and appraisals are true or false. There are moral properties which are genuine properties of things or actions.

Moral Relativism. The ethical theory which denies that there are moral standards which are binding on all persons.

Moral Rule. Articulation of a guide for conduct or character formation by means of a statement which prohibits or obligates one to behave in a certain way.

Moral Subjectivism. The theory which holds that morality is the creation of human persons functioning as a community to establish what conduct and persons are to be encouraged and which discouraged in order to further the overall project of making it more likely that all persons can realize a full and rewarding life.

Morality. The human activity which evaluates the conduct and character of persons by means of established conventions in language, making it possible to encourage or discourage various forms of life.

Nonappraisable. The status of persons under conditions of having no other choice, being coerced, being unavoidably ignorant (e.g., mental deficiency or moral innocence) according to which they are not morally accountable for their conduct or character (i.e., it is inappropriate to use moral language of them).

Noninstrumental Virtues. Those virtues valued because they are typical of persons who we wish to have relationships with because these persons enrich life and make it more satisfying, independent of the completion of any task itself.

Omission. Not to perform.

Original Position (The). An imaginary state in which one regards himself as free from any moral system whatever in order to determine what moral standards are justifiable to persons choosing rationally.

Philosophy. The rational activity of formulating and understanding questions which are of fundamental concern to human persons.

Prima Facie Duties. Those moral duties regarded as self-evident to all rational human persons (e.g., duties of fidelity, reparation, gratitude, justice, beneficence, self-improvement, and non-maleficence).

Principle of Responsive Adjustment. "I will not do it again, and I have taken steps to insure that it does not reoccur."

Rationalization. A responsibility description which resembles a justification or excuse, but is rejected by the moral community.

Responsibility Description. The use of moral language to establish a degree of blame or praise.

Self-deception. The intentional evasion of acknowledging a truth about oneself.

Special Role Standard. A moral concept or rule which applies only to those occupying a certain role or station in life, not to all persons.

Speciesism. A prejudice or attitude of bias toward the interests and desires of members of one's own species and against those of other species.

Straight Rule of Responsibility. The rule according to which a person is morally responsible for all and only his intentional actions.

Supererogation. Conduct which goes above an beyond one's moral obligations or prohibitions (e.g., heroes and saints).

Teleological Suspension of the Ethical. A notion expressed by Soren Kierkegaard, according to which one's ultimate obedience to God may sometimes require that one suspend ordinary moral beliefs or act contrary to them.

Utilitarian Calculus. An estimate of the possible consequences of one's conduct, predicting which of these is most likely to occur, and choosing from the ones that are most probable, those which are also most desirable for the greatest number.

Utilitarianism. That ethical theory according to which what is morally praiseworthy is the conduct which will actually produce as its consequences the greatest amount of pleasure or happiness for the greatest number of persons.

Value Indicator Words. Highly general terms used to identify that some sort of value appraisal is being made (e.g., right, wrong, should, ought, good, and bad).

Veil of Ignorance. In John Rawls' philosophy, the bracketing of one's knowledge about one's class, gender, nationality, race and such, in order to eliminate bias which might interfere with a fully rational choice of moral standards.

Vices. Moral concept words which are condemnations or blame of a person's conduct and/or character traits.

Virtues. Moral concept words which are commendations or praise of a person's conduct and/or character traits.

Zone of Permission. The area of activity not covered by moral rules or concepts according to which persons are free to conduct themselves as personal preference and taste lead them.

BIBLIOGRAPHY

Action and Responsibility. Edited by Michael Bradie and Myles Brand. Bowling Green, OH: Bowling Green State University, 1980.

Action Theory. Edited by Myles Brand and Douglas Walton. Dordrecht: D. Reidel, 1976.

Adams, Robert M. "A Modified Divine Command Theory of Ethical Wrongness." In Religion and Morality: A Collection of Essays. Edited by Gene Outka and J. P. Reeder. New York: Anchor Books, 1973.

Antony, Louise. "Why We Excuse." Tulane Studies in Philosophy 28 (1979).

Audi, Robert. "Intending." Journal of Philosophy 70 (1973).

_____. "Moral Responsibility, Freedom, and Compulsion." American Philosophical Quarterly 11 (1974).

_____. "Weakness of Will and Practical Judgment." Nous 13 (1979).

Austin, J. L. Philosophical Papers. Edited by J. O. Urmson and G. J. Warnock. Oxford: Oxford University Press, 1970.

Baier, Kurt. "Action and Agent." Monist 49 (1965).

Bates, Stanley. "The Responsibility of 'Random Collections.'" Ethics 81 (1970-71).

Bayles, Michael. Contemporary Utilitarianism. New York: Anchor Doubleday, 1968.

Beardsley, Elizabeth L. "Moral Worth and Moral Credit." Philosophical Review 66 (1957).

Bennett, Jonathan. "Accountability." In Philosophical Subjects. Edited by Zak van Straaten. Oxford: Clarendon Press, 1980.

Blatz, Charles V. "Mitigating and Meliorating Defenses." American Philosophical Quarterly Monograph Series 7 (1973).

Blumenfeld, David. "The Principle of Alternate Possibilities." Journal of Philosophy 68 (1971).

Brandt, Richard B. A Theory of the Good and the Right. Oxford: Clarendon Press, 1979.

_____. "A Utilitarian Theory of Excuses." Philosophical Review 78 (1969).

Brink, David. Moral Realism and the Foundation of Ethics. Cambridge:
     Cambridge   University Press, 1989.

Broad, D. D. "Obligations, Ultimate and Derived." In Broad's Critical Essays in
     Moral Philosophy. Edited by David R. Cheney. London: George, Allen
     and Unwin, 1971.

Callahan, Joan C. Ethical Issues in Professional Life. New York: Oxford
     University Press, 1988.

Carr, Charles R. "Punishing Attempts." Pacific Philosophical Quarterly 62 (1981).

Castaneda, Hector-Neri. The Structure of Morality. Springfield: Thomas, 1974.

Coercion. Edited by J. Roland Pennock and John W. Chapman. Chicago: Aldine
     and Atherton, 1972.

Cooper, D. E. "Collective Responsibility." Philosophy 43 (1968).

_____. "Collective Responsibility--Again." Philosophy 44 (1969).

Cummins, Robert. "Could Have Done Otherwise." Personalist 60 (1979).

_____. "Culpability and Mental Disorder." Canadian Journal of Philosophy
     10 (1980).

D'Arcy, Eric. Human Acts: An Essay in Their Moral Evaluation. Oxford: Oxford
     University Press, 1963.

Danley, John R. "Corporate Moral Agency: The Case of Anthropological Bigotry,"
     in Ethical Issues in Professional Life. Edited by Joan C. Callahan. Oxford:
     Oxford University Press, 1988.

Danto, Arthur. "Basic Actions." American Philosophical Quarterly 2 (1965).

Davidson, Donald. Essays on Actions and Events. Oxford: Clarendon Press,
     1980.

Dennett, Daniel C. "Conditions of Personhood." In Identities of Persons. Edited
     by Amelie Rorty. Berkeley: University of California Press, 1976.

_____. Elbow Room. Cambridge: The MIT Press, 1984.

The Divine Command Theory of Ethics. Edited by Paul Helm. London: Oxford
     University Press, 1979.

Donagan, Alan. The Theory of Morality. Chicago: University of Chicago Press,
     1977.

Downie, R. S. "Collective Responsibility." Philosophy 44 (1969).

Duff, Antony. "Psychopathy and Moral Understanding." American Philosophical Quarterly 14 (1977).

Dworkin, Gerald and Blumenfeld, David. "Punishment for Intentions." Mind 75 (1966).

Ethical Relativism. Edited by John Ladd. Belmont, C.A.: Wadsworth, 1973.

Feinberg, Joel. Doing and Deserving. Princeton, N.J.: Princeton University Press, 1970.

_____. "The Rights of Animals and Unborn Generations," in Rights, Justice and the Bounds of Liberty. Princeton, N.J.: Princeton University Press, 1980.

Fingarette, Herbert. The Meaning of Criminal Insanity. Berkeley: University of California Press, 1972.

_____. On Responsibility. New York: Basic Books, 1967.

_____. Self-Deception. Atlantic Highland, N.J.: Humanities Press, 1969.

Finnis, John. Natural Law and Natural Rights. New York: Oxford University Press, 1980.

Fischer, John Martin. "Responsibility and Control." Journal of Philosophy 79 (1982).

_____. "Responsibility and Failure." Proceedings of the Aristotlean Society (1986-1986).

Flew, Antony. Crime or Disease? London: Macmillan, 1973.

Foot, Philippa. Virtue and Vices. Cambridge, M.A.: Basil Blackwell, 1978.

Frankena, William K. "Obligation and Ability." In Philosophical Analysis. Edited by Max Black. Englewood Cliffs, N. J.: Prentice-Hall, 1963.

Frankfurt, Harry G. "Alternate Possibilities and Moral Responsibility." Journal of Philosophy 66 (1969).

_____. "Coercion and Moral Responsibility." In Essays on Freedom of Action. Edited by Ted Honderich. London: Routledge and Kegan Paul, 1973.

_____. "What are We Morally Responsible for?" In How Many Questions. Edited by H. Cauman. Indianapolis: Hackett Publishing Company, 1988.

French, Peter. Collective and Corporate Responsibility. New York: Columbia
        University Press, 1984.

_____. The Scope of Morality. Minneapolis: The University of Minnesota
        Press, 1979.

Gauthier, David. Morality by Agreement. Oxford: Clarendon Press, 1986.

Geach, Peter. The Virtues. Cambridge: Cambridge University Press, 1977.

Gert, Bernard. The Moral Rules. New York: Harper and Row, 1970.

Gewirth, Alan. Reason and Morality. Chicago: University of Chicago Press,
        1978.

Glover, Jonathan. Responsibility. London: Routledge and Kegan Paul, 1970.

Guilt and Shame. Edited by Herbert Morris. Belmont, C.A.:. Wadsworth, 1971.

Haksar, Vinit. "The Responsibility of Psychopaths." Philosophical Quarterly 15
        (1965).

Hare, R. M. "Adolescents into Adults." In Aims in Education. Edited by T.H.B.
        Hollins. Manchester: Manchester University Press, 1967.

_____. Freedom and Reasons. New York: Oxford University Press, 1970.

Harman, Gilbert. "Moral Relativism Defended." Philosophical Review 84 (1975).

Heintz, Lawrence L. "The Logic of Defenses." American Philosophical Quarterly
        18 (1981).

Held, Virginia. "Moral Responsibility and Collective Action." In Peter French,
        Individual and Collective Responsibility. 1972.

Hornsby, Jennifer. Actions. London: Routledge and Kegan Paul, 1980.

Hospers, John. Human Conduct: Problems in Ethics. New York: Harcourt, Brace,
        Jovanovich, Inc. 1982.

Hughes, Graham. "Attempting the Impossible." In Feinberg and Gross, 1975.

_____. "Omissions and Mens Rea." In Freedom and Responsibility. Edited
        by Herbert Morris. Stanford: Stanford University Press, 1961.

Husak, Douglas N. "Omissions, Causation and Liability." Philosophical Quarterly
        30 (1980).

Individual and Collective Responsibility. Edited by Peter A. French. Cambridge:
        Schenkman, 1972.

Introduction to Aristotle. Edited by Richard McKeon. Chicago: The University of
    Chicago Press, 1973.

Kant, Immanuel. Foundations of the Metaphysic of Morals. Translated by Lewis
    White Beck. New York: Liberal Arts Press, 1959.

Kim, Jaegwon. "Supervenience and Nomological Incommensurables." American
    Philosophical Quarterly 15 (April 1978).

Kovesi, Julius. Moral Notions. London: Routledge and Kegan Paul, 1967.

Lombardi, Louis G. Moral Analysis: Foundations, Guides and Application.
    Albany: State University of New York Press, 1988.

Lyons, David. Forms and Limits of Utilitarianism. London: Oxford University
    Press, 1965.

MacIntyre, Alasdair. After Virtue. Notre Dame, I.N.: University of Notre Dame
    Press, 1981.

_____. Whose Justice? Whose Rationality? Notre Dame, I.N.: University
    of Notre Dame Press, 988.

Mackie, J. L. Ethics: Inventing Right and Wrong. New York; Penguin Books,
    1977.

Martin, Mike W. Everyday Morality: An Introduction to Applied Ethics. Belmont,
    C.A.: Wadsworth Publishing Co., 1989.

_____. Self-Deception and Morality. Lawrence, K.S.: University of
    Kansas Press, 1986.

McDowell, J. "Aesthetic Value, Objectivity, and the Fabric of the World." In
    Pleasure, Preference and Value. Edited by E. Schaper. Cambridge:
    Cambridge University Press.

McNaughton, David. Moral Vision: An Introduction to Ethics. Oxford: Basil
    Blackwell, 1988.

Mele, Alfred. Irrationality: An Essay on Akrasia, Self-Deception, and Self-
    Control. New York: Oxford University Press, 1988.

Mill, John Stuart. Utilitarianism. Edited by Oskar Piest. Indianapolis: Bobbs-
    Merrill, Co. 1957.

Moral Concepts. Edited by Joel Feinberg. Oxford: Oxford University Press.

Moral Responsibility. Edited by John Martin Fischer. Ithica, N.Y.: Cornell
    University Press, 1986.

Morris, Herbert. On Guilt and Innocence. Berkeley: University of California Press, 1976.

Murphy, Jeffrie. "Moral Death: A Kantian Essay on Psychopathy." Ethics 82 (1972).

The Nature of Human Action. Edited by Myles Brand. Glenview: Scott, Foresman, 1970.

Neil, Ornora. Acting on Principle: An Essay on Kantian Ethics. New York: Columbia University Press, 1975.

Nesbitt, Winston and Stewart Candlish. "On Not Being Able to Do Otherwise." Mind 82 (1973).

Nicomachean Ethics. Edited by Richard McKeon. Chicago: University of Chicago Press, 1973.

Nozick, Robert. "Coercion." In Freewill. Edited by S. Morgenbesser, P. Suppes, and M. White. New York: St. Martin's Press, 1979.

Pahel, Kenneth. "The Public Process of Moral Adjudication." Social Theory and Practice 2 (Summer 1988).

Pence, Gregory. "Recent Work on Virtues." American Philosophical Quarterly 24 (1984).

Pincoffs, Edmund L. "Are Questions of Desert Decidable?" In Justice and Punishment. Edited by J. B. Cederblom and William L. Blizek. Cambridge: Ballinger, 1977.

_____. Quandaries and Virtues: Against Reductivism in Ethics. Lawrence, K.A.: University of Kansas Press, 1986.

Quinn, Philip. Divine Commands and Moral Requirements. Oxford: Clarendon Press, 1978.

Quinton, Anthony. Utilitarian Ethics. New York: Macmillan, 1973.

Rawls, John. A Theory of Justice. Cambridge, M.A.: Harvard University Press, 1971.

The Republic. Translated by F. M. Cornford. New York: Oxford University Press, 1945.

Rescher, Nicholas. Risk. Lanham, M.D.: University Press of America, 1983.

Resnik, Michael D. Choices: An Introduction to Decision Theory. Minneapolis: University of Minnesota Press, 1987.

Responsibility. Edited by Joel Feinberg and Hyman Gross. Encino: Dickenson, 1975.

Ross, David. The Right and the Good. Oxford: Clarendon Press, 1930.

Ruf, Henry. Moral Investigations: An Introduction to the Study of Current Moral Problems. Lanham, M.D.: University Press of America, 1978.

Singer, Peter. Animal Liberation. New York: Random House, 1975.

Smith, Holly. "Culpable Ignorance." Philosophical Review 92 (1983).

Snyder, C. R., Higgins, Raymond L., and Stucky, Rita J. Excuses: Masquerades in Search of Grace. New York: John Wiley and sons, 1983.

Sokolowski, Robert. Moral Action: A Phenomenological Study. Bloomington: Indiana University Press, 1985.

Taylor, Paul. "The Ethics of Respect for Nature." Environmental Ethics 3 (Fall 1981).

Thalberg, Irving. "Remorse." Mind 72 (1963).

Thomson, Judith Jarvis. Acts and Other Events. Ithaca: Cornell University Press, 1977.

Trainosky, Gregory. "Supererogation, Wrongdoing and Vice: On the Autonomy of the Ethics of Virtue." Journal of Philosophy 83 (1986).

_____. "Virtue, Action and the Good Life: a Theory of the Virtues." Pacific Journal of Philosophy (1988).

Van Inwagen, Peter. "Ability and Responsibility." Philosophical Review 87 (April 1978).

VanWyk, Robert. Introduction to Ethics. New York: St. Martin's Press, 1990.

Velasquez, Manuel G. "Why Corporations are not Morally Responsible for Anything They Do." In Ethical Theory and Business. Edited by Tom Beauchamp and Norman Bowie. Englewood Cliffs, N.J.: Prentice-Hall.

Vice and Virtue in Everyday Life. Edited by Christina Hoff Sommers. San Diego: Harcourt, Brace, Jovanovich, 1985.

The Virtues. Edited by Robert Kruschwitz and Robert Roberts. Belmont, C.A.: Wadsworth, 1987.

Wallace, James D. Virtues and Vice. Ithaca: Cornell University Press, 1978.

Warnock, G. J. The Object of Morality. London: Methuen and Co. Ltd., 1971.

Watson, Gary. "Skepticism about Weakness of Will." Philosophical Review 86
      (1977).

Weakness of Will. Edited by G. W. Mortimer. New York: St. Martin's Press,
      1971.

Weinryb, Elazar. "Omissions and Responsibility." Philosophical Quarterly 30
      (1980).

Zimmerman, Michael. An Essay on Moral Responsibility. Totowa, N. J.:
      Rowman and Littlefield, 1988.

_____. "Intervening Agents and Moral Responsibility." Philosophical
      Quarterly 35   (1985a).

_____. "Moral Responsibility, Freedom, and Alternate Possibilities." Pacific
      Philosophical Quarterly 63 (1982).

_____. "Negligence and Moral Responsibility." Nous 20 (1986a).

INDEX

DATE DUE

FEB. 1 4 1994			
JUN 1 4 95			
MAR 1 8 96			
GAYLORD			PRINTED IN U.S.A.